Joseph Lathrop

Sermons on Various Subjects

Evangelical, devotional, and practical adapted to the promotion of Christian piety,

family religion, and youthful virtue. Vol. 1

Joseph Lathrop

Sermons on Various Subjects
Evangelical, devotional, and practical adapted to the promotion of Christian piety, family religion, and youthful virtue. Vol. 1

ISBN/EAN: 9783337114251

Printed in Europe, USA, Canada, Australia, Japan

Cover: Foto ©Lupo / pixelio.de

More available books at **www.hansebooks.com**

SERMONS

ON

VARIOUS SUBJECTS,

EVANGELICAL,

DEVOTIONAL AND PRACTICAL,

ADAPTED TO

THE PROMOTION OF

CHRISTIAN PIETY,

FAMILY RELIGION,

AND

YOUTHFUL VIRTUE.

BY JOSEPH LATHROP, D.D.
PASTOR OF THE FIRST CHURCH IN WESTSPRINGFIELD.

PRINTED AT WORCESTER, MASSACHUSETTS,
BY ISAIAH THOMAS.
Sold by him in WORCESTER; and by said THOMAS, and ANDREWS, at
Faust's Statue, Newbury Street, BOSTON.

MDCCXCIII.

CONTENTS.

Sermon		Page
I.	GOD *glorified in Heaven for the Works of Creation and Providence.*	6
II.	GOD *works not for our Sakes only, but for his Name's Sake.*	22
III.	*The same Subject, continued.*	37
IV.	*The Work of Redemption marvellous, but divine.*	56
V.	*The same Subject, improved.*	69
VI.	*Shepherds glorifying* GOD, *for the Birth of a Saviour.*	84
VII.	*John leaning on Jesus's Bosom.*	98
VIII.	*The Spectators of the Crucifixion smiting their Breasts.*	112
IX.	GOD'S *Works, as King of Saints, great and marvellous.*	126
X.	*The same Subject, continued.*	140

XI. GOD

Sermon		Page
XI.	GOD *glorified in the Punishment of Sinners.*	156
XII.	*The same Subject, improved.*	173
XIII.	*Jesus rising early for secret Prayer.*	192
XIV.	*Family Prayer.*	209
XV.	*The same Subject, continued.*	224
XVI.	*A Christian Family helping their Minister.*	240
XVII.	*Children in the Temple praising the Redeemer.*	256
XVIII.	*The Necessity of early Religion.*	272
XIX.	*The Youth assisted in forming his religious Sentiments.*	289
XX.	*Samson shorn of his Locks.*	305
XXI.	*Reflections on Abraham's Artifice with Abimelech.*	320
XXII.	*The Kingdom of God without Observation.*	335
XXIII.	*The same Subject, improved.*	347
XXIV.	*Innumerable gone to the Grave, and every Man drawing after them.*	359
XXV.	*Reflections on Harvest.*	374

God glorified in Heaven for his Works of Creation and Providence.

REVELATION 4, xi.

Thou art worthy, **O Lord,** *to receive glory, and honour, and power; for thou haſt created all things, and for thy pleaſure they are and were created.*

T. John, in this chapter, deſcribes a viſion which he had of the heavenly worſhip. He ſaw a throne placed in heaven, with the appearance of divine glory upon it; and ſeats diſpoſed around, on which ſat the elders, clothed in white raiment, with golden crowns on their heads; and in the midſt, and round about the throne, were the principal angels. Theſe began the worſhip with celebrating the infinite purity of the divine nature, and aſcribing all glory to him, who ſat on the throne; and then the elders joined their

A   voices,

voices, falling before the throne, casting down their crowns, and saying, *Thou art worthy to receive glory, and honour, and power; for thou hast created all things, and for thy pleasure they are and were created.*

In these words we may observe,

I. That all things were created by God.

II. That they were created, and are upheld *for his pleasure.*

III. That all rational beings are to *glorify him* for his creation and providence.

I. The heavenly church acknowledge that *God created all things.*

If the world was created, there was a time when it did not exist. Though it received its present form from preexisting matter, yet this matter must, at some time or other, have received its existence from the same hand which moulded it into this wondrous form. *The worlds were framed by the word of God; so that things which are seen, were not made of things which do appear.* If the world were eternal and self existent, it would be immutable; for that which exists necessarily, is necessarily what it is, and not liable to change or dissolution. But we see these material things continually subject to alteration and decay; we may therefore conclude that they are the creatures of time.

As all creation had a beginning, so this part of it had a *late* beginning. The scriptural account, which dates it but a few thousand years back, is in some measure confirmed by observation. The lateness of our most ancient histories, the imperfection of arts and sciences, and even of the geography of the world, and the vast tracts, which still remain unpopulated, or but sparsely inhabited, though mankind have, in general, been in a state of increase, make it credible, that the world cannot have existed much longer than the Mosaick account represents.

"But, ¿ Can we suppose, that the Deity, who is eternal, would suffer such a long duration to pass away, before he employed his power, wisdom, and goodness, or made beings to know, enjoy, and praise him?"

This question has been asked, and urged as an objection against the lateness of creation.

But the objection, if it may be called one, can respect only that part of creation of which Moses has given an account. Space is boundless, as well as duration endless. Beyond our system—beyond these visible heavens, there is room for innumerable worlds to have existed, millions of ages before this part of the universe rose into being. Besides, the objection itself, when it is examined, vanishes into nothing. If the world was created, there was a time when it began. And if, for its origin, you go back as many millions of ages as there are sunbeams in the heavens, still there was a time, when it had not existed six thousand years. And this objection might then be made, as well as now; for it was then as true, as it is now, that there had paſſed a duration without beginning. The difficulty in ſuch caſes is, we attempt by time to meaſure eternity; and the meaſure is not adequate to the object.

From the things which exiſt, we know there is a God. *The inviſible things of God, from the creation of the world, are clearly ſeen, being underſtood by the things which are made, even his eternal power and godhead.*

If God created *all things*, then a creating power belongs not to creatures. It is a power, which we may ſuppoſe them incapable of receiving; for creation is the higheſt act of Divinity that we can conceive of; probably there can be none higher.

By human ability and ingenuity many things have been done, which to the unexperienced appear ſurprizing. The combined ſkill and power of a number have produced works far greater ſtill. But all their works are only giving a new form to things which already exiſt. They cannot originate matter, nor animate it when it is made. There are beings above us endued with ſuperiour powers; but to none of theſe does the ſcripture aſcribe the power of creation. On the contrary, it expreſsly tells us, *all things* were created by God. But our apoſtle, in his goſpel, ſays, " All things were made by Jeſus Chriſt, and without him was not any thing made, that was made." Hence then we muſt conclude, that he is not merely an exalted creature,

but

but properly divine, possessed of divine power, and entitled to divine honour.

How vast is creation! Even this world, when we view it in comparison with the little creatures which inhabit it, appears a mighty thing. But, what is this, with all its innumerable inhabitants, to the universe! When we step abroad, and cast our eyes up to the heavens, what an astonishing scene do we behold! What multitudes of worlds do we there see scattered around, and sunk in the depths of space! At what an amazing distance are they placed from us, and from one another! How small is the spot which our sight commands, compared with unlimited space! How inconsiderable the number of bodies which we see, compared with those which may be supposed to exist! After imagination has taken its most distant flight, still, How far is it from having reached the bounds of creation! And yet all these things were created and are upheld by one almighty, omnipresent, eternal Being. He spake, and they were made; he commanded, and they stood fast. By his word the heavens and the earth were created, and all the host of them by the breath of his mouth. He still upholds them all by the word of his power. The thunder of his power, who can understand!

We proceed to our second observation.

II. All things are and were created for *God's pleasure;* or for his *will,* as the word properly signifies.

If you aſk, why God made the world, and upholds it; why he framed the univerſe, and formed this globe, in ſuch time and manner, as he has; the ſong of angels gives the proper anſwer. "All things were made for his pleaſure." The apoſtle Paul expreſſes the ſame ſentiment: *He works all things according to the counſel of his own will.*

There has been much inquiry, and ſome controverſy among Chriſtians, concerning God's ultimate end in the work of creation; whether it was his own glory, or the exerciſe of his goodneſs in the communication of happineſs. But the apoſtle, in the text, cuts the matter ſhort. He introduces the ſpirits in heaven as celebrating the wonders of creation, and aſcribing them all to God's *will.* Here is a plain intimation, that theſe ſpeculations on the ſupreme and ultimate end of an infinite and all perfect Being, in the formation of all his works, are too high for mortals. Angels, with greater modeſty, bow down and adore unſearchable wiſdom. Wiſe ends he certainly has in all his works. But, farther than he has given us an account of his matters, his counſels are too deep for us.

Creation is a vaſt and ſtupendous work. It is but a ſmall part of it which comes within our obſervation; and even this we know but imperfectly. And if we know not the work itſelf, much leſs can we know all the purpoſes for which it was intended. For us it is enough to know, that all things were made by a moſt perfect Being,

and

and that for his pleasure they are and were created.

But though we cannot comprehend the works of God, nor determine that they were made for this or that purpose solely or supremely, yet there are certain uses to which we see many of them adapted; and *these* it becomes us to observe.

The heavens declare the glory of God, and the firmament sheweth his handy work. The earth also is full of his riches. His power and goodness every where appear. Manifold are his works; in wisdom he has made them all.

As the works which we behold, display his perfections, and manifest, in a particular manner, his wisdom, power and benevolence; so it is certainly his will, that intelligent creatures should attend to the displays and manifestations which he has made of himself, and exercise toward him correspondent affections and regards. Though we cannot affirm, that this, that, or the other, was the only or ultimate end of all creation, yet we know that God made rational creatures to serve him; discovers to them his character, that they may love him; bestows on them his goodness, that they may trust him; and calls them to himself, that they may enjoy him. The language of angels, is the voice of reason. *Thou art worthy to receive glory, and honour, and power; for thou hast created all things, and for thy pleasure they are and were created.*

This

This brings us to our last observation,

III. That all intelligent beings are bound to glorify God for his works of creation and providence.

1. These works should lead us to the knowledge and contemplation of their great and glorious Author.

God's works are wonderful, sought out by them who have pleasure in them. While the philosopher explores them for the enlargement of his mind, the amusement of his fancy, and the investigation of their uses in common life, the good Christian will regard them in a higher view. He will look into them, that he may gain a juster knowledge, and raise a nobler conception of the Creator. He will behold God in them, and contemplate the wisdom, goodness, and power which they display. When he sees the works, he will see God working. He will consider himself as surrounded by the Deity; animated by his breath; inspired with reason by his spirit; sustained by his hand; supplied by his goodness; guided by his counsel; and protected by his power.

Of the wicked it is said, God is not in all their thoughts. What stupidity is this! ¿ Is God always with them, and working before them? ¿ Does he manifest himself in the heavens, in the earth, in rain and sunshine, in winds and storms, in succeeding their labours, and blessing the works of their hands? And, ¿ Can they banish him
from

from their thoughts? If we live without God in a world, which is every where so full of him, ¿ What are we better than the heathen? We know God, but we glorify him not as God, neither are thankful. ¿ *Better* than the heathen? Nay, we are inferiour to the mere animal. "The ox knows his owner, and the afs his master's crib."

2. We should glorify God in his works, by improving them to awaken in our souls pious affections to him.

The Being who made and upholds so vast a system; who supplies such innumerable multitudes; who has given understanding to many; who has provided for their subsistence in this state, and their happiness through eternity, must be great, and wise, and good. To him then are due our highest regards. We should tremble at his presence, reverence his majesty, submit to his pleasure, trust his care, admire his character, thank him for his benefits, and acknowledge him in all our ways.

In tracing the connexions, and investigating the causes of things, the philosopher is led up to the Deity as the grand first cause of all. But if he introduces into his scheme the agency of a God, only as he admits the power of attraction, magnetism and electricity, to solve the phenomena of nature, he stops far short of the proper end of his researches. The Christian will contemplate
the

the Deity, not merely as a power producing great effects; but as a Being, whose power is guided by wisdom, justice and benevolence. While he admires the works, he will love and fear, trust and adore the God who made them.

3. The works of God should invite us to him in the humble exercises of devotion. He who offers praise, glorifies God. The Being who made all things, must himself be independent. The things which are made must be dependent on him. When we look up to this glorious Being, we should sink down into the most humble thoughts of ourselves. What are we amidst this vast creation! How wonderful is his condescension, that he attends to our wants, and visits us every moment! When we consider the heavens, the work of his fingers, the moon and stars, which he has ordained, ¿ How just is the reflection, What is man that he should be mindful of him?—¿ Does it not become such dependent and indebted creatures daily to call on God for what they want, and daily to thank him for what they receive? He is not indifferent to us: ¿ Shall we be indifferent to him? We daily stand in his presence, and receive bounties from his hand: ¿ Shall we pay no reverence to his character, and make no returns for his beneficence? From just apprehensions of God, and of ourselves, a spirit of devotion must arise.

4. We

4. We are to glorify God for our own existence.

If we are to praise him for creation in general, surely some gratitude is due for our distinguished rank in the creation. *I will praise thee, for I am fearfully and wonderfully made. How precious are thy thoughts to me! How great is the sum of them!*

God has given us a rational existence; made known to us his will; taken us under his particular care; furnished us with the means of virtue in this state, and eternal happiness in the next; and all along the passage through this to the future world, the blessings of his goodness attend us. Is not existence, under these circumstances, to be regarded as a privilege? If a happy existence is to be valued, an existence accompanied with present enjoyments, and with the means of obtaining higher enjoyments hereafter, is to be contemplated with gratitude and joy.

Perhaps, in the gloom of a discontented mind, you complain of life as a burthen.

Impatience may undoubtedly draw up a long list of grievances. But from this list, let your sober reason make proper deductions.

In the first place, strike out your *imaginary* troubles—those which arise from pride, vanity, avarice, habit, irregular passion, and extravagant expectation. Strike out next the troubles which are merely *negative*, consisting only in the removal of blessings which you have enjoyed for a while, and which, if you had never enjoyed them, you never would have defired. Strike out alfo your *comparative* evils, which owe their exiftence to an apprehenfion, that your neighbours poffefs benefits denied to you—benefits, which you would not have thought of, if you had not feen them in poffeffion of others. Make thefe deductions, and your lift of grievances will be much reduced. Call gratitude to make the eftimate, and your bleffings will be found to exceed your troubles.

You have more days of health and comfort, than of ficknefs and pain. In a courfe of regular induftry, you have more fuccefs than difappointment. In your connexions, you have many friends; few enemies—perhaps none. Remember alfo, that your real troubles, rightly regarded, are preparatives for a ftate of pure enjoyment; and that death, which of all things here you moft dread, is your paffage to that ftate. Confider thefe things, and then fay, *Our light afflictions, which are but for a moment, will work for us a far more exceeding and eternal weight of glory.*

But ftill perhaps fome will conclude, that their exiftence is to be regretted: " For revelation informs us, that a great part, yea much the greater part of the human race will be miferable forever. It is then, with refpect to each one who comes on this ftage, more probable that he will be miferable than happy. And if this is his ftate, ¿ What ground is there to be thankful for exiftence?"

Now

Now, without entering on the question, whether the proportion of the saved will be great or small, a question not subject to human calculation, we are to consider, whether we have the means and offers of happiness, and whether we have them from a Being who may be trusted. If we have, then there is cause of thankfulness for our existence; for we may be happy, if we will be wise. It is only the abuse of divine goodness, that makes us miserable. Happiness is proposed to our choice; and whether we accept or reject it, still God is good. Our folly alters not the nature of goodness, nor diminishes the obligation of gratitude.

You are not to consider the plan of the gospel, as the scheme of a lottery, in which each man's chance for success is according to the proportion of prizes to blanks; but as a moral and rational plan, in which each one's success will be determined by his own choice. Be the number of the saved ever so small, this diminishes not the probability in favour of those, who seek for glory by a patient continuance in well doing. Be it ever so great, this gives no additional hope to those who neglect their salvation. To determine the probability of your success, you need not inquire how many, or how few will be saved: You are only to inquire, what you yourselves are doing. In the destruction of the old world, Noah and his household, though few, only eight souls, were preserved.

preferved. At the wedding fupper, the one unworthy gueft was caft into utter darknefs. Whatever may be the number of the righteous, or of the wicked, the Lord knoweth how to deliver the godly out of temptation, and how to referve the unjuft unto the day of judgment to be punifhed.

The apoftle fays to the Corinthians, *They who run in a race, run all; but one receiveth the prize. So run, that ye may obtain. I fo run, not as uncertainly.* In a race, there is only one prize; and whatever exertions the combatants make, it is only the foremoft who wins. In the Chriftian race it is otherwife. Here is a prize propofed to each; and all may obtain, if they will run well. Therefore the apoftle fays, *So run, that ye may obtain.* Ye may all obtain, who enter on the race, and finifh the courfe. Your fuccefs will not be influenced by the good or ill fuccefs of others: It will be determined by your own fincerity, activity and perfeverance. *I fo run, not as uncertainly; fo fight I, not as one who beateth the air; but I keep under my body to bring it into fubjection, left by any means, when I have preached to others, I myfelf fhould be a caftaway.*

5. If creation deferves our praife, redemption deferves it ftill more, for this is our hope.

Creation difplays God's wifdom, power and goodnefs; redemption difplays his holinefs, juftice and grace. If it is matter of gratitude, that we were called from nothing into rational exiftence; it is matter of higher gratitude, that we are recovered from darkness, bondage and fear, to a state of light, liberty and hope. If we are to give thanks, that, when we were nothing, God called us into being, to behold and contemplate his works; much rather should we give thanks that when, by perverting the design of our creation, we had ruined ourselves, in him was our help; that when we were without strength, in due time Christ died for the ungodly.

Finally, we are to glorify God for the prospects which are opened before us.

Here we may know something of God's works; for creation is all around us, and providence is working before us. Angels and saints above know more of God's works than can be known here. They have a stronger sight, and can look to more distant objects. They are raised to higher ground, and can command a more extensive view. Their sight is not bounded by the circle of our horizon, nor their prospect terminated by the canopy of our skies. They see more than we can see, and they admire and love more than we can do. But delightful is the hope, that we shall one day be with them, and be like them; see as they see, and praise as they praise.

We behold many wonders of God's wisdom and goodness in this earth, and in those heavens. But, ¿ What are these compared with the wonders which will crowd upon our sight, when we shall tread the new earth, and contemplate the new heavens?

heavens? At the opening of these new scenes, all former glories will be extinguished, like a lamp before the rising sun. *Behold*, says the God of glory, *I create new heavens, and a new earth; and the former shall not be remembered, nor come into mind. Be glad and rejoice forever in that which I create. Behold, I create Jerusalem a rejoicing, and her people a joy.*

The new heavens and earth will need no sun or moon to shine upon them. The glory of the Lord shall lighten them, and the nations of them who are saved shall walk in the light thereof, and there shall be no night there.

While we dwell in this lower creation, let us raise our thoughts to the superiour world, and here begin the devout and holy exercises which are to employ us there.

If all things were created for God's pleasure, let us remember, that for his pleasure we were created too. We are to live, not to ourselves, but to him—to make, not our own, but his will, the rule of our actions—to please, not ourselves, but him whose will is perfect—and to expect happiness, not in the world, but in his favour.

Be not then conformed to this world, but be ye transformed by the renewing of your mind, that ye may prove what is the good, acceptable and perfect will of God.

END OF THE FIRST SERMON.

SERMON II.

God works, not for our Sakes only, but for his Name's Sake.

EZEKIEL 36, xxxii.

Not for your sakes do I this, saith the Lord God, be it known unto you;——

TO the Jews, now in captivity at Babylon, the prophet, in this chapter, communicates God's gracious promise of their restoration to their own land; and describes the happy circumstances which should attend it. They should be reinstated in their former privileges—should receive plentiful effusions of the Holy Spirit—should be blessed with all temporal and spiritual good things—in a word, the Lord would be their God, and they should be his people. But lest, on hearing such rich and gracious promises, their hearts should be lifted up in pride and selfconfidence, the caution in the text is subjoined—*Not for your sakes do I this, saith the Lord God, be it known unto you; be ashamed and confounded for your own ways.* The same caution is before given in the 22d verse;

Thus

Thus faith the Lord I do not this for your fakes, O houfe of Ifrael; but for my holy name's fake, which ye had profaned among the heathens, whither ye went. I have had pity for my holy name. I will fanctify my great name, which ye had profaned. The heathen fhall know that I am the Lord, when I fhall be fanctified in you before their eyes.

The reafon of God's granting to the captive Jews, a reftoration to their country, and fo many attending privileges, was founded, not in their worthinefs, but his own mercy—not in a partial regard to them, but in a general regard to the human race.

We will illuftrate our text—

Firft, As it refpects the cafe of the Jews in particular.

II. In its more general application to others.

I. We will confider the text as it immediately refpects the cafe of the Jews.

Their deliverance from Babylon was eminently the work of God.—*It was He, who did this.* Taken in all its circumftances, it evidently appears to have been wrought by a divine hand.

The duration of their captivity was exactly foretold, before it began; and Cyrus, the prince who granted their releafe, was exprefsly named in prophecy, before he was born. During a period of feventy years, they were preferved a diftinct people in the land of their enemies, while other nations were fwallowed up and loft. They enjoyed fome peculiar privileges in their captivity, efpecially the privilege of exercifing their own religion,

religion, and attending the miniſtrations of their prophets. Some of their prophets and prieſts, men of diſtinguiſhed abilities, gifts and virtues, were, by a wonderful concurrence of circumſtances, admitted to great honour and influence in the court of Babylon, where, uncorrupted by their preferment, they retained their zeal for the religion, and concern for the intereſt of their nation, for whom they procured ſome ſignal favours. In this period Cyrus the Perſian is born. Under him are united the Perſian and Median powers. He proves a wiſe and virtuous, as well as a warlike and victorious prince. A little before the time predicted for the deliverance of the Jews, he makes a conqueſt, and obtains the government of the Chaldean empire. He favours theſe captives, and grants them liberty to return to their own land. Under the authority of the decree paſſed in his reign, his ſucceſſors continue to them this indulgence, and aſſiſt them in reſettling their country, and rebuilding their city and temple. Some of their countrymen, now in honour and affluence at Babylon, ſacrifice all their worldly poſſeſſions and proſpects to the intereſt of this deſpiſed people, and not only aid, but accompany them in their return. Here, under the ſmiles of Providence, they increaſe in number, ſtrength and importance, and ſoon become reſpectable among the nations around them.

In this great event, utterly improbable to human foreſight, ſo conſpicuous was the divine hand, that when God turned again the captivity of Zion, it was said among the heathen, *The* Lord *hath done great things for them.*

God would have them consider, that all this was done, not for their sakes, but for his name's sake.

It was done, not on account of their *worthiness*, but from pure *mercy*.

They had been sent into captivity for the sins which they committed in their own land; and these sins they carried with them and still retained in the land of their captivity. Thus God complains of them in the preceding part of this chapter. " When the house of Israel dwelt in their own land, they defiled it by their own way, and by their doings; wherefore I poured out my fury upon them, and I scattered them among the heathen.—And when they entered unto the heathen, whither they went, they profaned my holy name, when it was said unto them, These are the people of the Lord, and they are gone forth out of his land." As if it had been said, " By their evil practices they have brought a reproach on my name, and given occasion to the heathen to say, See what profligate and impious wretches these Jews are, who call themselves the servants of a holy God! No wonder he has expelled them out of the country, which he gave them." When God promises their restoration, he calls upon them to remember all that they had done, and to be ashamed and confounded for their own ways.

This deliverance was not intended principally for their benefit; but for a more general and extensive tenfive good. "I do this," fays the Almighty, "for my name's fake, and that the heathen may know that I am the Lord."

In this work God glorified his great name. He gave a ftriking difplay of his *power*, by refcuing thefe feeble captives from the hands of fuperiour enemies—of his *wifdom*, in fo difpofing events as to accomplifh this mighty purpofe—of his *foreknowledge*, in pointing out the time, manner and circumftances of their deliverance—of his *faithfulnefs*, in fulfiling the promifes, which had long before been made in their favour—of his *goodnefs*, in watching over this unworthy people, and pardoning their numerous provocations—of his *holinefs*, in chaftifing their iniquities—of his *juftice*, in punifhing the oppreffions of their enemies—of his *fovereignty*, in cafting down a fuperiour nation to make way for their deliverance—and of the *truth* of the *religion* inftituted among them, by accomplifhing the predictions of his prophets.

God did not at firft fet his love upon them, becaufe they were more in number than any people; for they were then the feweft of all people. Neither did he overturn the empire of Babylon in order to their deliverance, becaufe they were the greateft nation in the world; for they were but an inconfiderable company, compared with the nation now conquered. He muft have had fome higher end than merely the advancement of this fmall number of captives, fcarcely amounting to fifty thoufands.

God's ways are not as our ways, nor his thoughts as our thoughts. It is by a variety of means, and by a laboured procefs, that we effect a fingle purpofe. A variety of vaft and wonderful purpofes God accomplifhes by the fame means. There is a connexion which runs through his works. The end, which feems firft intended, is one ftep in the procefs, in order to bring about fome diftant and more important defign.

1. The captivity and deliverance of the Jews were the means of fpreading in the world the knowledge of God, and of the true religion.

The heathen were thus made to know that he was the Lord.

The benefits of the revelation, which God gave to the Jews, were not wholly confined to them. They reached to other nations. The frequent captivities and difperfions of this enlightened people, as well as the travels of their prophets, contributed to diffeminate far and wide the knowledge of the truth. Babylon was the moft celebrated city, and the capital of the moft powerful empire in the world; fo that by means of this long captivity, the knowledge of the true God was more extenfively fpread, than it would have been, had his profeffed worfhippers been fuffered to continue in their own land. By various other calamities, as famines, plagues, ftorms and earthquakes, God could have punifhed their manifold iniquities; but judgments of this kind were not fo well adapted to diffufe the knowledge of his name.

The

The means made use of in Providence for their deliverance, conduced to the same great end. To make way for this event, the empire of Babylon is subdued by the Medes and Persians, who of course now become acquainted with the Jews, with the religion which they profess, and with the God whom they worship. The information which Cyrus received concerning the predictions of the prophets, and the conviction which he felt of their truth and divinity, were doubtless the motives which first prompted him to release these captives. It is evident that he, as well as some preceding and following kings of Babylon, acknowledged the God of Israel to be the true and supreme God. If *they* acknowledged him, many of their subjects would follow their example. So that the Jewish revelation was, in fact, more extensive than some imagine. That which at first looks like partiality in their favour, was, in its effects, the exercise of general goodness.

2. The return of the Jews was a strong confirmation of the truth of their religion, adapted to give conviction to all who were witnesses of it.

The wonderful steps of Providence in accomplishing this event, and the exact fulfilment of the many predictions and promises which had been made concerning it, were undeniable proofs, that the God whom they worshipped, was the only true God.

3. God preserved this people, because to them were committed his sacred oracles.

Though they were a sinful nation, yet as the only instituted church, and the only written revelation, were among them, he would not utterly destroy them. He spared them, because a blessing for mankind was in them. As the scriptures, which they enjoyed, were ultimately designed for general benefit, God would preserve the nation to whose care he had committed them. Had these sacred writings been extinguished by the destruction of the present possessors of them, the world would have sustained a loss, which could, by no human means, have been repaired.

4. God restored and preserved this people, because from them was to proceed the great Saviour of the world.

To Abraham was a promise made, that among his descendants, the Redeemer should be born, and in his seed all nations should be blessed. As the time was not yet come for the appearance of the promised Saviour, the nation from whom he was to spring, and who were first to be blessed with his presence, must be preserved. Accordingly we find, that until the time of his coming, this nation was God's peculiar care; though he often chastised them, he forsook them not utterly; though he delivered them up to captivity, he dissolved not their national state. But this singular care of them was not for their sakes; it was for the sake of mankind in general, that the blessing promised to Abraham might come on the Gentiles. And therefore,

fore, after the Saviour's death, this special care for them is withdrawn.

They are soon given up to the power of the Romans, by whom they are completely subdued, and scattered over the face of the earth; and even to this day they no where subsist in a national capacity.

5. The captivity and deliverance of this people, were events which conduced much to prepare the world for the reception of the Saviour.

By these means, many learned men, in the most respectable nations of the earth, were brought to the knowledge and belief of the Jewish scriptures, and of the prophecies concerning the Messiah. The prophecy of Daniel, which was delivered toward the end of the captivity, expressly pointed out the time of his appearance. This must have been known to many besides the Jews; and from hence probably arose the prevailing expectation in those parts of the world, that some extraordinary person would appear, who should have a general dominion. Hence he is called the desire, or expectation, of all nations. And doubtless the great success, which the apostles found in preaching the gospel among the Gentiles, was, in some measure, owing to these preparatory means.

The time is coming when the knowledge of God shall cover the earth, and all nations shall see his salvation. The gospel will not always be confined to a small part of the human race. It will have a universal spread. Those means which

have

have introduced, and hitherto maintained it, were designed for the benefit of generations to come, as well as of those which are past. God's particular favour to the Jews, will eventually prove a blessing to all nations.

REFLECTIONS.

1. This passage, in its connexion, teaches us, what is intended by the phrase, so often used in scripture, of God's working *for his own sake*, and *for his name's sake.* It is working, that his name may be more extensively known and regarded among men.

This is evidently the sense, in which it is used in this chapter. *I do this for my name's sake, and I will sanctify my great name; and the heathen shall know, that I am the Lord.* So it is repeatedly used in the 20th chapter. *I wrought for my name's sake, that it should not be polluted among the heathen, in whose sight I made myself known.*

When we meet with such phrases, we must not understand them, as if the independent, allperfect, selfsufficient God, had some design diverse from, and opposite to, the good of his creatures. For as he is completely happy in himself; and as nothing can increase, or diminish his felicity and selfenjoyment, so it is impossible, that, *in this sense*, he should do any thing *for his own sake.* But his acting *for his name's sake,* is acting for the sake of making his *name,* or *character,* known among

his

his rational creatures, and bringing them to acknowledge, fear and obey him. What he does for his own sake, has respect to their good, and is suited to render them virtuous and happy. So that the phrase, in the strongest manner, expresses his free and disinterested goodness.

When a man is said to do any thing for his own sake, we consider him as acting selfishly, and without regard to the interest of others. But the phrase is, in scripture, applied to the Deity in a higher and nobler sense, as imparting his kind and gracious intentions toward moral beings. When he makes his name known, it is, not that he himself, but that his creatures, may be better and happier.

In like manner we are to understand the similar phrase of God's acting *for his own glory.* This is not to make himself more glorious; for he is infinitely glorious in his nature: His gloriousness consists in his unlimited and immutable perfection: But it is to manifest and display among his creatures his glorious character, that they may know and love him, adore and serve him. And he requires them to admire and worship him, not because he is benefited by their affections or praises; for he is not worshipped by men's hand, as though he needed any thing from them—their goodness cannot extend to him; but because these regards are due from them as rational creatures, and are necessary to their own happiness.

In

In a sense consistent with this, we must understand the command, *to do all things to the glory of God*. We must not imagine, that our righteousness is gain to him—that our services turn to his real benefit—that our praises add any thing to his excellency. Such ideas of him would be impious. But we then act to his glory, when we imitate his goodness by doing good to mankind—when **we obey** his commands **on** the motives which he proposes—and when we shew forth the glory of his character, in such a manner as to promote the virtue and happiness of our fellow creatures. *Herein is our heavenly Father glorified, that we bring forth much fruit.* We are to *abound in the fruits of righteousness, which are by Jesus Christ, to the praise and glory of God. Our light is to shine before men, that, seeing our good works, they may glorify God.* We are to *give glory to God, by exercising repentence and making confession of our sins. Whatever we* **do, we** are to *do it to his glory, giving no offence to any man, and* **not** *seeking our own profit, but the profit of many, that they* **may** *be saved.*

2. Our subject leads us to admire the grand scheme of **God's** providence.

His dispensations, both of mercy and correction toward particular persons **and nations**, look beyond those **who** are the immediate objects of them; and produce effects more distant than we can trace—more extensive than we can comprehend—more numerous than we can conceive. The mercies granted to the Jews, were not for their

sakes

fakes only, but for his name's fake, that it might be known among the heathen. When we contemplate the hiftory of his dealings toward them, we fee confquences of great and general importance produced by means, which feemed at firft to refpect them only. The ways of his providence are ftill as wife and gracious—ftill as complex and interefting, as thofe which are the fubject of facred hiftory.

. When we review thofe difpenfations, which more immediately concern ourfelves, we often find great effects produced by caufes which to us feemed fmall—happy confequences following, at a diftance, from events which, in the time of them, promifed nothing—fubftantial good iffuing from occurrences, which had a contrary afpect—and trouble growing out of meafures, which we fondly adopted and eagerly purfued. And befides this connexion of things, which we are able to difcover, there is doubtlefs a more remote and important connexion, which, in the prefent ftate, we never difcern. "What God does we know not now, but fhall know hereafter."

We fee, or think we fee, worldly good and evil diftributed with great inequality. Some are rich, and others poor. Health of body and fuccefs in bufinefs, attend one man; ficknefs, difappointment and perplexity, are the painful lot of another. We wonder why there is this difference. Impatience complains, that God's ways are not equal. But thefe are matters concerning which we are not

capable

capable of judging. We see but in part. The inward pains which corrupt the rich man's enjoyments and the hidden consolations which refresh the spirits of the poor and afflicted, may essentially alter the balance. The external difference which we observe, may be more owing to men's different tempers, aims and manner of conduct, than we imagine. And even so far as this difference is properly and directly providential, it is the effect, not of partiality in the Supreme Disposer, but of his general goodness. The circumstances of a particular person are ordered, not for his sake only, but for the sake of others. These circumstances may be productive of consequences which we cannot foresee, and do not even suspect. Until we can comprehend the various relations and connexions of things, and discern how one man's condition will affect another, and what consequences will issue from particular events, we are incompetent judges of the wisdom and equity of Providence. He who governs the world, is a God of truth, and without iniquity. He is a rock, his way is perfect; just and right is he. Let us never suspect his ways are unequal. Let us never indulge an impatient, murmuring spirit; but learn in every state to be content.

3. We see the proper foundation of submission and gratitude under all the dealings of God. It is a humble sense of our unworthiness. *Be ashamed and confounded for all your ways,* says the prophet.

If

If you enjoy prosperity, imagine not, that heaven gives it *for your sake*, either for your worthiness, or *solely* for your use; but remember that God distributes the bounties of his providence, with a sovereign hand, to the just and unjust, as his wisdom sees best—that his bounty is the source of all your enjoyments—that you are not worthy of the least of all the mercies which he has shewed you—and that you are to glorify him by an imitation of his goodness, in promoting virtue and happiness among your fellow mortals.

If you suffer adversity, utter no complaints—indulge no impatience; but be confounded for all your iniquities. These have forfeited the blessings which you have lost; and merited the pains which you feel. Every good is undeserved—every affliction is less than you deserve. The more humble thoughts you entertain of yourselves, the more contented and thankful you will be, and the less disposed to complain of Providence, and to envy or despise your fellow men.

Humility in the heart, is the groundwork of religion. Till we know ourselves, we shall neither love God, nor our duty. When we know ourselves, we shall be humble, for we can find nothing within us—nothing done by us, which will justify a spirit of pride. The more clearly we see our own unworthiness, the more highly we shall admire God's goodness. The deeper sense we have of our own ignorance, the more we shall confide in his wisdom—the more sensibly we realize our

impotence

impotence and dependence, the more readily we shall submit to his sovereignty.

The proper effect of God's mercies, is to melt us into a godly sorrow for our sins. Not for our sakes does he grant them, but that we may be ashamed and confounded for all our ways. His goodness will lead an ingenuous mind to repentance. The humble penitent takes serious notice of the ways of God, and sees mercy in those dispensations, of which he once complained. He examines himself, and discovers iniquity in those works of his own, in which once he gloried. He was formerly alive without the law; but when the commandment comes, sin revives, and he dies. When the law enters, the offence abounds. He sees that his remedy is not in himself—he repairs to the mercy of God. He remembers, and is confounded, and never opens his mouth any more because of his shame, when God is pacified toward him for all that he has done. Let us consider and know ourselves, and contemplate the the ways of God's providence and grace, and we shall admire his wisdom and love, and shall condemn our own folly and ingratitude. *Not unto us, O Lord, not unto us; but unto thy name be glory, for thy mercy, and for thy truth's sake.*

END OF THE SECOND SERMON.

SERMON III.

God works, not for our Sakes only, but for his Name's Sake.

EZEKIEL 36, xxxii.

Not for your sakes do I this, saith the Lord God, be it known unto you;———

THE deliverance of the Jews from their captivity in Babylon is the work of God here referred to. This was attended with such circumstances, as proved it to be eminently *his* work. When the captivity of Sion was turned, then said they among the heathen, "The Lord hath done great things for them." Under such a sudden and surprising change of condition, there was danger, that, being lifted up with pride, they would vainly imagine, their own virtue had entitled them to so great a favour, and God had too high a regard for them to punish them any more. This caution is therefore repeatedly given them, *Not for your sakes do I this, be it known unto you, but for my holy name's sake, which ye had profaned among the heathen. Be ashamed and confounded for all your ways.* These

C   words,

words, as they refpect the cafe of the Jews, import two things: Firft that God delivered them, not for their own *worthinefs*, but in mere *goodnefs and mercy*. And, Secondly, that he reftored them, not with a primary view to their national benefit and importance, but rather in order to the general good of mankind, and that his great name might be more extenfively known.

The fame may, with equal truth, be faid of every favour which God grants, either to *particular perfons*—to *communities*—or to the *human race*.

I. The benefits which God beftows upon us *perfonally*, are the fruits of *his benevolence*, not of *our defert*; and intended, not merely for *our* advantage, but for the glory of *his name*, by rendering us more ufeful in our fphere.

The apoftle fays, " None of us liveth to himfelf, and no man dieth to himfelf; for whether we live, we live to the Lord; and whether we die, we die to the Lord; whether we live therefore, or die, we are the Lord's." As we were not made merely for ourfelves, fo we ought not to live folely to our own ends. We are the fervants of him who made us at firft, and who preferves us ftill: And by his will, not by our own humour, are our lives to be governed. We then do his will the beft, and advance his glory the moft, when we direct our abilities and opportunities to the promotion of virtue and happinefs among his rational creatures.

No man dieth to himfelf. God orders the time, manner

manner and circumstances of each man's death, to serve the great and benevolent purposes of his providence. The good man's death brings him indeed to that happiness, which is the reward of his virtuous life. In this sense, as he lived, so he dies, to himself. But his death, at the same time, answers other more general ends. It may impress on survivors those serious sentiments, which he taught and inculcated in the course of his life. And in the other world, where he enjoys the fruits of his piety and goodness, he may still, in ways unknown to us, do much to advance the felicity of moral beings—may perhaps do more than he ever did, or could do, here below. *As he lived to the Lord, so he dies to the Lord.*

"Ye are not your own," says the Apostle, "for ye are bought with a price: Wherefore glorify God in your body, and in your spirit, which are God's."—"The love of Christ constraineth us, because we thus judge, that if one died for all, then were all dead; and that he died for all, that they who live should not henceforth live to themselves, but to him who died for them, and rose again."

If we are wholly God's property, then such is every thing that we possess. If our life and death are not for our sakes only, but for his name's sake, then all his particular gifts are to be regarded in the same light, and improved to nobler purposes than our own immediate interest.

Thus we are to regard all the gifts of *Nature.*

As God hath made different orders of intelligences, so in each order there is a gradation; and all to promote the general happiness. The singular genius of a *Newton* was given, not merely that he might amuse and gratify himself in stating the tides, measuring the distances of planets, and tracing the paths of comets; but that he might explore the vast fields of science, and collect treasures for the general benefit of mankind.

¿ *Who is a wise man,* says St. James, *and endued with knowledge? Let him shew out of a good conversation his works with meekness of wisdom—And the wisdom, which is from above, is full of mercy and good fruits.*

You have nothing, but what you received; and if you received it, ¿ Why should you glory, as if it were your own? Consider it as bestowed not merely for your benefit, but for the benefit of others; and use it accordingly. To whom much is given, of him much is required. Every man is bound to be useful according to his ability; and the greater the ability given, the greater the usefulness demanded.

Thus also we are to view the gifts of *Providence*. And thus we all view the gifts which others possess.

When men are exalted to an eminent station, we at once see, that not for their sakes God has done this, but for his name's sake. The civil ruler is promoted, not that he may live at ease, wallow in luxury, acquire boundless wealth, and pride
himself

himself in honour; but that he may do good to mankind. As the minister of God for their good, he is to attend continually on this very thing. A teacher in the church is to watch for souls—to take heed to the flock over which he is made an overseer—to feed them whom Christ has purchased with his blood. He is Christ's servant for their sakes, and must seek not theirs, but them—not his own profit, but the profit of many, **that they may be saved.**

But, ¿Are rulers and ministers the only men who are bound to act on disinterested principles? ¿May every body else be selfish? No: The same obligation which lies on them, extends to all. If you have a larger portion of worldly goods than those around you, remember you received it from God. If you acquired it by your industry, it is his providence, that succeeded you. It is he who giveth power to get riches. And not for your sake hath he done this; but for his name's sake, that you might imitate his goodness in works of beneficence to mankind. "Charge them, who are rich in this world," says Paul to Timothy, "that they be not high minded, neither trust in uncertain riches; but in the living God, who giveth us richly all things to enjoy; that they do good; that they be rich in good works, ready to distribute, willing to communicate, laying up for themselves a good foundation against the time to come, that they may lay hold on eternal life."

If

If we are to live, not to ourselves, but to God; we are to use our property, not to our own ends, but to his glory. To his glory we apply it, when we improve it for the benefit of our fellow men. "He who hath pity on the poor," says Solomon, "lendeth to the Lord." The words of our Saviour are to the same purpose. "What ye have given to my brethren, ye have given to me." What we thus give to God, we give him out of his own. So David acknowledges. "¿ Who am I? and, ¿ What is my people, that we should be able to offer so willingly after this sort? For all things come of thee, and of thine own have we given thee. All this store that we have prepared for thy name, cometh of thine hand; it is all thine own."

The poor man feels the justness of these observations, and he wishes the ruler, the minister, and the rich man would apply them. But, ¿ Is there nothing for which you are indebted to God? ¿ Nothing which you owe to mankind? If you have health or strength, or skill, this is also the gift of heaven, and you are under the same obligation as others to do good according to your ability. To you the Apostle says, "Labour with your hands the thing which is good." ¿ Why?—¿ For yourself only? No; but "that you may have to give to them who need;" i. e. to them who cannot work with their hands as you can. If you have been delivered from sickness, or from death; it is not merely for your own sake; but that you may glorify God in the improvement of life and health.

If

If the head of a family is spared; it is that he may guide and inſtruct his children, train them up in piety, and aſſiſt them in their preparation for uſefulneſs in this world, and happineſs in the next.

If a youth is preſerved from death; it is for the comfort of his parents in the declining period of life, or for the more extenſive benefit of mankind, in the preſent and ſucceeding generation.

Every inſtance of divine mercy ſhould be regarded as a new obligation, and a freſh call to a virtuous and uſeful life. We are not to imagine, that God keeps us night and day, guides our ſteps and protects our ſlumbers, merely for our own ends, that we may eat and drink, and ſport and ſleep; or that we may acquire wealth to be thrown into a uſeleſs heap while we live, and waſted as ſoon as we are dead. It is for the nobler purpoſes of his goodneſs and benevolence to mankind.

We may add farther—The gifts of *Divine Grace*, as well as thoſe of Nature and Providence, are for more general purpoſes, than the benefit of thoſe, on whom they are immediately beſtowed.

It is not owing to ourſelves, but to the ſelfmoving love of the independent God, that a Redeemer was ſent into our guilty world. It is not owing to our previous choice, but to the merciful diſpoſal of his ſovereign providence, that we are placed under the advantages of the goſpel. Why has he given us theſe advantages? One reaſon indeed is, that in the diligent improvement of them,

them, we may work out our own salvation. But this is not all—we are also to assist others in the same work. The parent is to communicate to his children that divine and all important knowledge, which he has received from the gospel of Christ. Christians are to consider one another, and provoke unto love and good works. They are to exhort one another, lest any be hardened through the deceitfulness of sin. They are to take heed, lest there be among them any profane person, whose evil communications shall corrupt good manners—lest any root of bitterness springing up, trouble them, and thereby many be defiled.

We of the present generation enjoy the gospel, not for our sakes only, but for the sake of succeeding generations. We are to transmit it to our children, and make such provision for its continuance, that they who come after us may enjoy it as amply as we have done before them. It is committed into our hands, as a sacred deposit, for the benefit of those around us, and those who shall succeed us. While we are working out our own salvation, we are to remember that this is but a part of our work. As it is not solely for our own sakes, that God has given us the means of salvation; so it is not singly on our own account, that we are to value and use them.

The Christian is to attend on the instituted worship of God, both for his own edification, and for the encouragement of others. He is to live in the practice of all good works, both that he may

obtain

obtain the reward of righteousness, and that others, beholding his example, may glorify God.

The conversion of a sinner is, in the wisdom and goodness of God, intended for the benefit of others, as well as for the salvation of him, who is the immediate subject of this grace. St. Paul says of himself, "I, who was a blasphemer, a persecutor and injurious, obtained mercy—and the grace of our Lord was exceedingly abundant. Howbeit for this cause I obtained mercy, that in me first Jesus Christ might shew forth all longsuffering for a pattern to them, who should afterward believe on him to life everlasting."

You wonder perhaps why some great sinners are, by the uncommon grace of God, recovered, while others, less guilty than they, are suffered to go on still in their trespasses.

We are not, indeed, very competent judges, who are the greatest sinners, and who have done most to abuse divine grace: But admitting this to be the case, as doubtless it may be, we must remember, that grace is free, and an undeserved benefit conferred on one, is no injury to another. Besides, when great sinners are thus mercifully distinguished, it is not merely for their sakes, but for God's name's sake. As it could not be at all for their worthiness, so neither is it altogether for their benefit; it is also that they may be influential in encouraging the repentance of others.

The conversion of one may be the means or the occasion of the conversion of many. So it
evidently

evidently was in the cafe of Paul. ¿ Who could be more injurious to the caufe of truth, than he was, while he continued a Pharifee?—¿ Who more ufeful than he, after he became a Chriftian? ¿ How much evil was prevented—how much good was done, by the converfion of this one man? ¿ What an encouragement to finners under a fenfe of guilt, is this example of divine mercy?—¿ How many were converted by Paul's preaching in the courfe of his miniftry?—¿ What lafting and extenfive benefit have mankind received from the writings which he has left? He was a chofen veffel to Chrift to bear his name among the Gentiles, as well as the Jews. His natural abilities, his education and accomplifhments, when his heart was fanctified by grace, eminently qualified him for fo great a work.

The converfion of every finner has its ufes, within a narrower fphere. Every convert is bound to improve, for the benefit of others, the grace of God toward him. " When thou art converted, ftrengthen thy brethren;" is Chrift's command to Peter. This was David's prayer and refolution, " Create in me a clean heart—uphold me with thy free fpirit; then will I teach tranfgreffors thy ways, and finners fhall be converted unto thee."

I proceed to obferve,

II. As *perfonal* bleffings are defigned for the benefit of many, fo bleffings granted to *focieties* are intended for the general good of mankind.

The

The national deliverance of the Jews from the Egyptian servitude, and afterward from the Babylonian captivity, was vouchsafed, not so much to render *them* important, as to display the glory of God's name among the heathen. The publick institutions of religion enjoyed by them, were made subservient to the happiness of many other nations.

Revolutions in favour of liberty, in a particular country, may be productive of interesting consequences in lands far remote, and in ages long to come.

The revolution, which has taken place in America, is operating to great, and we hope, happy events elsewhere. What God has done for us, was not only for our sakes, but for the benefit of mankind in other regions of the globe, and in other periods of time. And though Liberty in her progress, will meet with violent opposition, and, in her conflicts, will suffer dire calamities, yet we cannot doubt, but she will finally triumph.

We trust also, that this revolution will prove friendly to the interest of pure religion.

It is indeed complained, that infidelity much prevails. But perhaps its prevalence is more in appearance, than in reality; and it rather throws off its former disguise, than gains additional strength. There is greater freedom of inquiry, and more liberality of sentiment, than in years past: Learning is also more cultivated, and knowledge more generally diffused. That spirit of liberty, which sprang up here, and is now spreading

in

in the world, will probably render the civil governments of nations more tolerant to free religion, as well as more congenial to the rights of mankind. As learning becomes more common in the body of the people, it will of course be deemed a more requisite qualification in the publick teachers of religion; and ignorant pretenders, and designing impostors, will be more easily discerned, and more effectually discountenanced. As the light of truth beams on mankind, superstition and enthusiasm will retire to their primeval darkness; and rational, substantial religion will stand forth confessed in all its divine beauties. The truth will bear the strictest inquiry. And though, in an inquisitive age, some novel opinions may be started and pursued for a while, yet truth will eventually be more extensively known, and more firmly believed.

The changes, which we have seen, probably will never answer all the purposes, which worldly wisdom has contemplated; but they will answer the greater and better purposes of divine wisdom. They have already contributed much, and doubtless will contribute more to the advancement of useful knowledge, liberality of sentiment, and the intercourse of nations: And as these are advanced, there will be more room for religion to have free course and be glorified.

We are apt to contemplate events on the partial scale of self interest. The Deity views them on the extended scale of benevolence. Our selfish

ish expectations are usually disappointed. The purposes of divine goodness will be accomplished. If we regard events only in reference to our private interest, we shall never find them agreeable to our wishes. But if we believe that the divine government is good, and will extend to all nations and ages, looks forward to the most distant connexions of things, and moves the whole chain of events, then we may acquiesce in its dispensations, however unfavourable to our private views. Benevolence will rejoice in the belief of God's general goodness, when selfishness murmurs at the disappointment of its own grovelling designs.

Farther—The gospel, which is given to a particular people, is given them for the benefit of other nations—not merely for their own.

The Apostle observes, that the preaching and reception of it in Thessalonica, proved the means of its general diffusion; for from thence sounded out the word of God, through Macedonia and Achaia; yea, in every place the faith of the Thessalonians was spread abroad. He says to the Ephesians, "God who is rich in mercy—hath quickened us together with Christ, that in the ages to come, he might shew forth the exceeding riches of his grace in his kindness to us by Jesus Christ." "He hath made known unto us the mystery of his will, according to the good pleasure which he purposed in himself, that in the dispensation of the fulness of times, he might gather together in one all things in Christ, both

which

which are in heaven, and which are in earth." To the Romans, he fays, " The fall of the Jews," who rejected the Saviour, " was the riches of the Gentiles." The perfecutions which the Apoftles fuffered from the Jews, drove them to other nations, and thus proved the occafion of the general fpread of the gofpel. " But, ¿ How much more their fulnefs ?" The final converfion of the Jews fhall conduce to the ingathering of the fulnefs of the Gentiles. " As in time paft the Gentiles have not believed God, but now have obtained mercy through the unbelief of the Jews," which has occafioned the diffufion of knowledge among them, " even fo alfo have *thefe* not believed, that they through God's mercy to the Gentiles, may finally obtain mercy." The gofpel, which, through the infidelity of the Jews, is come to the Gentiles, will be preferved in the world, and one day be communicated from the Gentiles to the Jews. " Behold, the depth of the riches both of the wifdom and knowledge of God ! How unfearchable are his judgments, and his ways paft finding out! But,

III. We may rife ftill higher in our contemplation of this wonderful connexion of God's works.

As favours to particular perfons may be publick bleffings ; and national bleffings may extend their influence to mankind in general ; fo God's mercies to the human race may operate to the benefit of other intelligences ; as the fun beams, which enlighten the earth, are reflected back to the fkies.

When God fent his Son from heaven to redeem

us

us from guilt and ruin, it was not for our fakes only, but for his name's fake, that the glory of his wifdom, grace and holinefs might be difplayed throughout the whole intellectual world. The angels in heaven praife God for the wonders of his redeeming love to mankind. They give glory to him, that there is on earth peace, good will to men. They defire to look into this aftonifhing fcheme, which, by the publication of the gofpel is opened to *their* view, as well as *ours*. Paul was fent to preach among the Gentiles the unfearchable riches of Chrift, not only to make *men* fee what is the fellowfhip of the myftery, which had been hidden from ages; but alfo to the intent, that *now unto principalities and powers in heavenly places* might be known by the church the manifold wifdom of God. Angels now join with faints in the new fong to him who was flain, and has redeemed us by his blood: And every intellectual and virtuous being, through the creation of God, afcribes, and will afcribe, riches and blefling, and glory and honour to him who fits on the throne, and to the Lamb forever and ever.

REFLECTIONS.

1. Our fubject teaches us, that God's moral government is a fcheme of moft aftonifhing benevolence.

The calamities, which he fends among men, are defigned to promote that virtue and righteoufnefs, on which the happinefs of rational beings depends. His mercies to particular perfons terminate

minate not with the immediate receivers; but, in their operation, run on and spread around, beyond the reach of imagination. Yea, blessings bestowed on the human race, contribute to the improvement and joy of angels.

Under such a government, ¿ Who shall complain? In obedience to it, ¿ Who can but be happy? The Lord reigns; let the earth rejoice, and the multitude of the isles be glad. This is the united voice of the myriads which surround his throne; " Praise our God, all ye his servants; and ye who fear him, both small and great. Give praise, for the Lord God omnipotent reigns. Be glad and rejoice and give honour to him.

2. We learn that benevolence is an essential part of true religion. If the blessings which God bestows on us, are not for our sakes only, but for the sake of others, then we should apply them to the benefit of others, as well as our own. To the nature and intention of God's government we no farther conform, than we act with a regard to his name, in imitation of his goodness, and with a view to the happiness of our fellow creatures, in conjunction with our own. All injustice, avarice, ambition, cruelty, fraud and selfishness, are contrary to the design of God's government, and to the nature of pure religion. The kingdom of God is righteousness and peace, and joy in the Holy Ghost; and he who in these things serveth Christ, is accepted of God, and approved of men.

3. We learn farther, that under all the adversities

sities of life, we have reason to confide in God's care, and submit to his will.

There is, in the works of God, an extensive connexion, which *we* cannot comprehend, but which *his* wisdom perfectly understands. Events, which appear to us adverse, may, in their operation and design, be blessings. Dispensations, which seem to be against us, may be intended for us. No good thing will God withhold from them, who walk uprightly. All things are working together for their good. To know God's will, and stand approved in his sight should be our only solicitude. Secure of his favour, we have nothing to fear. Let us trust in him and do good, and no evil will happen to us. He careth for us; we may cast our cares upon him. He is a faithful Creator, unto him we may commit ourselves in well doing.

4. We learn from our subject the folly and impiety of envy and discontent.

¿ Do you envy the man who possesses a larger portion of earthly good, than yourself? Remember, it is given him, not for his own sake, but for a more general purpose. If he has a larger portion, he has also a greater trust committed to him, and a more difficult part to act. There is more required of him, and he will have a greater account to render. ¿ Is this an enviable situation? You wish for his honour, or his wealth. ¿ Do you wish too for his obligations to discharge, his duties to perform, his accounts to settle, when he shall close his stewardship? No: But still you desire his worldly ly condition. You desire then to have riches and honours for your own sake—to have them without an obligation to do good with them, or render an account for them. ¿ What is this, but to desire the scheme of God's government were changed, or you were made independent of it?—¿ Do you wish that others were free from their obligations to mankind, or their accountableness to God?—If not, ¿ Why should you covet such a situation for yourself?—¿ What advantage is there in earthly things, but as they are means by which you may supply your real wants, relieve the miseries and promote the happiness of those around you, and provide for yourselves treasures unfailing in the heavens?

You look on the superiour condition of another, and are discontented with your own. But why discontented? The abundance given him is not for his sake only: It is for your sake also, if you need it, and Providence sees best that you should receive it. The riches of one are a benefit to many. If he has not that benevolence, which becomes his ability, yet heaven is wise and good. Things are so constituted, that even from the miser's fountain some involuntary streams will run, at which others may drink and be refreshed. Whatever the rich man's heart may be, the God who gave him riches is as kind to others as to him. This man is as really dependent on his fellow men, as the poorest of his neighbours, and can, no more than they, subsist without aid. The variety which we see in men's outward circumstances, is intended ed for general good. A perfect equality would be inconsistent with human happiness. It would put a stop to mutual succour and assistance; to the reciprocation of benefits. It would weaken the springs of industry, and check the spirit of enterprise and invention. It would tend to poverty, rudeness and misery. The bounties of Providence are dispensed with wisdom; and all, though possessed by the sons of men in different measures, tend to the general good. Every virtuous and industrious man draws from the common treasury a share according to his wants. The poor have this; the rich can have no more. Let every man study to be quiet, to do his own business, and to be content with such things as he has.

To conclude: How glorious will God's providential government appear, in the result, when all its designs, connexions and effects shall be unfolded to our view!

Now we see through a glass darkly; then we shall see with open face. Then we shall rejoice in that, which now is matter of complaint, and discern wisdom in that, which now looks like confusion. Let us acquiesce in the ways of God's providence, and submit to the terms of his gospel, and then all things are ours. Whether the world, or life, or death, or things present, or things to come, all are ours, for we are Christ's, and Christ is God's. To him be glory. Amen.

END OF THE THIRD SERMON.

SERMON IV.

The work of Redemption marvellous, but divine.

MATTHEW 21, xlii.

This is the Lord's doing, and it is marvellous in our eyes.

THE work here pronounced marvellous in the eyes of men, is the Redemption of our fallen race by the Son of God, sent down from heaven, appearing in human flesh, dying on the cross, exalted afterward to glory, and exalting believers with him.

This work, faintly exhibited in prophecy, was a subject of admiration; displayed in the actual execution, it was a subject of higher admiration; but its final result in the salvation of believers, will raise to greater height, and spread to wider extent, the admiration of God's manifold wisdom, and unsearchable grace.

However the Redeemer may be despised and rejected now, the day is coming, when he will be glorified in his saints, and admired in all them who believe. The stone, which has been set at nought

nought by the builders, is made, and will appear to have been made, the head of the corner. God has laid in Sion a chief corner stone, chosen and precious; and he who buildeth thereon shall not be confounded. But to many it is a stone of stumbling, and a rock of offence. They who fall on this stone shall be broken; but on whomsoever it shall fall, it will grind him to powder.

The Apostle observes, that the doctrine of Christ crucified for the sins of men, to some is foolishness; but to others it appears to be the power and the wisdom of God.

The scheme of salvation opened in the gospel, all who contemplate it, must acknowledge to be wonderful. And some have thought the wonder too great to be believed. " Mankind," they say, " are an inconsiderable race of beings—probably the lowest in the rational scale. God is perfectly happy and glorious in himself, and cannot be made more or less so by the conduct or the condition of his creatures. ¿ Can it then be thought, that he would take all that concern for men which the gospel represents him to have done; that he would so pity them in their guilt, as to send a *Divine* Redeemer, in a human form too, yea, in the lowest condition of men—would subject him to an infamous death, number him with transgressors, and appoint him a grave with the wicked—would afterward raise him to heaven in this same human body, and there place him at the head of his kingdom to manage the affairs of it for the benefit of believers?

believers ?—¿ Is there in man any dignity or importance which deserves such a singular interposition ?—¿ Are not the means out of proportion to the end ?—¿ Can we see any thing in the whole economy of Providence at all resembling this ?"

Thus the mercy, which appears in the gospel, and which surely ought to recommend it to guilty creatures, has been urged as an objection against the truth of it.

The examination of this matter will lead us to some profitable meditations, and prepare the way for some serious reflections.

1. The wonderfulness of the scheme of redemption, exhibited in the gospel, is a presumptive evidence of its divinity.

The farther it lies beyond the reach of human invention, the more reason is there to believe that it came from God. If it is quite a singular plan, and there is nothing in the whole system of nature that bears a resemblance to it, then there is nothing that could suggest it to the wit of men, or give a hint from which to frame it in the imagination; consequently it must be wholly the contrivance of divine wisdom, and the discovery of divine revelation.

That men are guilty and impotent, is obvious to experience. This has ever been their acknowledgment and complaint. To inform them of this unhappy state, they have not needed revelation. How they may be recovered, is a natural inquiry. But, ¿ Could it, without any intimation, have

have entered into the heart of man, to imagine such a scheme as the gospel lays before us?—If any had been disposed to frame a scheme for the amusement, or deception of their fellow creatures, Could they possibly have conceived so great, so singular a scheme, as the incarnation, crucifixion, and resurrection of the Son of God? Man is indeed an inventive creature; but his invention appears rather in improving on suggestions already made, than in originating things entirely new. The greatest discoveries, which have been made in arts and sciences, are the fruits of some fortunate accident, from which a hint was first taken, and afterward ripened by experiment. But as there could be nothing in nature to suggest the idea of the death of the Son of God for the sins of men, so it is absurd to suppose it a human invention. It can rationally be ascribed only to the wisdom of God.

2. Though, in the works of nature, we see nothing similar to the redemption of man, yet we see great preparation made for him, and great goodness exercised toward him; and hence we may conclude, that he is an object of God's special care.

The provision made for our present accommodation, might as well be said to be disproportioned to the end, as that which is made for our future happiness; for there is at least as much difference in the ends, as there is in the means.

If we consider man in relation to the present life, What is he? He is born, grows up, eats and

and drinks, labours and sleeps, provides him a successor, and soon retires to be seen on earth no more. Yet behold what God has done for him. Here is a spacious world for his habitation; numerous tribes of animals subjected to his dominion; a mighty sun kindled up in the heavens to enlighten and warm him; a vast firmament stretched over his head, and thousands of luminaries scattered through it for his comfort and convenience; the clouds deposite their treasures, and the sun emits its beams to fructify the earth for his support. ¿Is it not strange that such mighty preparation should be made for so inconsiderable and transient a creature as man? Strange it would seem indeed, if his existence ended with his life. But we see, that all this is done for him. Other purposes may probably be answered by these works; but the good of man is one purpose which they evidently answer, and one purpose for which they were certainly designed. *When I consider thy heavens,* says the Psalmist, *the work of thy fingers; the moon and stars which thou hast ordained; ¿What is man, that thou art mindful of him; and the son of man, that thou visitest him? For thou hast made him little lower than the angels, and hast crowned him with glory and honour; thou madest him to have dominion over the works of thy hands; thou hast put all things under his feet, the beasts of the field, the fowls of the air, and the fish of the sea. O Lord, our Lord, how excellent is thy name in all the earth!*

This vast preparation for so small and unworthy

thy a creature, the Pſalmiſt confiders, not as an objection againſt the wiſdom of Providence, but as an evidence of its boundleſs goodneſs.

Now if God has done all this to accommodate man, during the preſent ſhort term of his exiſtence, ¿ Is it incredible that he ſhould do much more for his happineſs in the future, eternal ſtate of exiſtence?—¿ Is the work of redemption more difproportioned to man's importance, as an immortal creature, than the works of providence feem to be, when we confider him only as a mortal creature? The works both of providence and of grace, are marvellous. When we trace them, we meet wonders, which aſtoniſh us. But let us remember, they are the works of God. While we admire the works, let us adore the author, and rejoice in his wiſdom and goodneſs.

3. Though man confidered in relation to this world, may feem but a contemptible creature, yet, confidered in relation to another world, he is a creature of vaſt importance.

Let us contemplate him in this light, and furely it will not appear ſtrange, that a God of infinite wiſdom and benevolence ſhould do great things for his redemption.

Here is a creature formed by God's own hand, infpired with his breath, and endued by him with an intellectual mind. This mind, made for immortality, is capable of continual improvement through all the ages of eternity. Though this creature is now fmall, yet who can conceive the

extent

extent to which his capacity may be enlarged; the dignity to which his nature may be raised; and the degree to which his virtue and happiness may be improved, in some distant period of his existence? Man, considered as a rational and immortal creature, rising and continuing to rise, in the scale of being, for ever, and for ever, has a kind of infinity annexed to him.

¿If one rational and immortal soul is so important, What shall we say of the human race at large? When we view men as mortal, they appear in a diminutive figure; but this mortality, which seems to lessen the importance of the individual, increases the importance of the race; because the race is multiplied by this quick succession. Contemplate the vast number, which composes one generation—consider how soon one generation passes away, and another comes—reflect how many such successions must already have passed—look forward, and think how many more will follow in the unknown ages, that the world will continue—realize that all these beings will exist forever in happiness or misery—that eternal misery is the natural consequence of incurable vice, and that happiness can result only from a holy and virtuous temper—contemplate these things, and then say, ¿ Whether the redemption of mankind was a business too small to be undertaken by the Son of God?—¿ Is not the end to be accomplished so amazingly great, that we may believe a divine Saviour would be employed in the work?—¿ Is

not

not the work too great and arduous to be undertaken by a feebler hand?

When we confider the Saviour as dying for the redemption of a mortal creature, there seems to be a disparity between the means and the end. But when we confider this mortal creature as having an immortal soul, which will exist through eternity in happiness or misery; and confider also, that there are innumerable millions of such creatures, and will be innumerable more of the same kind, and in the same condition; then our views must be altered. It can no longer seem a thing incredible, that God should redeem the world by his Son.

4. We know not but the human race is essentially connected with other parts of the moral world; and their redemption productive of interesting consequences to other beings. And doubtless it is so.

In that part of the creation which falls within our notice, we see a dependence of one thing upon another. If one part was struck out, confusion would immediately follow. We see an easy gradation from the lower creatures to higher, until we come up to man. We are told, that, above man, there are intelligent beings, and that among these there are orders and degrees. The gradation may probably be continued beyond all our conceptions. However we may view the human race, when we confider it by itself, yet if we confider it in its relation to other beings, and to the

the creation of God, we muſt think it to be of infinite importance. Should this link, in the chain of God's works, be broken, the whole order of the ſyſtem might be deſtroyed.

God certainly had ſome wiſe and great end in making ſuch a race: The preſervation of the race, when made, and the redemption of it, when fallen, might, in the plan of God's government, be as neceſſary as its creation.

We are aſſured from ſcripture, that the redemption, though it immediately relates to man, is a work in which other intelligences have ſome concern. Our great Redeemer has all power given him in heaven and earth; principalities and powers are made ſubject to him; the multitude of the heavenly hoſt rejoiced and ſang praiſe at his birth; angels, on divers occaſions, miniſtered to him; they aided him in his perſecutions—ſtrengthened him in his temptations—attended him at his reſurrection and aſcenſion—and are ſubject to him in his kingdom; they learn from the goſpel diſpenſation the manifold wiſdom of God; they join with thoſe who are redeemed from the earth, in ſongs of praiſe to him who ſitteth on the throne, and to the Lamb who was ſlain. The work of redemption is far more important than we are apt to conceive it, when we conſider it only in relation to ourſelves. Though it primarily relates to us, yet we have reaſon to believe, that it is adapted to anſwer other great purpoſes in the moral world. And until we know how

many

many and how great these purposes are, let us not pretend to say, The means are unsuitable or disproportioned to the end. When we enter into another state, new scenes will open; new displays of divine wisdom and goodness will be made. Then we shall see and admire that proportion in the works of God, which now lies beyond our search.

5. When we consider the works of God we should remember what a being he is.

¿ Does it seem strange, that so great a Being should do so much for so small a creature as man? To an Infinite Being all things are alike easy; and the exercises of his power will always be guided by his perfect wisdom. But how perfect wisdom will judge, we can no more determine, than we can comprehend what infinite power can do. Man, small as he is, was formed by God's hand; and a creature which was not too small for him to make, is not too insignificant for him to preserve. There are innumerable creatures below us. These are also the objects of his care. A sparrow falls not to the ground without him. We are of more value than many sparrows. The hairs of our head are numbered. ¿ Will our souls be neglected? A rational soul is of more value than the world.

When we consider the greatness of God, we must remember, that goodness belongs to greatness. In the contemplation of human greatness, we often leave out the idea of goodness, because we see that the thing itself is often wanting. Men of
great

great wealth and power defpife thofe who are placed below them. If we fee much condefcenfion joined with earthly dignity, we admire it as fomething rare. But thefe partial conceptions of greatnefs we muft not apply to the Deity. Goodnefs is his glory, and the exercife of it is his delight.

That man is unworthy of fuch a work as has been done for him, is undeniable; yea, he is unworthy of the daily bounties of Providence. But if the goodnefs of God is equal to the work, then we may believe, that it has been done. As God is an infinite and allperfect being, his goodnefs muft exceed all our thoughts. However our guilt may abound, his grace much more abounds.

We fee and know that God has made kind provifion for our prefent fupport :—¿ May we not from hence reafonably hope, that he has done more for our future happinefs? We feel that we are weak, and need the care of his Providence, and we perceive that we enjoy it. We are confcious too, that we are guilty, and dependent on his grace :—¿ May we not hope for *this* ? The gofpel tells us, that he has fent his Son to redeem and fave us, and given his fpirit to fanctify and preferve us :—¿ Is it not a faithful faying, and worthy of all acceptation ? We are finners, but ftill God loads us with his benefits :—¿ May not his daily bounty encourage our hope in his everlafting mercy ? We cannot have too humble thoughts of ourfelves, nor can we have too exalted thoughts of God.

If he had never revealed his mercy to save us, we could never have been assured how he would deal with us. Mercy is free; it may do for sinners more or less, as wisdom shall direct. The hopes of nature are doubtful hopes. At most they can only say, ¿ Who can tell, if God will be gracious? If human reason, without revelation, could not gain assurance of pardon, much less could it conceive such a method of dispensing pardon, as the gospel discovers. But since the discovery is made, and fully attested by signs and miracles, we have good reason to receive it; and we ought to receive it with gratitude and joy. It is the Lord's doing; let it be marvellous in our eyes.

How great soever the work of redemption is, it is not too great for perfect wisdom to contrive, boundless mercy to adopt, and infinite power to execute. Man, however small, is the creature of God, a rational and immortal creature; and his race is an innumerable multitude. God, whose goodness extends to the brutal tribes, which exist but a few days, may well be supposed to regard such a race as the human, created to exist forever. We see the race to be important; and, in its connexion with other beings, it may be vastly more important than we can conceive; and the work of redemption, though it immediately relates to man, may answer other grand purposes in God's moral government. The works of grace then, though marvellous beyond conception, are rational

tional and credible—rational, as suited to the wants of man, and agreeably to the goodness of God—credible, as revealed in his word, and attested by signs and wonders, and gifts of the Holy Ghost.

It becomes us then seriously to contemplate, and devoutly to admire these works of God; and with thankfulness and joy to take the benefit of them. For our salvation God has marvellously interposed. ¿ Shall we despise his grace, and neglect our salvation?—¿ How then shall we escape? Jesus has offered himself a sacrifice. If we reject this, there remaineth no more sacrifice for sin.

END OF THE FOURTH SERMON.

SERMON V.

The work of Redemption marvellous, but divine.

MATTHEW 21, xlii.

This is the Lord's doing, and it is marvellous in our eyes.

AMONG all the works of God which have come to our knowledge, the redemption of fallen men by Jesus Christ, is by far the most marvellous. Into this the angels desire to look, and from this they learn the manifold wisdom of God.

When we behold the glorious Creator and Governour of the universe, giving his own Son to death, that through him we might live—when we behold this divine Saviour compassed with our infirmities, bearing our sorrows, and dying in our cause—when we behold him, for the suffering of death, crowned with glory, and bringing many to glory with him—we cannot but say, *This is marvellous in our eyes.*

In the contemplation of this work, some have thought it too marvellous to be believed, and have

have made the greatness of it an objection against its credibility.

This objection we have examined; and our examination, while it removes the objection, and confirms our faith in the great and admirable plan of the gospel, suggests to our minds various useful and important reflections.

1. The scheme of our redemption is a subject worthy of our frequent contemplation.

The scheme is wonderful; the more we view it, the more wonderful it appears; and the more wonderful, the more evidently divine; and if it is divine, it demands our attention and regard.

A design so grand in itself, so graciously adapted to human weaknesses and wants, and so clearly manifesting the glories of the Divine Character, will acknowledge no author less than God. All the works of the Lord are great, sought out by them who have pleasure in them. *This* work is peculiarly honourable and glorious. In this he appears gracious and full of compassion. In this he has abounded toward us in all wisdom and prudence. Let this be forever remembered.

Meditation is a rational exercise, and the proper employment of an intelligent being. We have intellectual, as well as animal faculties, and the former as well as the latter ought to be applied to their proper objects. The contemplation of grand and noble subjects swells the soul, enlarges its capacity, exalts its powers, and purifies its affections. No subject can so usefully or agreeably employ

ploy our thoughts, as the work of our redemption; for there is none so great and wonderful, so solemn and awful; none in which we are so deeply interested, and in which the glories and perfections of the Deity are so clearly displayed. If the angels, who need no redemption, desire to look into the plan of *ours*, how much should it engage *our* attention, for whose benefit it was immediately designed!

That we may have more admiring apprehensions of this great work, we must become acquainted with ourselves. The reason why many think of it so seldom, or so indifferently, and discern in it so little wisdom and grace, is their ignorance of their own character, and their insensibility of their own condition. Christ came to seek and to save them who are lost. Had not men been lost, they would have needed no redemption. Until they feel themselves lost, they will not value nor accept redemption. To them, who realize their ruined and helpless state, a Saviour will be precious.

Humility is a necessary preparative for the kingdom of God. The knowledge of ourselves is the ground work of humility. Convinced that we are guilty before God, and condemned by his justice; that we can make no satisfaction to his justice, nor resistance to his power, we shall adore his wisdom and grace in giving a Saviour for us, and laying our help on one, who is mighty to save; we shall admire the compassion of the Saviour

iour in bearing our sins on the cross, that we might live through him; we shall rejoice, that he was delivered for our offences and raised for our justification; that he is gone into heaven to prepare a place for us, and has sent down his Spirit to prepare us for a place with himself.

Men's different apprehensions of the gospel scheme, are chiefly owing to their different views of themselves. The self confident and careless sinner will not submit to it, for he feels no need of it, and sees no excellency in it. The convinced and humbled sinner, realizing his own impotence and unworthiness, admires the salvation of the gospel, and earnestly desires to become a sharer in it. To him the invitations, calls and promises of the gospel, come with peculiar acceptableness.

That we may be better prepared for meditation on this marvellous work of God, we must be conversant with ourselves, search our hearts, try our ways, know our guilt, and learn our weakness. The weary, the hungry, the thirsty, the poor, and the sick, are called to the Saviour, that they may receive relief, comforts and supplies. They who fancy themselves to be full, and in want of nothing, will despise the call: To men of an opposite character it will come as tidings of great joy.

2. Our subject opens to us most glorious and astonishing prospects.

What a marvellous work God has wrought for the redemption of men! The end was certainly ly worthy of the means. The redemption then contains in it something far beyond all our conceptions. How vast must be that happiness, which was purchased by the death of the Son of God! It must be more than eye hath seen, or ear hath heard, or human heart conceived.

Our worldly prospects are low, confined and precarious. This life is short; the good which the world affords is but small, and only suited to the body. To obtain this, our endeavours are of uncertain success; and the little which we obtain is of uncertain continuance. Soon we must relinquish all, and lie down in the dust. Had rational beings nothing more to expect than what this world can give, deplorable would be their condition.

But the gospel opens to us brighter prospects. It assures us, that there is a future life; that the life to come is eternal, and the happiness of it complete. It does not yet appear what we shall be. But to raise our hopes and expectations, let us remember, that we are not redeemed with corruptible things, such as silver and gold, but with the precious blood of Jesus the Son of God. More than this cannot be said. Contemplate the greatness of the price, and you will have some idea of the value of the purchase. View yourselves as rational beings, designed for immortality—as soon to mingle with angels, in the presence of God and the Redeemer—as there continually to grow in knowledge, improve in virtue, rise in dignity, and advance

advance in glory and happiness, through endless ages—as, by and by, to become equal to angels, and, in the remoter periods of your existence, to be raised above the present perfection of angels—view yourselves in this light, and, ¿ Will you not be transported with the prospect before you? ¿ Will you not feel yourselves already on the wing, and elevated far above this earth?—¿ Will you not, from this exalted height, look down with indifference on all the little and lessening glories of the world; and, like the eagle, with strong and steady pinion, bear through this terrestrial atmosphere, full on the sun; rising, and rising, until you reach that glorious rest, which awaits you in yonder world?

3. What a firm and immoveable foundation has the Christian for his faith and hope!

When we consider ourselves as guilty, and the Almighty God as perfectly just and holy, we tremble in his presence. ¿ If thou, Lord, shouldst mark iniquity, O Lord, Who can stand? If thou shouldst contend with us, we cannot answer thee. When our iniquities take hold on us, ¿ How shall we look up?—But we will turn our eyes to the work of redemption. Here we see, that God is gracious and merciful, as well as holy and righteous. Here we see pardon and life purchased by the blood of his Son, for fallen and guilty men. There is forgiveness with him. We will wait for the Lord, and in his word we will hope, for with him is mercy and plenteous redemption. He will

redeem

redeem us from all our iniquities. He who spared not his own Son, but delivered him up for us all, How shall he not with him also freely give us all things? He who has sent his only begotten Son, that we might live through him, will give eternal life to as many as believe in him. His mercy is unto all, and upon all who believe in Jesus, and there is no difference. We cannot imagine, that the all wise and unchangeable God, who, for the salvation of sinners, has performed a work, marvellous in the eyes of all holy beings, will drop his great design, throw aside all that he has done, and leave repenting, believing, hoping sinners, to perish. We cannot imagine, that the God, who has displayed such astonishing mercy in laying the ground work of our happiness, will frustrate the humble expectations of those, who build on this foundation. Thus reasons the Apostle:—" God commended his love toward us, in that, while we were yet sinners, Christ died for us. Much more, then, being now justified by his blood, we shall be saved from wrath by him. For if, when we were enemies, we were reconciled to God by the death of his Son, much more, being reconciled, we shall be saved by his life." Impressed with a sense of guilt, we may confidently repair to that God, who gave his Son to expiate our sins by his death, and who raised him from the dead, and gave him glory, that through him our faith and hope might be in God. There is laid in Sion a corner stone, elect and precious. He who believeth, will not be confounded.

4. Our

4. Our subject reminds us of the great evil of sin, and teaches us the utter inconsistency of a vicious temper with the happiness of rational beings.

What a work God has done for the recovery and salvation of apostate men! Having revolted from him, they could not be restored to the hope and prospect of happiness, without such a divine work, as fills heaven with wonder. The Son of God came down from heaven, took part of our flesh and blood, and offered himself on the cross a sacrifice to God for human guilt. ¿ Could any thing give so striking a demonstration of the contrariety of sin to the will of God, and to the design of his moral government?—We can think of nothing—¿ Had it not been opposite to the nature of God, inconsistent with the happiness of man, and destructive of the beauty and order of the rational world, Can we suppose, any thing like this would have been done?

If you think lightly of sin, look to Jesus suffering on the cross to expiate your guilt, and be convinced of your mistake.

If sin is of such a detestable nature, and ruinous tendency, then entertain not the hope of salvation without repentance.

The gospel tells us, *God would not that any should perish.* At the same time, it tells us, *He would that all should come to repentance.* Without repentance, there can be no salvation. *Christ bare our sins in his own body on the cross, that we, being dead to sin, should live to righteousness.* He shed his blood,

that

that he might redeem us from our vain conversation. He gave himself for us, *that he might purify us to himself, a peculiar people, zealous of good works.* He came *to call sinners to repentance,* and thus to *save them who are lost.* The gospel displays the purity, as well as the mercy of God; and, while it brings us the hope of pardon, it shews the necessity of a renovation of our nature. Christ died to deliver us from the wrath to come; but he delivers us from wrath only in a way of holiness. Notwithstanding all that has been done, still cometh the wrath of God on the children of disobedience.

5. We are taught our obligation to universal benevolence.

The gospel is a plan of benevolence. Here we see the independent Creator exercising his compassion to fallen creatures. Here we see the Saviour coming down from heaven, to accomplish, by his labours and sufferings, the wonderful design which divine wisdom and goodness had formed. Here we see angels rejoicing and giving glory to God, that there is peace on earth, and good will to men. Here we see the richest blessings held forth to the most unworthy creatures. Here we see heaven expanding its gates to receive us, and an eternal weight of glory there prepared for us. The whole scheme of the gospel is goodness and love; and it is perfectly adapted to teach us our obligation, and inspire us with a disposition, to do good, as we have opportunity.

Whoever

Whoever really falls in with the gospel, partakes of that spirit of benevolence, which it exemplifies and inculcates. The man of an envious, malicious, haughty, unforgiving temper, whatever regard he may profess, is, in heart, an enemy to the gospel of Christ. To receive the gospel, is to receive the genius and spirit of it, which is love and good will. That regeneration, which is our preparative for the happiness revealed, is a transformation of our souls into the temper required in the gospel; and of this temper, an eminent and distinguishing part is love. " Be ready," says the Apostle, " to every good work ; speak evil of no man ; be gentle, shewing all meekness to all men. For we were sometimes foolish, disobedient, living in malice and envy, hateful, and hating one another; but after the kindness and love of God our Saviour toward man appeared, he, according to his mercy, saved us by the washing of regeneration, and by the renewing of the Holy Ghost.— Thus we are made heirs according to the hope of eternal life." The change, which the gospel produces, where it takes effect, is a change from a temper of envy, malice and hatred, to a temper of gentleness, meekness, and good will toward all men. This change is effected by the kindness and love of God our Saviour ; not by works of righteousness which we had done, but according to the mercy of God, who through Jesus Christ hath shed forth his spirit abundantly. By this change we become heirs according to the hope of eternal life.

They

They who have seen such an example of love in the Saviour of the world, and have felt the power of his love on their own hearts, will put on, as the elect of God, bowels of mercies, kindness, humbleness of mind, meekness and longsuffering. They will rejoice in the happiness, and sympathize in the miseries of their fellow creatures. They will look with concern on stubborn sinners, who appear to be hastening their own destruction, in contempt of all the grace of the gospel. They will wish the universal spread of true religion, and rejoice in the hope of its future power and prevalence among the nations of the earth. They will pray for all men, knowing, that this is acceptable in the sight of God our Saviour, who will have all men to be saved, and come to the knowledge of the truth.

If the benevolence of the gospel inspires our hearts, we shall not only desire and pray that others may share with us in its blessings, but endeavour, within our sphere, to promote its influence. We shall openly profess it before men, and, by a conversation agreeable to it, shall recommend it to all around us. We shall encourage an attendance on its institutions, not forsaking the assembling of ourselves together, but considering one another, to provoke unto love and good works. We shall regard, with particular attention, the young who are placed under our care; shall lead their tender minds to some just apprehensions of the gospel; shall inculcate on them the tempers

and

and duties which it enjoins, and aid their preparation for that glorious state which it reveals; and great will be our joy, when we see them walking in the truth.

Did the kind and friendly spirit of the gospel generally prevail, how greatly would it diminish the miseries, and advance the happiness of the world! It is the nature of true religion to make men happy. Its work is peace, and its effect is quietness and assurance forever.

6. Awful is the danger of those who reject the gospel.

A way of salvation so marvellous, as this, which the gospel reveals, we may be assured is the only way. They who refuse it, must perish; and marvellous will be their destruction. Hear the Apostle's warning to the contemptuous, unbelieving Jews:—" Know ye, that through Jesus Christ is preached to you the forgiveness of sins; and by him, all who believe, are justified from all things, from which they could not be justified by the law of Moses. Beware therefore lest that come upon you, which is spoken of in the prophets:— *" Behold, ye despisers, and wonder, and perish."*—Ye shall perish wonderfully—" for I work a work in your days, which ye will in no wise believe, though a man declare it to you." As the way of salvation is wonderful, so will be the destruction of those, who despise it. It will be wonderful, as it will come upon them by surprise—will exceed all human apprehension—will be inconceivably
aggravated

aggravated by their abuse of God's grace—will be distinguished, by its severity, from the punishment of other sinners.

A like warning follows our text. Our Saviour tells the Jewish rulers, that in them would be fulfilled the prophecy of the Psalmist:—" The stone, which is rejected of the builders, is made the head of the corner." Though they despised him, and would soon put him to death, yet he was to be exalted to glory, and made the Head of God's moral kingdom. " Whosoever shall fall on this stone, shall be broken." Whoever, through ignorance, prejudice, or an implicit confidence in false leaders, shall stumble at the gospel, will be grievously wounded by his fall, and unless he recovers himself, will finally perish. " But on whomsoever this stone shall fall," after its elevation in the building, as vengeance will hereafter fall, with accumulated weight, on those who continue in unbelief, " it shall grind him to powder." Christ, you see, here makes a distinction between different kinds of sinners; between those who stumble at the stone, and those who despise and reject it. And he makes an answerable distinction in their punishment: The former are wounded by their fall; the latter are ground to powder. There are some heedless, inattentive creatures, who walk on in the way in which they chance to be led, and seldom consider whither they are going, or where their course will end. These are like men, who stumble at the stone. There are
others,

others, who hate the truth and will not come to it; who despise the gospel, and labour to infuse their own prejudices into the minds of others. These are the mad builders, who push away the chief corner stone and set it at nought. The former will meet a punishment proportionable to their guilt: On the latter, wrath will come to the uttermost. The stone, which in contempt, they roll aside, will fall back upon them, and crush them into ruins. Awful will be the doom of the careless—more so that of the avowed enemies of truth. Since God has wrought so great a work for the salvation of guilty men, to them who neglect this salvation there can be no escape. But a still sorer punishment awaits those who tread under foot the Son of God. To them who sin wilfully, after they have received the knowledge of the truth, there remaineth no more sacrifice for sin, but a fearful looking for of judgment, and fiery indignation, which shall devour the adversaries.

Let sinners, invited by the grace, and warned by the terrors of the gospel, flee from the wrath to come, and lay hold on eternal life. ¿ If you reject the Saviour, To whom will you go?—¿ If you refuse the salvation proposed, What other will you find?—As sinners, you are dependent on mercy. The mercy of God is revealed—the terms of it are stated—assistance is offered—patience is waiting—the Spirit of Grace is striving—the day of your probation is hastening to a close.

Know,

Know, in this your day, the things which belong to your peace, before they are hidden from your eyes.

Marvellous is the work which Jesus has done for you.—Let it not be said of you, as was said of the contemptuous Jews—He marvelled, because of their unbelief.

END OF THE FIFTH SERMON.

SERMON VI.

Shepherds glorifying God for the Birth of a Saviour.

A COMMUNION SERMON.

LUKE 2, XX.

And the shepherds returned, glorifying and praising God for all the things that they had heard and seen, as it was told them.

THE birth of Jesus Christ was attended with circumstances of solemn majesty and grandeur, as well as of singular poverty and meanness. His parents were in a low condition, but of royal descent. The place of his birth was a small village, but worthy of notice in ancient prophecy. The apartment was a stable, but attended by angels. The first who received intelligence of his birth, were shepherds in the field; but the heralds, who announced the event, were a multitude of the heavenly host.

Just before the Saviour's birth, an order from the Roman Emperour, that the whole empire should be be numbered and enrolled, obliged all the people to repair to their respective cities. Joseph and Mary, the parents of Jesus, being of the lineage of David, went, on this occasion, to Bethlehem, which is called the city of David. So great was the concourse of people, that persons, in the poor condition of this happy pair, could find no accommodation in the publick houses. They were therefore compelled to seek a shelter in a stable. Here was born that glorious person, who was to redeem a guilty world.

In the neighbouring country, were shepherds attending their flocks: While in their turns they kept the watches of the night, they were suddenly surprised with a light which blazed around them, and the presence of a superiour being standing near them.

The heavenly messenger soon calmed their fears. *Behold*, says he, *I bring you good tidings of great joy, which shall be to all people; for unto you is born, this day, in the city of David, a Saviour, who is Christ the Lord. And this is the sign by which ye shall know him, He is wrapt in swaddling clothes, and lies in a manger.*

Scarcely had he delivered his message, when he was joined by a multitude of the heavenly host, who celebrated the wonderful event in an anthem of praise—*Glory to God in the highest; and on earth peace; good will to men.* Having finished their hymn, they disappeared; they became again invisible; the glory, which shone around, vanished away, and Nature resumed her nightly aspect.

The wondering swains confer together on the unusual scene. They say one to another, *Let us go to Bethlehem, and see the things which are come to pass, and which God has made known to us.* They believed the heavenly message, but to confirm their faith, they went with haste to the place where the infant lay. Here they found the parents, and here they beheld the person of the newborn Redeemer. They saw him lying in a manger, as the angel had described him. The correspondence of circumstances, with the description, put it beyond a doubt that this was the promised Messiah. They returned, publishing the joyful news, and glorifying and praising God for all that they had heard and seen.

We will contemplate *the things* for which, and the *manner* in which, they glorified God, and will intermingle some practical reflections.

I. We will consider the matters for which they glorified and praised God. These were *the things, which they had heard and seen.*

1. They glorified God, that the promised Saviour was now *born.*

They seem to have been some of those pious people, who looked for redemption in Israel. In their rural occupation they enjoyed leisure for spiritual contemplation, and for converse with the book of prophecy. Hence they learned, that a Redeemer was promised to Israel and to the world. Free from that pride and ambition, which possessed the minds of the opulent and great men of the

nation,

nation, they formed more juft ideas of the defign and manner of his appearance. That he fhould be born in fuch humble circumftances, fhocked not their faith, for they were looking, not for temporal grandeur, but for fpiritual falvation.

Worldly affections are oppofite to the genius of Chrift's religion. *How can ye believe,* fays he to the Pharifees, *who receive honour one of another, and feek not the honour which cometh only from God?* They who receive Chrift as their Redeemer and Lord, muft crucify the flefh, and renounce the world. The fimple manners and humble views of the fhepherds, were better fuited to the fpirit of the gofpel, than the profpects and refinements of the great.

2. They rejoiced that this Saviour was born *for them.* The angel fays, UNTO YOU *is born this day a Saviour.*

Confcious of their impotence and unworthinefs, they felt their need of a Saviour, and efteemed it matter of great joy, that he was come to bring falvation to them.

They doubtlefs admired the diftinguifhing grace of God, in vifiting them firft of all with the glorious tidings. While the rich and great were paffed by, humble fhepherds were regarded. Not many mighty, not many noble, are called. Things which are hidden from the wife, are revealed to babes. The pride and parade of courts, are the contempt of angels; but the cottage of the fhepherd is honoured with their prefence. Let no man

man repine at the meanness of his own condition, or envy the superiour circumstances of another. God dwells with humble souls. He has chosen the poor in this world, rich in faith, to be heirs of his kingdom. He fills the hungry with good things, but the rich he sends empty away.

How joyous the message to these humble swains, *A Saviour is born to you !* Every penitent soul may apply the gracious declaration. ¿ Do you perceive your own guilty, helpless condition ?—¿ Are you anxious for deliverance ?—¿ Do you feel your incapacity to effect your own salvation ? Here are tidings of great joy : A Saviour is born— and born to *you*. His gospel is come to you, and the invitations and promises of it are directed to you. He came to save *sinners*—the *chief* of sinners ; to comfort them who mourn ; to bind up the broken hearted ; to ransom the prisoners ; to give sight to the blind ; to bring salvation to the poor. The weary, the thirsty, the naked, destitute and forlorn, he calls to himself, that they may receive rest, refreshment, and every needed supply ; and receive them freely, without money, and without price. Be of good comfort, arise, he calleth thee.

3. The shepherds rejoiced that the Saviour was born for *others*, as well as themselves.

I bring you good tidings, says the angel, *which shall be to* ALL PEOPLE. The heavenly host subjoin. *Peace on earth, good will to men.*

When the good man looks around, he sees the world lying in wickedness. In the hours of serious contemplation, he feels a painful solicitude for his fellow mortals. He considers, that they, as well as he, are soon to quit this transitory scene, and enter on a state of everlasting retribution. He is deeply affected with the thought of that dreadful end, to which multitudes, with little concern for themselves, appear to be hastening. It is, however, a joyful consideration, that a Saviour has been born, and has lived and died for mankind, and that the benefits of his death are of extensive design; that through him pardon is offered without distinction of nation, age or character; through faith of him, the mercy of God is unto all, and upon all who believe, and there is no difference. While he laments that so many nations of the earth are strangers to the Saviour, and among those who have heard of him, so many live regardless of him, he rejoices in the persuasion, that a time is coming, when salvation shall be proclaimed through the world, and meet with general acceptance among a fallen race. In the mean time, he is solicitous to work out his own salvation, and by his example and conversation, to awaken to so important an object, the attention of all around him. By his daily prayers he implores divine grace for those at a distance, whom he has never seen; for his country; for the church of God; for all mankind in the present, and in succeeding ages.

4. The shepherds glorified God for what they had *seen*, as well as what they had heard.

They had seen the Saviour—seen him in the very place and condition in which the angel had described him. They had seen full evidence, that this was indeed the promised Messiah. They had seen in him the accomplishment of the ancient prophecies, which foretold, that he should be born of a virgin, of the lineage of David, in the city of Bethlehem, and in an obscure condition; should grow up as a tender plant, and as a root out of dry ground. The manner of his birth, and the circumstances which preceded it, they doubtless learned in conversation with Joseph and Mary. When they saw the predictions of scripture, and the information of the angel, so exactly verified, they could no longer doubt but this must be the Saviour, who was come to accomplish the great and good things foretold of him.

Happy were they, that they should live in a time, when the Saviour was born, and in a place near the city, which was honoured with his birth—that they should be notified by angels concerning this glorious event—that they should have an opportunity to behold him, pay their honours to him, see the prophecies fulfilled in him, and confirm their faith, by a sight of this wondrous babe, now wrapt in swaddling clothes, and lying in a manger; but ordained to be the Saviour and Lord of the world.

These were the *things* for which they glorified God. Let us now,

II. Consider the *manner* in which they glorified him.

1. They

1. They glorified God by *faith* in the Saviour, whom he had sent.

They believed the heavenly message, that a Saviour was born; they sought him in the place pointed out to them; and when they saw him, they received him with joy.

By faith in the Redeemer, we give glory to God. His first appearance was attended with evidence of his heavenly descent. When he entered on his publick ministry, more full demonstration was given of his mission from God. We have not seen him in the flesh, but his gospel is come to us, in a manner, under circumstances, and with characters, which prove it divine. We have as full evidence for the ground of our faith, as they who lived when Jesus was on earth—much fuller evidence than those shepherds who had only seen him in his infant state. If they, on the first notice of his birth, so readily sought him, and believed in him, How inexcusable are we to reject the great salvation, which began to be spoken by the Lord, and was confirmed by the testimony of those who heard him, by the signs and wonders which were wrought in his name, and by the completion of a series of prophecies uttered from his own mouth and the mouth of his Apostles? If, after all the light which we have received, we reject this Saviour, disbelieve his gospel, and despise the salvation purchased with his blood, we make God a liar, and judge ourselves unworthy of eternal life.

2. They

2. They glorified God by a *ready obedience.*

Being informed by a heavenly meffenger, where the Saviour lay, *they came to him with hafte.* They made no delay, but immediately obeyed the divine intimation.

Faith operates **in a way of cheerful obedience.** ¿ If thefe fhepherds had refufed to repair to Bethlehem, Would you have thought that they believed the tidings fent them ?—¿ If the care of their flocks had now detained them from the Saviour, Would you have imagined that they regarded him more than thefe ?—The faith which produces no obedience, is unprofitable and vain. How many practically deny the Saviour, whom they profefs to honour! You fay, you believe that the Son of God has come into the world, been manifefted in our flefh, died on the crofs, rifen from the dead, and afcended to heaven; that he is able to fave to the uttermoft, and that there is falvation in no other. Thefe indeed are important truths. But, ¿ Do you really believe them ?—¿ Have you repaired to Jefus for falvation ?—¿ Have you received him in all his characters ?—¿ Have you renounced fin and the world ?—¿ Have you chofen his religion, and given yourfelves up to the direction of his gofpel ? Then you believe indeed ; but if not, your faith is but mere pretence.

3. They glorified God by *confeffing* and *fpreading* the Saviour's name. "When they had feen him, they made known abroad what had been told them concerning the child."

They were not ashamed to own him as the Messiah, even in his infant state. They waited not to see what would be the current opinion; they confessed him early; they were the first who acknowledged him in his high character.

You see, that true faith will prompt you to honour Christ before men. ¿ Do you believe that he came to save a lost world, and still do you decline, or neglect to confess him in this character, to dedicate yourself to him, and to attend his ordinances?—¿ Where is your consistency? ¿ Do you delay to profess your faith in him, because others are in a different practice?—¿ Do you wait to see what they will do?—¿ Are you restrained by the apprehension of contempt? ¿ Where is your sincerity? These humble, honest shepherds, waited not for example: They only waited for time to confirm their faith. They would not confess him implicitly, nor fully rely on the word of an angel. They first sought the token, by which the angel's information was to be verified; and when they had found it, they spread abroad the tidings.

4. They glorified God by an *attendance* on the *means* of faith.

The angel who announced the Saviour's birth, gave them a token by which they might know him. *This shall be a sign to you, Ye shall find the babe wrapt in swaddling clothes, lying in a manger.—And they came with haste, and found as he had told them.*

God gave them a particular sign for the confirmation of their faith; and he has appointed standing means to strengthen and enliven ours. Jesus Christ is exhibited to us in his word, in his sanctuary, and at his table. Here we are to seek him, and converse with him, that we may increase our faith and warm our loves. ¿ Had the shepherds refused to see the newborn Saviour in Bethlehem, and to accept the offered confirmation of the angel's word, What would you have thought of them?—¿ Would not such a conduct have been marked with ingratitude, unbelief and contempt?—¿ Will you neglect the more easy means of awakening into exercise, your faith in, and love to, the crucified and ascended Saviour? ¿ Shall his gospel lie by you unread and unregarded?—¿ Shall the doors of his house in vain be thrown open for you to enter?—¿ Shall his table, from time to time, be spread, and this King of Glory take his seat there, and will you turn away your faces, and retire with cold indifference? How unlike are you to these pious swains! ¿ Would you have ran with them from a neighbouring field to Bethlehem, to see your Redeemer in his manger, wrapt in his infant robes? And, ¿ Will you not come to his table to behold him dressed in all the bright ornaments of grace and love—to behold him offering himself a sacrifice to God for your salvation, and stretching forth the arms of his mercy to invite you to his affectionate embraces? The same faith and love, which

winged

winged the feet of the shepherds on their way to Bethlehem, would waft you to the house, where Jesus has appointed to meet you, and place you down at the altar, where he exhibits himself crucified for you.

5. They glorified God with *the voice of praise.*

It is said, They *returned*—returned to their fields and flocks, to the business of their calling: But they returned *praising* God. Their rural occupation could not engross their thoughts. While they attended the duties of their secular calling, their thoughts ran on higher themes. The sight of the Saviour left their minds replete with sentiments of gratitude, admiration and praise. Pious affections and devout contemplations sweetly mingled with their worldly employment. They conversed together on the things which had passed, and they praised God for the wonders they had seen. The main subjects of their private meditation and mutual discourse, were Jesus, and his salvation.

When you have beheld the Lord at his table, return not to the world with unaffected hearts. Suffer not the devout thoughts suggested here, to languish into indifference, or to be lost in earthly cares; nor the warm affections kindled at the altar, to die away as soon as you retire. Continue to glorify and praise the God of wisdom and grace, for the wonders, which you have seen and heard.

Great was God's condescension to the shepherds, in sending them a message by angels: Greater is his

his condescension to our fallen race, in sending them salvation by his Son. This is grace, which angels contemplate with astonishment. ¿Shall we be unaffected? When the Redeemer was born, joy and admiration strung their harps and tuned their voices: On wings of benevolence they flew to bear the happy tidings, and teach mortals how to praise. The multitude of the heavenly host sang, *Glory to God in the highest; and on earth peace; good will to men.* These ministering spirits still visit the churches, and hover around the worshipping assemblies of Christians, though invisible to mortal eyes. ¿If when the Saviour came, they, transported with joy, flew in eager haste to proclaim the news, as what, above all things, should be welcome to guilty mortals, What think you?—¿Are they not astonished to see our ingratitude and indifference?—¿To see in a Christian land the number of professing Christians so small?—¿To see the assemblies in Christ's house so thin?—¿To see so few gathering round his table?—¿To hear our songs of praise to the Redeemer rise with so partial, and so faint a sound? ¿If mere benevolence so deeply interested them in this great event, What must they think, when they see us, whose eternal salvation depends upon it, so indifferent to it—so negligent to secure to ourselves its infinite and everlasting benefits? ¿Shall the air ring with angelick praises for man's redemption, and earth not catch the sound?—The shepherds in the field heard the voice, and

Serm. VI. 97

and felt the devotion—¿ Shall we, under advantages for superiour knowledge and stronger faith, be dead to all sense of gratitude?—¿ Shall we never learn the song of those who are redeemed from the earth?—¿ Shall the fields and cottages of Israel's shepherds be more vocal in the Redeemer's praise, than the churches of Christians?

END OF THE SIXTH SERMON.

SERMON VII.

John leaning on Jesus's Bosom.

A COMMUNION SERMON.

JOHN 13, xxiii.

Now there was leaning on Jesus's bosom one of his disciples, whom Jesus loved.

OUR blessed Lord, having nearly finished his work on earth, and knowing that the time of his death was just at hand, expressed an earnest desire to celebrate the passover once more with his disciples. Preparation being made, according to his instructions, he sat down with them to the feast. This precious season he employed in such discourse as was adapted to their present circumstances. When the first meal was made ready, he, to teach them condescension and love, went round among them, and washed their feet; giving them notice, at the same time, that he should soon be delivered into the hands of his enemies, and be betrayed by *one of them*. This he knew would be surprising intelligence; he therefore

fore communicated it with caution. When he had washed their feet, he said, *Now ye are clean, but not all.* An intimation this, that there was among them one who was not clean, and who had no part in him. He had reference to the traitor; but the disciples did not fully comprehend his meaning. He therefore, a little after, speaks more plainly. *If ye know these things, which I have done, happy are ye, if ye do them. I speak not of you all; I know whom I have chosen: But that the scripture may be fulfilled, He that eateth bread with me, hath lift up his heel against me. Now I tell you before it come, that when it is come to pass, ye may believe that I am he.* This premonition put them on thinking. But that one of his own family should join his enemies, seemed so incredible, that they scarcely yet understood him. While he dwelt on the melancholy subject, his spirit was greatly troubled: But painful as it was, he at length speaks not the matter fully—*Verily I say unto you, that one of you shall betray me.* Struck dumb with horror, *the disciples sat, and looked on one another, doubting of whom he spake.*

Now there was leaning on Jesus' bosom one of his disciples, whom he loved. This, as we learn from the last chapter in this gospel, was John himself. He is often called *the beloved disciple.* At supper he sat next to Jesus, and reclined on his bosom. Peter, seeing John in this attitude, beckoned to him, that he should ask Jesus, which was the disciple of whom he spake. John then lying on Jesus's breast,

breaſt, ſays to him, probably in a low voice, *Lord, Who is it?* Jeſus, in the ſame manner, anſwered, *It is he, to whom I ſhall give the ſop, when I have dipped it.*—And *he dipped the ſop and gave it to Judas.* That this converſation between Jeſus and John was unheard by the other diſciples, is evident; for they knew not that Judas was the traitor, until afterward, when Jeſus pointed him out by his dipping his hand with him in the diſh.

The circumſtance of John's leaning on his Lord's boſom at ſupper, is ſeveral times mentioned, and may be ſuppoſed to import ſomething worthy of our notice. Surely it was not by accident that he ſat in that poſture, nor without deſign that it is ſo often marked in the hiſtory.

It will doubtleſs ſuggeſt to us ſome thoughts pertinent to the ſimilar occaſion now before us: And happy the diſciple, who, at this ſupper, ſhall by faith and love, lean on the breaſt of his Redeemer.

1. Chriſt, by admitting this diſciple to lean on his boſom, ſhewed a *ſpecial* and *peculiar affection* for him.

It is obſerved in the text, that he who leaned on his breaſt, was the one *whom he loved.* He loved the others; but this he loved with ſuperiour affection. In the temper and behaviour of John, there was ſomething which recommended him to his Lord's particular eſteem, and entitled him to this endearing appellation, *the diſciple whom Jeſus loved.*

The

The writings of this Apostle shew him to have been a man of a warm and affectionate turn of mind. This sensibility of his heart, and his constancy and fidelity in duty, pointed him out as a person capable of the strictest and most endearing friendship. None of the sacred writers dwell so much on benevolence and brotherly love; introduce the subject so often, or urge the temper with so much earnestness. The argument from which he principally deduces our obligation to love one another, is the wonderful example of love exhibited by Jesus Christ, in giving himself for our sins. As this argument seems ever to be uppermost in his mind, we may conclude, that he felt it to an uncommon degree. None were more strongly affected with a sense of the love of Christ, or had more of the same mind which was in him. That benevolence which operated so powerfully in his own breast, he wished to see transfused through the hearts of all.

As he was distinguished by a kind and friendly disposition, so he shared largely in the love of Christ, and was admitted to special intimacy with him. He was one of the three disciples, who accompanied Jesus, when he went to heal the ruler's daughter—when he ascended into the mountain to display the glory of his transfiguration—when he retired to the garden for prayer, just before his crucifixion. This was the disciple to whom he, on the cross, committed the care of his aged mother. He placed particular confidence in John, as one who would faithfully execute the tender charge.

Every sincere Christian is an object of the Redeemer's love. But some are admitted nearer to him than others. His love is not, like human affection, arbitrary and capricious; it is guided by a clear discernment of the comparative degrees of holiness in his different disciples. As the graces of religion, especially the more amiable graces of humility, meekness, condescension, constancy, fidelity and benevolence, abound in them, they share more largely in his approbation and regard. We are often attached to persons by things foreign to their character; by the comeliness of their form, the dignity of their station, the politeness of their manners, the brilliancy of their wit, the pleasantness of their natural temper, or the elegance of their dress and appearance. But these are circumstances on which the love of Christ will never turn. It is real virtue and righteousness, rectitude of heart, and purity of life, which entitle us to his esteem. The more we have of that mind which was in him, the greater and stronger interest have we in his friendship and regard.

John was highly honoured in being the disciple whom Jesus loved. But let us remember, that the same temper which was so pleasing to Jesus in this disciple, will equally meet his approbation wherever it is found.

2. John's leaning on Jesus's bosom, denotes *intimacy* and *familiarity*.

Between Christ and his other disciples there was an endearing friendship. He allowed them near access to him, and communicated to them many things, which he imparted not to the world. He says, *I call you not servants, for the servant knoweth not what his Lord doth; but I have called you friends, for all things which I have heard of my Father, I have made known unto you.* To them he expounded in private many things, which he had publickly delivered in parables. To them he foretold many events, of which he gave no general notice. To them he opened the mysteries of the kingdom of God, before he saw fit to reveal them to the multitude. He admitted them to join with him in his prayers. He often retired with them for devotion, and they well knew the place whither he usually resorted. With them he celebrated the last passover, and the first supper. He conversed with them freely, attended to their inquiries, and resolved their doubts. Thus familiar was he with them all. But John enjoyed a peculiar intimacy. While they sat at the passover, he took his seat by Jesus's side, and reclined on his bosom: And in this nearness to his Lord, he enjoyed a converse which was unknown to his brethren.

When Christ testified to them, saying, *One of you shall betray me,* they knew not whom he meant. Peter beckoned to John, to ask him who the traitor was. His beckoning to John on this occasion, is an evidence that John had, before now, enjoyed special intimacy and freedom with his master. John asked him, of whom he spake this. Jesus said, *It is he to whom I shall give the sop,*

sop, when I have dipped it. This conversation was not heard by the other disciples. John was the first who knew Judas to be the traitor—the first who was relieved from the torturing anxiety, lest he himself were the unhappy man. When Christ had given Judas the sop, he said to him, *What thou dost, do quickly.* To what intent he spake this, none at the table knew, except John. Some of them thought, that, because Judas had the bag, Christ meant that he should go and buy the things which were necessary for the seven ensuing days of the feast; or that he should give something to the poor, as was customary at the time of the passover. As Christ's general premonition had pointed out no particular person, they were exceeding sorrowful, and began, each for himself, to inquire, ¿ *Lord, Is it I?*—¿ *Lord, Is it I?* Jesus now distinguishes the traitor. Judas's hand was in the same dish, out of which Jesus was eating: At this instant Christ says, *It is he, who is dipping his hand with me in the dish.* This was the first sign, by which they knew who should betray their Lord. John only knew this before, by the token of the sop.

We see, that Christ's beloved disciples enjoy the privilege of intimate communion with him. All sincere Christians have this privilege; but some have it in a more sensible manner than others. John, in this respect, was privileged above his brethren. The greater is our love and fidelity to Christ, the nearer access may we find. How happy is the devout, humble, fervent Christian!

Whatever

Whatever are his burdens, he may lean on Chriſt's boſom—may whiſper to him his inward ſorrows and ſecret deſires, and may receive from him kind and ſeaſonable anſwers, in a manner unobſerved by others. This intimacy with the Saviour depends much on our likeneſs to him. If we have in us that temper of love and goodneſs, humility and meekneſs, devotion and heavenlineſs, which was in him, we ſhall know where to find him—we may come even to his ſeat—we may expreſs our deſires in groans and aſpirations, which cannot be uttered—we may hear his ſtill ſmall voice, and feel the gentle illapſes of his grace; while thoſe around us, know not what is paſſing between us and our heavenly friend.

We think John was highly privileged in being admitted ſo near to Chriſt. But our Lord can hear us, as eaſily as he heard him. From his throne in the heavens, he bends down his gracious ear to receive our prayers. He attends to the ſincere, though ſilent language of the heart. His love to pious ſouls he manifeſts by the ſecret communications of comfort, ſtrength and peace. The ſecret of the Lord is with them who fear him, and he will ſhew them his covenant.

3. John, by leaning on Jeſus's boſom, expreſſed *his love to his Saviour.* He choſe to be as near him as poſſible; not only to take a ſeat by his ſide, but to recline on his breaſt.

In the writings of this Apoſtle, love to Chriſt is characteriſtick of a ſincere diſciple. Saint Peter, writing to believers, many of whom had not seen Christ in the flesh, says, *Though ye have not seen him, yet ye love him; and though now ye see him not, yet believing, ye rejoice in him.* Those who *love our Lord Jesus Christ in sincerity, are,* by Saint Paul, pronounced *the subjects of his grace.*

This love is not a sensitive passion, awakened by the imaginary view of a beautiful form, or of some resplendent external glory. It is a calm, rational approbation of that holy character in which the gospel represents the Redeemer—It is a deliberate choice of his doctrines, precepts and example—a grateful sense of his goodness and compassion to a perishing world—an esteem of him, and complacence in him, as the image of the invisible God, the only Mediator, an allsufficient and most suitable Saviour.

This love to Christ will express itself in obedience to his commands—in an imitation of his example—in doing good to his friends—in acknowledgments of his love—in promoting the interest of his kingdom—in frequent converse with him—and especially in a ready attendance on those ordinances, which are the appointed means of communion with him. It was at the ordinance of the passover, which immediately preceded the institution of the supper, that John was seen leaning on his Saviour. The paschal supper prefigured, and the sacramental supper commemorates, the death of Christ. They both had the same general design, with this difference only; one

looked

looked forward to a future event, the other respects that event already past. The gospel supper is appointed in remembrance of Christ's dying love. The Christian, under the influence of love to his Saviour, delights to attend on this institution, that he may have a more lively view of this once suffering, and now exalted friend—may stir up in his heart warmer affections to him, and more firmly fix his resolutions of obedience.

A careless neglect of so kind an institution, indicates a heart dead to pious and grateful sentiments. True love may indeed be attended with such selfdistrust, as will deter some timorous and tender minds from this ordinance. But a careless neglect of, and habitual indifference to this gracious and dying institution of Christ, proves the intire want of love to him.

4. John's posture at supper, bespoke *a grief of heart* under the apprehension of approaching trials. Leaning on the bosom of a friend, is an attitude expressive of *sorrow* and *languishment*.

Jesus had often warned his disciples, that he must suffer death at Jerusalem. As the time drew near, his warnings were more frequent and explicit. He had just intimated to them, that this was the last passover which he should celebrate with them. *With desire*, says he, *have I desired to eat this passover with you, before I suffer*. The thought of the approaching trial deeply affected them all, and especially the beloved disciple. His trouble was increased by the premonition, that

Jesus would be betrayed by one of his own family; and he knew not yet but himself might be the man. Contemplating the sad scene which was before him; compassionating his dearest friend who was soon to suffer in an unexampled manner; and, at the same time, anticipating the solitary and dangerous condition, in which he and his brethren would be left, he sunk into his Saviour's arms, unable to sustain the weight of his sorrow.

As his heart was more affectionate, and his love to Jesus more ardent, than that of his brethren, so his grief under present apprehensions, bore, with peculiar weight on his spirits. This might be one reason, why Christ saw fit to satisfy him before the rest, that he would not be the traitor.

The sincere believer is affected at the consideration of Christ's sufferings. But what especially affects him, in the contemplation of this subject, is, that Jesus suffered for the sins of men, and that he, by his own sins, has crucified the Son of God afresh. When he views the Redeemer dying on the cross, he reflects, "Jesus was wounded for my transgressions, and bruised for my iniquities. He has borne my sins, in his own body, on the tree, that with his stripes I might be healed." The contemplation of Christ's death, awakens in him an abhorrence of sin. While he meditates on this sad scene, his great consolation is a consciousness of his sincere repentance, a hope of his interest in the purchased salvation, and a

vigorous

vigorous resolution, that he will not offend any more.

5. John's leaning on Christ's bosom, expressed *faith* and *confidence* in him. Leaning on another is a posture of reliance. The bride, in the Canticles, is described, as *coming up from the wilderness, leaning on her beloved.*

This was a time of great anxiety and distress. The disciples were soon to see their Lord in the hands of his enemies. But John gives not up his hope. Still he rests on his Saviour's arm, casts his burden on him, and trusts that he will sustain him.

Here is the Christian's refuge. Pressed with affliction, conscious of weakness, burdened with a sense of guilt, he repairs to the Saviour for pardon, consolation and support. In the sufferings of Christ, he sees the great evil of sin, and sees also ground of hope. The same blood, which displays the wrath of God against sinners, manifests also the mercy of God to pardon the believer. While he beholds the suffering Saviour, he reflects—¿ *If these things were done in a green tree, What will be done in the dry ?* But at the same time, his soul gathers hope and confidence from this thought—*He who spared not his own Son, but delivered him up for us all ¿ How shall he not with him also freely give us all things ?*—¿ *Who is he that condemneth ? It is Christ who died.* He glories in Christ Jesus, and has no confidence in the flesh.

6. The

6. The particular *time*, when John leaned on Jesus's bosom, deserves to be remarked. It was while he was sitting with him, *at the paschal supper*.

His attendance with him, at this solemnity, awakened those sentiments of love, faith, gratitude and hope, which he expressed by leaning on his breast.

While he looked back to that great national salvation, which was represented in the passover, we may suppose, his thoughts reached forward to the spiritual salvation typified therein. He saw, at the table, the Lamb of God, who, by his blood, was to take away the sin of the world, and who was prefigured in the paschal lamb. While he ate at this table, his eyes, his faith, and his affection, were fixed on the Redeemer by his side, who was now giving his flesh to be meat indeed, and his blood to be drink indeed, for hungry and thirsty souls.

Such exercises were certainly proper in a disciple, who sat by his Saviour, and ate with him at the same table, in the evening before he gave himself a sacrifice for the sins of the world.

We see then with what meditations and affections we should approach this table now spread before us. This ordinance was instituted in the same evening, when Christ celebrated the last passover with his disciples. It was designed as a memorial of his sufferings. Herein we shew forth his death. We are to attend it in remembrance of him. He sat with his disciples in the
first

first supper. He is now on his throne in the heavens; but his eyes look down on us; his ears are attentive to hear what we speak—what is the voice of our lips, and the language of our hearts. We may here view him as near us. When we take our seats at this table, let us consider, that our Saviour is by our side. Here is his spiritual and gracious presence. Let us sit down, leaning on his bosom. He admits the humble believer near to himself; allows him to speak in his ear—to whisper the complaints and desires of his soul. While we sit by him, let us converse with him, confess to him our sins, lament our unbelief and hardness of heart, seek the supports of his grace, and the pardoning efficacy of his blood. Let our souls go forth toward him in love of his divine excellencies, in thankfulness for his wonderful goodness, and in desires of a nearer conformity to him, and of a clearer interest in his salvation. Under a humble sense of our sins, and of the imperfection of our best works, let us lean on his bosom; for in him we have righteousness and strength. By thus leaning on him, let us gain a more familiar acquaintance with him, and grow in our preparation to be received into his bosom in heaven, and to eat bread with him in the kingdom of his Father.

END OF THE SEVENTH SERMON.

SERMON VIII.

The Spectators of the Crucifixion smiting their Breasts.

A COMMUNION SERMON.

LUKE 23, xlviii.

And all the people, that came together to that sight, beholding the things which were done, smote their breasts and returned.

How exceedingly changeable were the affections and sentiments of the Jews with regard to Jesus of Nazareth! In the course of his ministry, they had expressed the highest esteem of him. They had followed him to the remotest corners of the country, to hear his doctrines and see his works. When he entered into Jerusalem on a publick occasion, they received him with loud acclamations. There was a time, when they intended to take him by force and make him their king. But after they perceived, that his kingdom was not of this world, and that their earthly views were likely to be disappointed, their affection soon turned to resentment and hatred. Now they

they joined in the attempts to deftroy him, and were inftant with loud voices to have him crucified. When the governour declared him innocent, and propofed to releafe him, they fpurned the propofal, and repeated their demand, *Crucify him! Crucify him!*

Their clamours prevail. He is fentenced to death, and carried to execution. As he hangs on the crofs, they feaft their eyes, for a time, with the difmal fpectacle. They pafs by him, wagging their heads, and faying, "Ah! Thou, who deftroyeft the temple, and buildeft it in three days, fave thyfelf, and come down from the crofs." They caft on him a fcornful eye, and fay, "He faved others; himfelf he cannot fave. Let him fave himfelf, if he is a king."

But foon the fcene changes. The fun withdraws his beams, and the heavens, at noon day, are wrapt in darknefs; the earth trembles; the rocks are rent afunder; the repofitories of the dead are difclofed; and the infulted Saviour, commending his fpirit to God, bows his head, and, in exclamations of anguifh, expires.—Look on the multitude now—fee how they appear—They, who before had triumphed in his mifery, are ftruck with deep aftonifhment. One fays, "Surely this was a righteous man." Another fays, "This is the Son of God." *And all the people, who came together to that fight, feeing what had paft, fmote their breafts and returned.* They came to the execution with eager hafte, and bitter zeal.

They

They retired flow, silent, and pensive, with downcast looks and labouring thoughts.

Their smiting their breasts indicated some painful sensations within.

1. It expressed their *conviction* of the innocence and divinity of this wonderful sufferer.

Whatever sentiments they had entertained in the morning, they had now seen enough to extort from them an acknowledgment, that this was a *righteous man*—this was the *Son of God*.

This character Jesus had openly assumed; and with unwavering constancy he maintained it to the last. Through all his trials he never once dissembled it; nor, in the least degree, departed from it, to prevent danger, or avoid death.

Observe his *calmness*. Amidst the rudest and most provoking insults, he discovered no malice or resentment toward his enemies; but all his language and behaviour was mild and gentle. When he was reviled, he reviled not again; but committed himself to him who judgeth righteously.

See his *benevolence*. He attended to the case of his afflicted mother, and commended her to the care of his beloved disciple. He wrought a miracle to heal an enemy wounded in the attempt to seize him. He extended mercy to a malefactor, who was suffering by his side. He implored pardon for those, who were torturing him to death, and urged in their behalf, the only excuse which their case could admit—*They know not what they do.*

Consider

Confider his *humble piety*. He maintained his confidence in God; called him *his* God and *his* Father; and into his hands committed his spirit.

Such distinguished piety, benevolence and constancy, under trials like his, shewed him to be a righteous man—to be more than man.

And heaven itself bare solemn testimony in his favour.

The darkness, which overspread the land, was evidently supernatural. It happened at the full moon, when there could be no natural eclipse of the sun. The total darkness, which, in a natural eclipse, can last but a few minutes, here continued for the space of three hours. At the time of his death, the great curtain of the temple, which separated the most holy place from the common sanctuary, was torn from top to bottom. The earth was thrown into convulsions. The rocks were rent in pieces, and the graves, made in the rocks, were of course laid open. The dead bodies there deposited were exposed to view, and many of them rose after his resurrection.

The concurrence of so many miraculous events at the time of his death, forced on the minds of the spectators a full conviction, that he was the Son of God.

2. Their smiting their breasts was expressive of their *compassion* for this innocent and glorious sufferer.

Their rage, which had been wrought up to the highest strain, now began to subside, and give
way

way to the tender feelings of humanity. They had discharged their malice, they had seen Jesus bow his head in death, and heard him groan his last; and their pity could sleep no longer. It was natural for them to reflect, how barbarously he had been used, and how serene he appeared—how horridly he had been injured, and how meek was his temper—how cruelly they had mocked him, and how fervently he prayed for them—how confidently they had declared him guilty, and demanded his death; and yet how innocent, how worthy of life. Here was the malicious execution of an innocent man.—Here was goodness in its real perfection, suffering death in all its tortures.

Amidst these reflections, which must now rush into their minds, no wonder if compassion swelled too big for utterance—no wonder if, in the anguish of pity, they smote their breasts and returned.

3. This action expressed a *deep remorse of conscience*.

When they had seen such convincing demonstration of the innocence of Jesus, and felt the return of natural compassion, they could not well avoid some reflections like these:—¿ Why did we so clamorously demand his death?—¿ Why so rashly and resolutely urge his crucifixion?—¿ Why did we not consider and examine, before we acted? ¿ Why did we not move for his deliverance; at least accept it, when it was offered?—¿ How could we prefer an infamous robber to this holy

and

and just one?—How shall we forgive ourselves in being so active to procure the death of one in whom no fault could be found?

With such selfupbraiding thoughts, they withdrew from the execution. The declaration of the soldiery, that he was the Son of God, and the deep sense of anguish which the spectators expressed in smiting their breasts, may justly lead us to conclude, that conviction, compassion, and remorse, now laboured in their minds.

We see what a mighty effect the sight of Christ's sufferings had on the multitude: Whether it operated in any of them to a real repentance, we are not informed. But from the great success, which the preaching of the Apostles soon after had among the Jews, it is probable, that what they saw, heard and felt, on the day of the crucifixion, prepared the minds of many for a more ready reception of the gospel.

" A proper view of the sufferings of Christ, in their circumstances and design, has a powerful tendency to move and affect the mind, and dispose it to religion."

To behold this divine Saviour in the flesh, and to see him expire on the cross, was the lot only of those, who lived in his day. But the frequent contemplation of his death, is a matter of so much importance, that he was pleased, just before he suffered, to appoint an ordinance for the purpose of exhibiting his death to our view, and bringing it to our remembrance.

¿ If Christ were now to suffer, in a place near at hand, Should we not choose to attend the scene, sad and mournful as it would be?—¿ Should we not wish to be near him, in his last hours, that we might testify our regard to him, obtain a blessing from him, hear his departing counsels, receive new confirmation of our faith, and feel fresh motives to obedience?—¿ If we would attend his sufferings, Why not attend an ordinance instituted to represent his sufferings?—¿ If it would have been useful to see him on the cross, Why may it not be useful to behold him in this solemnity?—Here he is set forth crucified before our eyes.—¿ Do we turn away from this ordinance? We have little reason to think we should have attended the crucifixion on any higher motive than mere curiosity. If a real regard to him would have invited us to follow him to the cross, the same regard will invite us to come and see him at his table.

This table some of us are now approaching. Let us come with the same seriousness and collection of thought, as if we were coming to the cross itself. Let us attend to the design of this institution, that our minds may be duly affected, and that proper convictions, desires and resolutions, may be awakened.

1. ¿ Have any of you entertained indifferent notions of Christ and his religion?—Come here, and reflect on those characters of divinity, which he exhibited.

When

When you consider the purity of his life—the variety of his miracles—the beneficence of his works—his patience under sufferings—his meekness under injuries—what wonders attended his death—how gloriously he was raised from the dead, and exalted to heaven—and what plentiful effusions of the Divine Spirit soon followed his ascension—you must confess, that he proceeded and came forth from God.

When farther you consider how excellent are the precepts which he gave—how sublime the doctrines which he taught—how perfect the whole system of religion which he left to his disciples—how full of benevolence this religion is—how adapted to enlarge the understanding, exalt the thoughts, elevate the affections, give peace to the conscience, and inspire with cheerful hopes—and how happy mankind will be in a conformity to his example, in a subjection to his commands, and under the influence of his doctrines, you cannot doubt, but his religion is all divine, and infinitely important. If you have before indulged different thoughts, smite your breasts with conviction, and return with juster sentiments, and better resolutions.

2. Here meditate on *the worth of your souls.*

¿ Have you, in the eager pursuit of earthly designs, forgotten your eternal interest, and neglected the salvation of your souls?—Here see what salvation is, what it cost, and how it ought to be valued. You are not redeemed with corruptible things, but with the precious blood of Christ. Think how the Son of God came down from heaven, assumed human flesh, dwelt among men, laboured, suffered and died. ¿ For what end was all this ?—To procure salvation for such as you. How precious is the soul, which could be redeemed by a price no less than this ! How criminal to neglect your own souls, for the redemption of which Jesus was willing to die ! How just, how aggravated the condemnation of those, who despise a salvation so dearly purchased ! You censure the Jews, who, when Pilate offered to release to them Jesus, prefered a murderer before him. ¿ How then will you excuse yourselves, in prefering the pleasures of sin, before that salvation which he has bought with his blood ?

¿ Does not their sin become yours ?—¿ Does not your censure upon them fall upon yourselves ?—Look upon your suffering Saviour. Smite your breasts with conviction of the worth of your souls—return with new resolutions—work out your salvation with fear and trembling.

3. Here behold *the great evil of sin*.

¿ Have you been disposed to excuse it—to make light of it—to flatter yourselves that God will not remember it—that he will admit you to happiness without repentance ?—Look here, and learn another sentiment. Jesus, the Son of God, once suffered and died. ¿ Why ?—It was for sin—not his own, but ours. He was wounded for our transgressions, that by his wounds we might be healed.

healed. He was made fin for us, that we might be made the righteoufnefs of God in him. ¿ Could not fin be forgiven without fo vaſt a facrifice? It is then exceeding finful—odious to God, and dangerous to us. It muſt be forfaken, or we cannot be accepted. The death of Chriſt has opened a way for our pardon, but it has not changed the nature of fin. We can no more be happy in the love and indulgence of it, than if Chriſt had not died. He bare our fins, that we, being dead to fin, fhould live to righteoufnefs. ¿ If Jefus thus fuffered, when our iniquities were laid upon him; What muſt they fuffer, who, continuing impenitent, finally bear their own iniquities?--¿ If thefe things were done in a green tree, What will be done in the dry? Look on a dying Saviour; confider how, and why, he fuffered; fmite your breaſts under a fenfe of guilt; implore forgiving mercy; return with penitent hearts, and refolutions of new obedience.

4. Here meditate on the *wonderful mercy of God*.

You fee the goodnefs of God in his daily providence. You feel his kindnefs in fupplying your wants, healing your infirmities, refcuing you from dangers, and relieving your pains. Great are thefe mercies in themfelves, but fmall in comparifon with *this* which you now fee.

Here you behold his own Son given to be *your* Saviour. Here you fee this Saviour *crucified* for *you*, *fuffering* in *your* ſtead, *dying* for *your* fins, that you might obtain pardon, life and glory. God sent his Son to be a propitiation for your sins, that you might live through him.

Here then is a sure foundation for your faith and hope. ¿ He who spared not his own Son, but delivered him up for us all, How shall he not with him also freely give us all things? Go to God with deep repentance, and be assured, he will not cast you away. The blood, which has been shed, is sufficient to expiate, and the mercy which has been displayed, is sufficient to pardon the most accumulated guilt. Look unto Christ, and be ye saved. Behold him suffering for sinners like you, smite your breasts in deep contrition, and say, *God be merciful to us sinners.* Thus may you return justified, while they, who trust in their own righteousness, and commit iniquity, will be surprised with aggravated condemnation.

5. Look here, and behold an instructive example of *patience* and *resignation.*

We live in a world full of adversity. ¿ Do we censure the ways of God, and think our lot undeservedly severe? Let us turn our eyes to the suffering Saviour—¿ How calm, how patient was he, under trials far greater than ours? He was brought as a lamb to the slaughter; as a sheep before her shearers is dumb, so he opened not his mouth. Yet he suffered, not for his own sins, or for his own benefit, but for *ours.* We are corrected for our own profit. It is only, if need be, that we are in heaviness through manifold temptations. Let us learn of him, who was meek and
lowly.

lowly. When we consider the patience of our Redeemer, let us rebuke our own complaints, and chide our fretful spirits; let us smite our breasts in shame, and learn to be like him.

6. Look to Christ and learn to *despise the world.*

¿ Are your affections set on things below? ¿ Are you anxious for future supplies?—¿ Do you distrust the care of Providence under your worldly straits and embarrassments?—Consider him, who gave himself for you, that he might deliver you from this present evil world. Think how he lived above it; how contented he was in the most humble condition; how he shewed the vanity of the world, by dying on the cross; what blessings his death has purchased for believers; and whither he is gone to prepare for them a place with himself. Consider these things, and smite on your breasts, and say, We are crucified to the world, and the world is crucified to us, by the cross of Christ.

7. Look to Christ, and learn *meekness* and *forgiveness.*

¿ When you meet with injuries, Do your passions rise?—¿ Do malice, and revenge, kindle and glow in your breasts? Think how different was the mind that was in Christ. How calm and gentle was he under the greatest provocations! Far from the thoughts of revenge, he prayed for those who shed his blood. In fervent intercessions for them he employed his dying breath. ¿ Can you, with this example before you, suffer anger to rest in your bosoms?—Come here, behold the most wonderful pattern of goodness and philanthrophy, that ever was exhibited on earth, and then bid every resentful passion be still.—Come here, and forgive your enemies, and pray for them, who despitefully use you.—Come here, with a spirit of peace and love. Be like minded one toward another according to Christ Jesus.

Finally, look to Christ on the cross, and learn how *to die.*

He died with full resignation. When nature recoiled, and wished, if it were possible, to be saved from the dreadful hour, he thought on the cause for which he came to that hour—he thought on his Father's will, and said, " Thy will be done— Father, glorify thy name." He died in the exercise of *benevolence,* in love to mankind, in the forgiveness of, and in intercessions for his enemies. He died, committing his spirit into the hands of the God of truth, and contemplating the joy that was set before him.—As we should live like him, so like him we should die, with resignation to God— with benevolence to men—with forgiveness of injuries—with prayers for our enemies—with faith in God's promises, and with heaven full in our view.

Thanks to our gracious Redeemer, who has given us such an example to conduct us through the paths of life, and to guide us through the valley of death. O send thy good Spirit into our hearts, to form us according to thine amiable pattern—

tern—to direct us in the way of peace—to comfort us in all our troubles—and to strengthen us in our last conflict.—And when it shall be thy will to call us hence, enable us to die like thyself, and receive us to thyself in glory.

END OF THE EIGHTH SERMON.

SERMON IX.

The Works of God, as the King of Saints, great and marvellous.

REVELATION 15, iii.

Great and marvellous are thy works, Lord God Almighty; just and true are thy ways, thou King of saints.

THIS is a part of the song of those, who, having adhered to the purity of religion, in times of great persecution, are now brought forth from their sufferings into a state of security and peace. Taking a review of God's dispensations toward his church, and his judgments upon her enemies, and contemplating the happy, but unexpected result of all, in the advancement of true religion, they are filled with admiration of his wisdom and goodness, and especially of his providence toward his saints, which had long been mysterious, but was now opening to their view. And, in the gratitude of their hearts, they break forth into this hymn of praise, a part of which has been read—*Great and marvellous are thy works—thou King of saints—¿ Who shall not fear and glorify thy name? For thou art worthy. All nations shall come and worship before thee; for thy judgments are made manifest.*

God is here acknowledged in the character of *King of saints.*

His providential kingdom is universal and everlasting. His dominion is without bounds, and without end. All creatures are under his care; all events under his direction. Even ungodly men and apostate spirits, are in some sense, his subjects. Though they obey not the laws of his kingdom, they are under the restraints of his power; and their actions and designs, though tending to mischief and confusion, are overruled to serve the great purposes of his government. "The wrath of man will praise him, and the remainder of it he will restrain." In this sense wicked men are called *his servants*. They are used, in his providence, as instruments to accomplish the purposes of his wisdom.

But he is King of *saints* in a more special and peculiar sense.

They yield a *voluntary* obedience to his government: And he administers his government in an immediate reference to their interest. They are the objects of his peculiar care, and he causes all things to work for their good.

And his works, as *King of saints*, are *great* and *marvellous*. Such indeed are all his works; but more eminently such, are the works which respect his saints.

We

We will illustrate this important and pleasing thought.

I. The work by which the saints are *redeemed*, is great and marvellous.

¿ For the human race, fallen into guilt and ruin, and lying under a sentence of everlasting death, What remedy can created wisdom find?—¿ Who can expiate their guilt?—¿ Who can reverse the sentence of God's law?—¿ Who can ransom them from misery, and restore them to forfeited life? In the view of all wisdom, but the divine, their case must appear desperate; be sure, when it is considered, that a superiour order of beings, having rebelled against their Sovereign, are cast down to hell, and reserved, in everlasting chains, under darkness, to the judgment of the great day.

When we behold the glorious Majesty of heaven, whose justice spared not offending angels, now moved with compassion to fallen men—providing for their recovery—appointing his Son to be their Redeemer—sending him into the world clothed in their flesh—laying on him their iniquities—subjecting him to death as a sacrifice for them, and raising him from the dead to be their advocate; we cannot but adopt the language of the inspired Psalmist—*This is the Lord's doing, and it is marvellous in our eyes.*

Every step in this divine work increases our admiration. It is wonderful that we should be redeemed, when apostate spirits were left unregarded—that a divine person should be constituted the
Redeemer—

Redeemer,—that he should assume humanity and dwell on earth—that, instead of appearing in worldly dignity and power, he should make himself of no reputation—that he should submit to all the pains and dishonours of a most infamous and cruel death—that he should suffer death from the hands, as well as for the sins, of men—that he should make his grave with the wicked in his death—that he should ascend to heaven with the body in which he suffered, and with this body should appear in the presence of God, as a continual advocate for us!

This is a scheme which angels behold with wonder, and which men should contemplate with grateful astonishment.

You will ask, perhaps, Why did God choose such a method for the redemption of men? But tell me first, why he chose to redeem them at all. You will say, He redeemed them because he is merciful. I will add, He redeemed them in *this* method, because he is wise. If we cannot discern the particular reasons of this dispensation, then let us acknowledge, that the counsels of infinite wisdom are too deep to be fathomed by the line of human understanding. The Apostle says, *Christ crucified is to the Greeks foolishness; but to them who are called, he is the wisdom of God; because the foolishness of God is wiser than men, and the weakness of God is stronger than men.*

The humble saint, convinced of his fallen state, feels his need of mercy; and the mercy offered,

he

he gratefully receives. He waits not to explore all the reasons of the gospel plan of grace, before he consents to take the benefit of it. He thinks it enough for him, that mercy is offered to unworthy men. He esteems it a faithful saying, and worthy of all acceptation, that Jesus Christ came into the world to save sinners. He adores that wisdom which has devised so marvellous a plan of salvation, a plan which human wisdom could not have devised, nor can fully comprehend, even now when it is revealed.

Some will ask, ¿ How can we place our dependence on a scheme of redemption, which is to us incomprehensible? But, let me ask, ¿ How can you depend on any thing else, which is beyond your comprehension?—¿ Can you tell, how your clothes warm you, or how your food sustains you? ¿ Can you tell, how the grain, which you sow in your field, springs up and bears fruit?—Will you neglect your husbandry, or abstain from the use of food and raiment, until you can unfold these natural mysteries? If not, then go, and, with humble gratitude, submit to the terms of the gospel—go accept of, and rejoice in, that great salvation which is offered you through the Redeemer, whose name, as well as work, is called *Wonderful*.

If we were to believe nothing, but what we perfectly comprehend, our creed would be very short. If we were to do nothing, until we had discovered all the connexions between causes and effects, our circle of action would be extremely contracted.

God

God governs us as rational creatures. In common life, we act rationally, when we rely on the providence of God, in that course of conduct, which experience shews to be successful. In the religious life, we act rationally, when we receive divine revelation on competent evidence, and trust in God for glory and immortality, in that course of humble obedience, which his sacred word prescribes.

However unsearchable the reasons of the great scheme of our redemption may be, the way in which we are to obtain the benefit of it, is plain and obvious. Repentance toward God, and faith toward our Lord Jesus Christ, are the conditions of salvation proposed in the gospel; and these we find no difficulty to understand. The only difficulty is, the evil heart of unbelief, which departs from God—the hard and impenitent heart, which treasures up wrath against the day of wrath.

The plan of redemption, though great and marvellous, is not so dark and mysterious, but that we discern in it much of the wisdom of him, who formed it. The sufferings of a Saviour for the sins of men, display, in the strongest light, the holiness and justice, the mercy and goodness of God. Nor can we conceive, how the danger of sin, and the encouragement to repentance and virtue, could, in any other way, be so strongly exhibited to sinners. If God spared not his own Son, but delivered him up for us all, How shall he not with him also freely give us all things? But if we we sin wilfully, after we have received the knowledge of the truth, which, through this Saviour, offers pardon to repenting sinners, there remaineth no more sacrifice for sin.

II. Great and marvellous are those works of the King of saints, by which he has *communicated the knowledge* of this plan of salvation.

It was the manifest purpose of God, to bring his subjects to glory in a way of obedience. Man, in his first creation, was placed under a law; obedience to this law was the condition of happiness; by transgression he incurred the penalty of death. It is neither agreeable to the character of God, nor to the nature of intelligent creatures, that they should enjoy happiness in a way of sin; for sin is contrary to the design of God's moral government; and, in its direct tendency, productive of misery.

When man had offended, it was necessary to his repentance, that hope should be set before him; for without the hope of pardon, there can be no sufficient motive to repentance. This hope cannot arise from the law; for law, as such, makes no provision for pardon. It cannot be the result of reason; for reason, uninstructed, cannot conclude that God will forgive. At most, it can but say, as the Ninevites, *Who can tell, if God will be merciful?* And perhaps, without some divine intimation, it would not proceed so far as this. The hope of the Ninevites, feeble as it was, probably might be rather the effect of revelation, than

of

of mere reason; for they had intercourse with the Jews, and visits from the prophets of God. A direct, positive hope of pardon, must come in a way of revelation; for if the offender deserves punishment, justice may inflict it; and whether mercy will interpose to remit the punishment, and on what terms it may be remitted, if at all, none but God himself can determine. God has therefore, in all ages, favoured mankind, at least a part of them, with revelation. And though, in some periods, it has been obscure, it has so far discovered the mercy of God to pardon repenting sinners, as to encourage their humble application to him.

The promise made to the parents of our race, immediately after their lapse, gave a general assurance, that their lives should be spared for a season—that they should have posterity—and that, in some future period, one of their posterity, and this, in a peculiar sense, the seed of the woman, should in a way of suffering, conquer that enemy who had brought sin and death into the world. This promise was, from time to time, renewed in terms more clear and explicit; particularly to Enoch, Lamech and Noah, before, and to the patriarchs, after, the flood. As the term of human life was contracted, revelations became more frequent, because the conveyance of religious knowledge by tradition, grew more uncertain. Repeated communications from heaven were made to Abraham, and the most express assurance given him,

him, that in his family a Saviour would arise, who should bless all the nations of the earth. In this family, the knowledge of the true God, and of a Saviour to come, was preserved, partly by instruction, and **partly** by immediate revelations, until the time of Moses, when a general system of laws and institutions was given from heaven, and committed to writing, for the benefit of the Jewish nation, and others, who would come and join themselves to them. Of these institutions a considerable number were designed to prefigure the Saviour, and point out the way of salvation through him.

In addition to this revelation, God continued **among the** Jews a succession of prophets, who being divinely instructed, often inculcated on them their duty, reproved them for their sins, warned them of judgments, and called them to repentance. And some of them in very plain and explicit terms, foretold the Redeemer, the time and manner of his appearance, his death and resurrection, and the way in which he would bring salvation to a guilty world. The word of prophecy was a light shining in a dark place, until the daystar arose; and as it approached nearer to the grand object, to which it pointed, it grew more bright and clear.

Though the Jewish nation were favoured beyond others, the benefits of revelation were not confined to them. In the patriarchal age, Melchisedek, Abimelech, Job, and several others,

were

were honoured with immediate difcoveries of God's will, and fome of them employed in communicating to mankind the difcoveries, which they had received.

Many of the divine difpenfations toward the Jews, were of fuch a nature, as might awaken the attention of all around them, and give general conviction of the fupremacy of the great JEHOVAH. The annual folemnities inftituted in their law, were adapted, and probably defigned, to excite the inquiry of their neighbours, and diffufe among them the knowledge of religion. The travels of the prophets, and the frequent difperfions of the Jews, contributed much to diffeminate this knowledge among thofe who were remote from the land of Judea. So that revelation was not fo much confined to this one nation, as fome have feemed to imagine. At the time of Chrift's appearance, there was a general expectation of fome extraordinary teacher and reformer to arife in Judea.

Though this divine perfon confined his miniftry chiefly to the Jews, yet he commiffioned his Apoftles to go forth and teach all nations.

He came not only to redeem mankind by his death, but to teach divine truths more fully, and confirm them more ftrongly, than had been done before. After he had finifhed his perfonal miniftry, and returned to the heavenly world, his Apoftles, under the guidance of his Spirit, went forth preaching the kingdom of God, and proving their commiffion and doctrine by figns and wonders, which none could perform, unless God were with them.

The Gospel Revelation stands now established on the firm basis of divine testimony. As it was communicated by inspiration, so it was confirmed by miracles evidently divine. And notwithstanding all the persecutions and changes, which the church has suffered, this revelation, by the wonderful providence of God, is still preserved. By this we may fully learn all, which concerns us to know, relating to the grand scheme of our redemption, and the way to eternal glory. By this, not only are displayed to men the unsearchable riches of Christ, but is also made known to principalities and powers in heaven, the manifold wisdom of God.

Great and wonderful are these works of the King of saints.

When we consider the allglorious God stooping from his throne to converse with sinful men, inspiring some with the knowledge of his will, and the foresight of futurity, empowering *them* to convey this knowledge to *others,* and endowing them with miraculous gifts to confirm the heavenly origin of their doctrine—when we behold him working wonders to awaken the attention of stupid mortals, and bring them to a belief of the truth—when we see not only men, but angels; not only angels, but the Son of God himself, employed in ministering to our fallen race—when we trace the gradual progress of Revelation from

the

the apostacy to the appearance of the Redeemer—when we observe how Revelation, granted to particular persons or nations, was made subservient to the instruction of numbers besides, in distant nations, and remote ages—when we reflect how the knowledge of religion has been preserved, and its total extinction prevented, even in times of great ignorance and superstition—we must admire the divine wisdom and goodness, and say, Marvellous are thy works, O King of saints.

But if God has done so many marvellous works to make known his will to men, some will ask, ¿ Why has he not made it known universally ?— ¿ If revelation is so important, as from these works it seems to be, Why has it, in all ages, been so partial ?

But, ¿ What is that to you ? God has granted you this privilege ; see that you improve it. If others are not favoured as highly, this cannot justify your neglect. Adopt the language and sentiment of the blessed Redeemer, when he rejoiced in spirit, and said, *I thank thee, O Father, Lord of heaven and earth, that, though thou hast hidden these things from the wise and prudent, thou hast revealed them to babes.*

¿ Is Revelation less useful to you, because there are many who have not known it ? Or, ¿ Will you be excusable in your contempt of it, because you have been preferred to them ? No : He who knows his Lord's will, and does it not, will be beaten with many stripes.

Will you queftion the truth of Revelation, becaufe it is confined to but a part of our fallen race? As well might you queftion the reality of human reafon, becaufe fome are deftitute of this; and among thofe who enjoy it, fome poffefs it in a much higher degree than others. Remember that God is fovereign in the diftribution of his favours, and divides them among his creatures feverally as he will. His works are marvellous and unfearchable. Infinite wifdom doubtlefs fees fufficient reafons, why fome, rather than others, enjoy Revelation, though thefe reafons are not obvious to us.

Perhaps the partiality of Revelation is more owing to men's own fault, than is generally imagined. There are few nations, but what have heard of the gofpel. Were there among mankind the fame folicitude to acquire, and to fpread the knowledge of religion, as to improve arts and commerce, the gofpel would be far more generally known. Many nations, now in a ftate of ignorance, once enjoyed Revelation, but have put it from them; and the infidelity of one generation has entailed ignorance on thofe which fuccceded; as we fee, in a Chriftian land, the impiety of the father often corrupts and deftroys the children.

After all, it muft be remembered, that God will finally judge all men according to the talents which they have received. To whom he has committed much, of them he will afk the more.

Some

Some perhaps will be curious to know, ¿ Whether they, who enjoy not the gospel, can be saved? But such curious questions need no answer, because they, in no respect, concern us. The Judge of all the earth will do right. That God who has given a Revelation, can, in such ways as he pleases, communicate himself to those who seek after him; for great and marvellous are his works.

There is another question more important, and more easily answered, ¿ Whether we who enjoy the gospel, can be saved, if we live in opposition to it? This is a question which the gospel has decided. They who put the word of God from them, judge themselves unworthy of eternal life. Behold, ye despisers, and wonder and perish. To such a question the same answer is to be given, as our Saviour gave to one who asked him a similar question—¿ Whether few should be saved? *Strive to enter in at the strait gate.* Be not curious to know, how it will fare with others. Be solicitous for yourselves. Work out your own salvation; for many who enjoy the offers and means of salvation, will, through their own neglect, perish, and be lost forever.

END OF THE NINTH SERMON.

SERMON X.

The Works of God, as King of Saints, great and marvellous.

REVELATION 15, iii.

Great and marvellous are thy works, Lord God Almighty; just and true are thy ways, thou King of saints.

GOD is here acknowledged in the character of *King of Saints*. And his works, as King of Saints, are called *great* and *marvellous*.

These works of God we are humbly attempting to illustrate.

We have shewn,

I. That the work of redemption, which God has wrought, and in which the saints are peculiarly interested, is a marvellous work.

II. That the various revelations, by which God has brought the saints, in the several ages of the world, to the knowledge of this redemption, are also marvellous.

I proceed now to a farther illustration of this grand and solemn theme.

III. The dispensations of God's providence toward the church, in correcting and punishing her

her for her declensions, and in delivering her out of dangers and afflictions, are great and marvellous.

These are the works, to which our text especially refers. When John saw the seven angels, having the seven vials of plagues, which were last to be poured on the earth, before the commencement of the glorious state of the church, then he heard the saints, who had gotten the victory over their enemies, singing this song—*Just and true are thy ways—great and marvellous are thy works, thou King of saints. ¿ Who shall not fear and glorify thy name? For thou only art holy. All nations shall worship before thee; for thy judgments are made manifest.*

The church has, in all ages, been the object of God's peculiar care. Amidst all the revolutions, and all the corruptions, which have been in the world, *this* has been supported, and in it the knowledge of the true religion has been preserved.

When all flesh had corrupted God's way on the earth, Noah was found righteous; and he, with his household, was saved in that general deluge, which destroyed the rest of the human race.

Afterward, when idolatry had almost overspread the world, Abraham was called forth from among his kindred, that in his family the worship of the true God might be maintained. His posterity, when they were exposed to extinction by a famine, were miraculously preserved by a call to settle in Egypt. Here, for several generations, they were kept a distinct people, and then delivered

by

by a mighty hand, and formed into a national and ecclesiastical state in the land of Canaan.

With a view to the maintenance of religion, God, for several hundreds of years, supported and defended this people, to whom he had committed his oracles; while other nations were destroyed, and the remembrance of them blotted out from under heaven.

When their iniquities were grown so great, that God gave them up to the power of the king of Babylon, still they were the objects of his providential care. While other captivated nations were lost among their conquering enemies, the Jews remained distinct; and, after a captivity of seventy years, were restored to their country, and reinstated in their privileges.

To make way for their return, a surprising revolution takes place in Babylon. This monarchy, which had long been the scourge and terror of other nations, becomes subject to the Persian power; and Cyrus, a just and benevolent prince, being exalted to the throne, proclaims liberty to the Jews, and encourages and assists them in rebuilding their ancient city and temple. Amidst all the changes of the great empires of the world, this small people were strangely preserved. And though they were always hated, and often conquered, they were never totally destroyed.

No reason can be assigned, why they were thus distinguished, but because God would not blot out the knowledge of the true religion from the world,

world, nor take from them his kingdom, until the time was come, when it should be given to other nations.

No less remarkable have been the dealings of Providence toward the Christian church.

The religion of Jesus was first preached by a small number of Apostles, who had nothing to recommend them, but the simplicity of their manners, the reasonableness of their doctrines, and the evidence of their miracles; while they were every where opposed by all the prejudices and powers of the world. But yet, under their ministry, the word of God mightily grew and prevailed. In a few years it spread over a great part of the then known world. Christian churches were planted in almost every province of the Roman empire: Yea, in the city of Rome itself, the seat of the empire, there was a church of Christ; and there were saints even in Cesar's houshold.

The Christian church, without worldly wealth, or secular power, lived and gained strength through ten violent persecutions, which under the heathen Roman empire, continued, with some intermissions, for the space of two hundred and forty years.

In the time of Constantine the Great, these bloody persecutions ceased, and the church enjoyed security and peace. It now mightily flourished and prospered. But its prosperity was only for a season. In a few years, gross corruptions of doctrine and discipline crept into it; and even

idolatry

idolatry itself began to rear its head. When idolatry appeared, the spirit of persecution returned with all its former virulence and malignity. They who preserved the primitive purity of religion, were now persecuted by antichristian Rome, as Christianity itself had before been persecuted by pagan Rome. But still there was a number of brave and pious souls, who, in contempt of worldly dangers and sufferings, invariably adhered to the true religion of Christ.

When vice, superstition and ignorance, had widely spread, and nearly established their gloomy dominion in the Christian world, God, by a wonderful providence, raised up some extraordinary men, who, animated with primitive fortitude and zeal, stood forth in the cause of truth, opposed the errors and corruptions of the age, braved the thunders of the Roman pontiff, and the terrors of the civil power, and in a few years carried their reformation to such a surprising extent, that even princes and potentates embraced it, and lent their aid in its support and defence.

Had half the power, which has been employed to subvert the Christian church, been directed against any other people, it would soon have swallowed them up, or worn them out. The greatest and most formidable empires of the world have been overturned from their basis, and utterly demolished. ¿ Where is now the Assyrian empire, once so terrible to other nations ?—¿ Where is the Persian empire, which extended from India to Ethiopia?—¿ Where is the Grecian empire, which boasted the conquest of the world? ¿ Where is the Roman empire, which succeeded, and was the mightiest of them all?—They have all lost their ancient figure and importance. The three former have scarcely a name: The last but little more. But amidst all the convulsions of kingdoms, and changes of empire, the church still lives. It has sometimes been brought low, but never has it wholly ceased. God remembers his ancient promise.—*Though I make a full end of all nations, I will not make a full end of thee—Though I correct thee, it shall be in measure.* He has often punished her for her declensions, but has not utterly forsaken her. He has removed her from place to place, but has never removed her from the earth. *Great and marvellous are thy works, Lord God Almighty: Just and true are thy ways, thou King of saints.*

¿ How manifest is it to observation, that there is a holy, just and wise Providence, which governs the world?

¿ How evident is the divine original of the sacred scriptures, whose predictions and prophecies are continually fulfilling before our eyes, as in other instances, so very remarkably in the preservation of the church?

How conspicuous is God's care for his church in all ages!—And how dangerous must it be to oppose her interest, corrupt her purity, and disturb

turb her peace! *He who toucheth thee,* fays her God, *toucheth the apple of mine eye.*

How deplorable muſt be the ſtate of a people, who, having enjoyed the difpenfation of the goſpel, fuffer it to be loſt in their hands!

How carefully ſhould a people, profeſſing the goſpel, guard **againſt** declenſions **in** religion? *Remember from whence thou art fallen,* fays Chriſt to his churches in Aſia, *and repent and do the firſt works. Be watchful, and ſtrengthen the things which remain. Remember how thou haſt received and heard, and hold faſt and repent. If thou ſhall not watch, I will come quickly, and remove thy candleſtick out of its place.*

From the gracious promiſes of ſcripture, and from the marvellous **works of** Providence, we may be aſſured, that the King of ſaints will maintain his kingdom in the world, as long as the ſun and moon ſhall endure. But of its continuance *with us* we can no longer be aſſured, than while we ſubmit to its laws, **and** attend on its inſtitutions. And if it **ſhould be continued,** we can on no other conditions obtain a perfonal ſhare in its eternal bleſſings. We are warned, that many of the children of the kingdom will be caſt into utter darkneſs, becauſe they have been workers of iniquity; while **other** ſubjects from unknown nations, and from all quarters of the globe, ſhall come and ſit down in the kingdom of God.

With what joyful aſſurance may we look forward to the **happy** period foretold in ſcripture, when

when the kingdoms of this world shall submit to the government of Jesus Christ, the fulness of the Gentiles shall come in, and all Israel shall be saved?

The great and marvellous works of God, in behalf of his church, are sure pledges and earnests of the accomplishment of those promises, which respect her glory and extent in the latter days.

The present condition of the Jewish nation, is a striking evidence both of the truth of the gospel, and of their future incorporation with the Christian church. Though they are dispersed among all nations; hated and despised of all mankind; often banished from one place to another, and oppressed where they are; though they no where subsist in a national capacity, and few of them possess lands of their own; yet they remain every where distinct, in respect both of their nation and religion, and have never mingled with their neighbours. They have had every motive, which a people could have, to drop their national and religious distinction; for, on account of both, they have often been oppressed, and always despised; and yet of both they are fondly tenacious. A similar instance never was known. The gospel which has expressly foretold so singular and improbable an event, must be divine. The design of Providence, concerning this people, cannot be doubtful. The time is coming, when they shall turn to the Lord, and be grafted again into his church, from whence they were broken off by unbelief.

We proceed to observe farther,

IV. That

IV. That work, by which God fits and prepares the saints for glory, is great and marvellous.

Mankind, in their fallen state, are represented as dead in trespasses and sins. While they are under the power of a vicious and corrupt heart, they are incapable of enjoying the felicities of God's heavenly kingdom. That change, by which they are made meet for this kingdom, is in scripture called *a work of God*. He begins, and he performs it. Not only the external means of this change are from him, but there is also a kindly operation of his Spirit, which accompanies them, and gives them their efficacy. The Apostle says, *The weapons of our warfare are not carnal, but mighty through God to the pulling down of strong holds.*

To express the greatness of this work, the gospel compares it to a *new creation*, a *heavenly birth*, a *resurrection* from the dead. " If any man be in Christ, he is a *new creature*." " Except one be *born from above*, he cannot see the kingdom of God." " You hath he *quickened*—" " Ye are *risen* with Christ, through the faith of the operation of God."

The conversion of a sinner, is a great work, as it makes in him a *mighty change*.

He is formed to a new temper—is made partaker of a divine nature—has the same mind in him, as was in Christ. He walks in newness of life. Once he walked according to the course of the world, and yielded himself a servant to uncleanness,

cleanness, adding iniquity unto iniquity: Now he yields himself to God, as one who is alive from the dead, and his members instruments of righteousness to God. Once he placed his affections on earthly things; now they ascend to things above. He was once under guilt and condemnation; now he is brought into a state of peace with God, and is made an heir of the heavenly inheritance.

This is a marvellous work, as it is a work of *marvellous grace.*

By grace are ye saved, says St. Paul, *and that not of yourselves; it is the gift of God.* With respect to himself, he says, *I obtained mercy; and the grace of our Lord was exceeding abundant.* When the saint reviews his former guilty life, his stupidity, hardness of heart, unbelief, abuse of privileges, resistance of the Spirit, and opposition to the sentiments and convictions of his own conscience, he admires that grace, which effectually wrought in him to awaken him, and bring him to repentance and newness of life. He says, *By the grace of God I am what I am.* And, *God hath shewn the exceeding riches of his grace in his kindness to me by Jesus Christ.*

This is a marvellous work, as it is wrought in a *marvellous manner.* Our Lord says to Nicodemus, *The wind bloweth where it listeth, and thou hearest the sound thereof; but canst not tell, whence it cometh, nor whither it goeth. So is every one, who is born of the Spirit.*

The *nature* of the change itself is very plain. It is the turning of the heart from the love of sin, to the love of holiness: The effects of it are also easy to be understood. These are putting off the old man with his deeds, and putting on the new man, which is created after God in righteousness and true holiness. But the *manner* in which the Spirit operates to effect this change, is, like other divine operations, wonderful, and, in a great measure, inexplicable. We know not how our own spirits move and actuate our bodies; much less can we explain, how the Divine Spirit influences and directs our minds. But we must believe, that that immense Being, who is above all, through all, and in us all; who compasses us around, and possesses our hearts and our reins, is able to excite in us pious thoughts and resolutions, to work in us holy and spiritual dispositions, to guide and assist us in a virtuous and heavenly course, without suspending the exercise of our rational faculties, or controlling our moral freedom.

This is a great work, as it is effected by *divine power*.

A soul habituated to vice, and opposed to holiness, is called enmity to God. To subdue this enmity and opposition, must be a divine work. The gospel is mighty, *through God*, to the pulling down of strong holds. The word, as the sword of the Spirit, becomes quick and powerful. Sinners are made willing subjects to God, in the day of his power. But though the Spirit works powerfully, it
works

works not mechanically or compulsively, but kindly and rationally, and in a manner adapted to the intellectual mind. We are to work out our salvation, because God works in us. It may be added,

This is a great and marvellous work, as it is *infinitely important.*

The unrighteous cannot inherit the kingdom of God. They must be washed and sanctified by the Spirit of the Lord. To be carnally minded is death: To be spiritually minded is life and peace.

How solicitous should we be to become the subjects of this great work; and to know whether we are the subjects of it?

Let none imagine conversion to be a small and trifling change; or religion to be a careless and superficial business.

Let none be satisfied with any evidence of their conversion, short of an habitual temper of holiness, discovering itself in a steady course of obedience to the gospel of Christ.

Let none delay the work of repentance, under an apprehension, that to accomplish it will always be at their own option, whenever they find occasion. If it is a work in which they are dependent on the grace of God, let them apply themselves to it now, when they have most reason to hope for this grace. There is such a thing as total hardness of heart. The longer the sinner neglects the concerns of religion, the greater is his danger of falling into this awful state. Therefore, seek the Lord, while he may be found, and call upon him while he is near.

V. The

V. The dispensations of God's providence toward *particular saints,* in bringing them to glory, are great and wonderful.

All things work together for good to them who love God. The eyes of the Lord are upon them, and his ears are open to their cry. He not only hears their prayers, but does for them exceeding abundantly above all that they ask or think.

He answers their prayers in ways unknown to them—grants them many favours beyond what they asked, or could even imagine—causes those events to operate for their spiritual good, which seemed to wear a different aspect, and to have a contrary tendency—conducts them along through dangers, which they thought it impossible to escape, and delivers them from many hidden evils of which they had no apprehension, until after they had past them.

He employs his angels as ministring spirits to the heirs of salvation, and directs all the methods of his providence to their ultimate safety and happiness.

When the saints, once arrived to the heavenly world, shall from thence take a review of past scenes, I question not, but they will be filled with thankful admiration of God's great and marvellous works towards them, while they dwelt below. They will then see, how they were delivered from such a danger, rescued from such a temptation, and carried safely above such a snare. They will then see, how such an adversity roused them to a sense of duty, such a disappointment prevented some fatal transgression, such a prayer was answered,

swered, which they thought had been loft in air, such a defire was in mercy denied, and such an event, though ftrongly deprecated, was productive of fubftantial good. They will then fee, how they have been myfterioufly conducted along through this dangerous and enfnaring world, and brought at laft to the realms of fecurity and joy. They will find the truth of the Saviour's promife—*What I do thou knoweft not now; but thou fhalt know hereafter.* It will be no inconfiderable part of their felicity, to fee the myfteries of Providence unfolded, and the intricate fcenes, which once perplexed their reafon, and tried their faith, all unravelled, and made plain to their view. They will then admire the order of thofe providences, which once looked like confufion; the wifdom of thofe difpenfations, which once appeared unaccountable; and the kind intention of thofe divine works, which once, they thought, were againft them. They will then tune their harps to the heavenly fong—*Great and marvellous are thy works, Lord God Almighty, juft and true are thy ways, thou King of faints.*

But the moft furprizing fcene of all, is the glory and felicity of the heavenly ftate into which they have entered.

While they dwell on earth, faith looks up to the fuperiour world, with high and lively expectation. It meditates with pleafure on the image of heaven drawn in the facred pages, and anticipates a fmall portion of the good which is there. It believes,

believes, that the boldest description of language—yea, the loftiest flight of imagination falls far short of the glorious reality. But when they actually arrive to yonder world, How will they be surprised to find the vast disparity between former conceptions and present enjoyments! When they perceive themselves in the immediate presence of the all glorious Jehovah, in the company of the blessed Jesus, and surrounded by congratulating angels and fellow saints: When they feel themselves discharged from their conflicts with sin and temptation, and freed from every perverse and untowardly motion: When they find every virtuous disposition suddenly ripened to its proper perfection; their minds expanding to admit new and vast ideas of God and the works of God; and their spiritual affections now purged from the foul dregs of sensuality and worldly care, and rising aloft in the purest and warmest devotion—¿ What will they say?—¿ With what songs will they express the rapture of their joy? They will know the truth of the Apostle's sentiment—a sentiment, which, under severe trials below, they could scarcely realize. *I reckon that all the sufferings of the present time, are not worthy to be compared with the glory which shall be revealed. These light afflictions, which are but for a moment, work for us a far more exceeding and eternal weight of glory.* Then the great Redeemer will be forever glorified in his saints, and eternally admired in them who believe.

Come

Come then, ye saints, commit all your cares to God. ¿ Why your anxiety about the events of time ?—¿ Why your fears of affliction, poverty and death ?—¿ Why fails your courage, when dangers seem to await you ?—¿ Why sink your spirits, when adversity presses upon you ?—Your God is *King of saints*. Just and true are his ways—great and marvellous are his works. ¿ Who shall not fear and glorify his name? Trust your God, and he will sustain you; call on him, and he will hear you; seek him, and he will deliver you in all your troubles. His grace is with you—his providence watches over you—his angels encamp around you. O taste and see that he is good. Blessed is the man, who trusteth in him. Fear him, ye his saints; for there is no want to them who fear him.

This troubled scene of things will soon be closed. Glory and joy await you in a purer and brighter world. There you will give praise to God for all his works; yea, for many of those works which now cause anguish and grief.

Let it be your only solicitude to walk worthy of him, who has called you to his kingdom and glory. You have set your faces toward heaven; go on with constancy and courage in the path of righteousness and truth, looking forward to the glory which will soon be revealed. Under every affliction and temptation, maintain your confidence and hope; for light is sown for the righteous, and gladness for the upright in heart.

END OF THE TENTH SERMON.

SERMON XI.

God glorified in the Punishment of Sinners.

REVELATION 19. i, ii, iii.

And after these things I heard the voice of much people in heaven, saying, Allelujah, salvation, and glory, and honour, and power, unto the Lord our God. For true and righteous are his judgments, for he hath judged the great whore, which did corrupt the earth with her fornication, and hath avenged the blood of his servants at her hand. And again they said, Allelujah; and her smoke rose up forever and ever.

THIS great whore, which corrupted the earth with her fornication, and which, in the 17th chapter, is called *Babylon the Great, the Mother of Harlots*, is supposed, by interpreters, to be *the Church of Rome*. She had been the chief promoter of idolatry and superstition, which, in the language of scripture, are often stiled fornication and adultery. The 18th chapter describes the destruction of this idolatrous power, and the general lamentation

lamentation, which, on that occasion, should be heard among the nations connected with her. But while those nations mourned, the church of God should give thanks, and heaven itself should join in the praise. In our text the heavenly church is introduced, as uniting with the church on earth, in a hymn of adoration and thanks to the great Ruler of the world, for the happy revolution which he had made in favour of true religion— for the great salvation which he had granted to his suffering servants—and for the righteous punishment which he had inflicted on their implacable enemies.

We will make some observations on this seraphick hymn which has now been read.

I. The number of the heavenly inhabitants is vastly great. John heard the voice of *much people* in heaven.

The angels, who kept their first state, are an *innumerable* company. The saints, who came out of great tribulation, are called *a multitude*, which no man can number. There are *nations* of them who are saved.

If in that period of Christianity, when idolatry and superstition most prevailed, and when the violence of persecution obstructed the influence of religion, there were such multitudes brought to glory, How inconceivably great must be the final number of happy beings, when all who were saved before that period, all who have been saved since, and all who shall be saved in the unknown

known succession of future ages, shall be collected in the heavenly world?

The time marked in the text, is when Babylon the great, or the antichristian church, is totally destroyed. After this Satan is bound a thousand years, pure religion spreads without opposition, the nations walk in the light of God's church, and into it the kings of the earth bring their riches and their glory. If there are much people in heaven at the time pointed out in the vision, how amazing will be the number at the consummation of all things!

It must be pleasing to a benevolent mind to look forward, and contemplate the vast sum of human happiness, which shall ultimately result from the gospel. When we look around, and see errour and vice abounding—many nations destitute of the gospel—among those who enjoy it, many living in direct opposition to it, and more treating it with utter neglect; we feel a melancholy pity for our fellow sinners, who appear to be in great danger for want of the gospel, or in danger still greater by their abuse of it. But our minds are much relieved in contemplating the brighter side of the scene, which exhibits to our view such numbers of the human race, who shall eventually become partakers of the offered salvation. Delightful is the thought, that truth will finally prevail against errour, and virtue triumph over vice. God will gather out of his kingdom all things which offend, and them who do iniquity,

and

and will caſt them into a furnace of fire; and then the righteous ſhall ſhine forth in the kingdom of their Father, numerous as the ſtars, and glorious as the ſun ſhining in his ſtrength.

II. The people in heaven are much employed in the ſocial exerciſes of **devotion**. John heard them calling on one another to " praiſe God," and aſcribe to his name " ſalvation, honour, glory and power."

The ſaints on earth are not entire ſtrangers to this employment. They ſee much of God's glory diſplayed in his works. They behold bright diſcoveries of his purity, goodneſs and wiſdom, in his word. They experience the power of his grace, and the riches of his mercy toward themſelves. And in the contemplation, their hearts are often warmed with gratitude, and their lips are tuned to praiſe. But, compared with the **heavenly ſtate**, this is a ſcene of darkneſs, ſorrow and ſin: Hence prayer, humiliation, repentance and watchfulneſs, make a great part of their work. In heaven it will be otherwiſe. Joy and gratitude will fill every ſoul; thankſgiving and praiſe will ſound through the vaſt aſſembly. They will have clear and diſtinct views of the divine glories and works. The myſteries which here perplex them, will be unfolded to their underſtanding. They will ſee juſtice, wiſdom and goodneſs, in thoſe diſpenſations which now are wrapt in clouds and darkneſs. They will be delivered from the incumbrance of the fleſh, and from the diverſions of

ſenſible

sensible things. They will animate and warm each other by mutual zeal and love. In that numerous assembly there will be no interfering designs, jarring affections, and discordant voices. John heard the voice of much people, and their voice was one. *Praise God—Salvation and glory to him.* ¿ How rarely do we find much people on earth joined together in the same mind, and speaking the same things? In civil society, men have their different worldly views; in religious society, Christians have their various sentiments, for which they contend with too bitter zeal, and too unyielding obstinacy. How often do we see those who have covenanted to walk and worship together, dividing into parties, withdrawing from each other's communion, and judging one another, instead of provoking to love and good works!— ¿ Will it be so in heaven?—No; if it were so, heaven would cease to be itself. Love is there made perfect: It is the life and soul of happiness. There will be different degrees of perfection and glory; but there will be no envy on the one part, or pride and insolence on the other; no unsocial passions, or malignant tongues. All voices will sweetly mingle in the praise of the common Creator and Redeemer; the voices of that innumerable multitude will be as one.

We see then how the worship of God on earth must be performed, that it may rise with acceptance to heaven. It must be performed, as it is in heaven, with social and benevolent affections.

There

There can be no complete happiness without society. Even heaven, if we were to be there in a state of solitude, would lose much of its delight. In society there can be no happiness without union. The saints in glory, are described, as acting with one design, and praising God with one voice. There is no acceptable worship without a spirit of peace and love. We must be like minded one toward another, that we may with one mind and one mouth glorify God. By a temper of love we are to prepare for heaven; and by union in divine worship we are to improve our love. This temper we must ever aim to carry with us into the worship of God; and with a view to strengthen and exalt it, all the parts of worship must be conducted. So capital in the Christian scheme is this grace, that we are directed, above all things, to put on charity—to have fervent charity among ourselves—to love one another with a pure heart fervently. It is by the love of the brethren, that we are to prove to ourselves that we have passed from death to life, and manifest to others that we are the disciples of Christ. While we worship God together in peace and love, we are preparing for the world of love. When we make the worship of God an occasion of disunion and contention, we pervert it to a contrary effect. To them who are contentious and obey not the truth, will be rendered indignation and wrath.

III. Here

III. Here is pointed out to us one principal subject of the heavenly devotion.—" Salvation, and glory, and honour, and power, unto the Lord our God, for true and righteous are his judgments." This hymn of praise is sung to God, in consequence of his judging that idolatrous power, which had corrupted the earth.

The angels and saints in heaven are attentive to the state of the church on earth. They observe the dealings of Providence toward her, give thanks for every interposition in her favour, and from the judgments which God executes, learn more of his righteousness and truth. Heaven is a state of improvement. Knowledge increases there. Every fresh display of divine glory is celebrated in new songs of praise.

Religion on earth is a matter which interests the blest above. Those benevolent spirits rejoice in the diffusion of truth, virtue and happiness, among our race of mortals. They love to see fresh accessions to their own number. There is joy in heaven, when one sinner repents; and greater joy, when religion generally prevails, and multitudes are continually rising to join their happy assembly. When the hundred and forty and four thousand, sealed out of the tribes of Israel, were followed by a great multitude, which no man could number, out of all nations of the earth, John says, he observed, and immediately *these* shouted—*Salvation to God and the Lamb;* and then all the angels, elders, and cherubs fell on their faces before the

the throne, and worshipped God, saying, *Blessing, and glory, and wisdom, and thanksgiving, and power, be unto our God forever.* Such a mighty increase of the church was recognised by a general song of praise in heaven.

The saints give thanks for their own salvation. They admire and adore the love of God, who has called them by his grace, and the love of the Saviour, who has redeemed them by his blood.

They give thanks for each other's salvation; for the conversion of sinners, the prosperity of the church, and the increase of its members.

They praise God for his judgments on the enemies of truth. They are represented in our text, not only as ascribing salvation to God, but also as celebrating the rectitude of his government, in judging them, who had corrupted the earth.

These pure minds are incapable of malice and revenge. They rejoice in the destruction of corrupt and persecuting powers, only as by this the great obstacles in the way of truth are removed, and a more effectual door opened for its general spread and increase. Their joy springs from benevolence. The suppression of those who have corrupted the earth, is the suppression of corruption itself, and the means of advancing the virtue and happiness of the world.

We may observe farther,

IV. The punishment of the wicked in the future world, will be eternal. *Her smoke rose up forever and ever.* There is nothing more plainly declared ed in the gospel, than a future judgment, and the distribution of rewards and punishments. The declarations of the gospel, on this subject, are fully agreeable to the dictates of human reason. There is an obvious difference between virtue and vice; and according to this difference we must suppose the righteous Governour of the World will finally treat his subjects. As there is no visible distinction at present made between the good and the bad, a distinction doubtless will be made in a future state.

Experience teaches us, that virtue tends to happiness, and vice to misery. This is evidently the divine constitution. To suppose that the latter should be made happy, as well as the former, is to suppose, that there is an inconsistency in the divine government, and that the future distribution of good and evil will contradict the settled course of things in the present world.

Reason teaches us to expect a difference. How great the difference will be, reason cannot conjecture—Revelation only can inform us. This opens to our view most astonishing scenes. On the one hand, thrones and kingdoms, honour and immortality, fulness of joy, and an inconceivable weight of glory, are the rewards reserved for the just; and, on the other, darkness, horrour and despair, the agonies of corroding guilt, and the torments of devouring fire, are the portion of a wicked man, from God.

And

And these different states are always, in scripture, represented as eternal. The righteous shall go into *everlasting life;* the ungodly into *everlasting punishment.*

The former we readily believe; for, as we flatter ourselves with the idea of happiness after death, we are willing to believe the happiness will never end. The latter we receive with reluctance, and sometimes with distrust. Every man entertains a secret hope, that if he is to exist, he shall be happy. The conscious sinner intends to repent; he hopes divine mercy will be extended to him at death; and he is willing to believe, that if he should miscarry, there may be an after remedy.

To guard us against such presumption and selfflattery, the scripture has expressed the endless duration of the punishment of the wicked in a great variety of unequivocal terms. Language affords not an expression more strong and emphatical than this in the text. *Her smoke rose up for* EVER *and* EVER. Correspondent to this is the current language of inspiration—They who obey not the gospel will be punished with *everlasting destruction.*—Their worm *dieth not,* and the fire is *not quenched.*—When God gathers the wheat into his barn, he will burn the chaff with *unquenchable fire.*—The unbelieving and abominable shall have their part in the lake which burns with fire and brimstone, which is the *second death;*

the laſt ſtate of puniſhment. There is no intimation of another probation, and a third death for them who abuſe their new trial. To prevent all expectations of this kind, God has ſworn in his wrath concerning the impenitent and unbelieving, that they ſhall not enter into his reſt. For the ſon of perdition, it had been good that he had never been born. Theſe expreſſions preclude all hope of an eternal happineſs to ſucceed a temporary puniſhment in the future world. Were this to be the caſe, unbelievers would finally enter into reſt; and it would, on the whole, be good for them, that they were born.

You will ſay, "An eternal puniſhment is vaſtly diſproportioned to temporary crimes."—But, ¿ How do you know, that crimes are temporary? The act indeed is tranſient; but the effect may be perpetual. ¿ Can you tell, how many you have corrupted by your wickedneſs?—¿ How long the corruption will continue?—¿ To what number of generations it will reach?—¿ How many will carry with them into the other world, the corruptions infuſed into them by your example in this world?—If we are to judge of the duration of the puniſhment by that of the wickedneſs, we can ſet no bounds to it. The ſhort continuance of the action can be no ſtandard for the puniſhment. It is not ſo in human judgments: ¿ Why ſhould it be ſo in the divine? We never think a criminal the more excuſable, becauſe he accompliſhed his villany with diſpatch; nor
will

will this circumstance be an excuse at the bar of God.

Some would persuade themselves, that an endless punishment is not consistent with the goodness and mercy of God. But the same argument might as well prove, that there will be no punishment at all; and if no punishment, then certainly no misery—no unhappiness among any of his creatures. And yet misery, we see, there is in this world. The goodness of God does not prevent all misery; and therefore, merely from his goodness, we cannot conclude that, in another world, bounds will be set to the misery of the incorrigible, or that any abatement will be made from the due reward of their deeds.

If you suppose it is inconsistent with the character of God to make sinners forever miserable, let me ask you, ¿ Whether it is inconsistent with his character to make rational creatures—endue them with moral agency—place them in a state of probation—allow them only one probation—and fix a period for this? If these things can be reconciled to the divine character, you may suppose, that a final abuse of the limited trial will be followed with unlimited punishment. If no other probation is granted, the punishment which follows is endless.

Besides; ¿ Is it inconsistent with God's goodness, to establish a connexion between wickedness and misery? This will not be pretended; for a connexion we see there is. ¿ If vice, without a

mixture

mixture of virtue, univerfally prevailed in this world, Would human life be tolerable? Only fuppofe, then, that wicked men carry with them into another world the vicious difpofitions contracted in this, and you fee, they will of courfe be miferable there. And if they are immortal, their mifery will be endlefs. The queftion then is fimply this, ¿ Whether the juftice and goodnefs of God require him to annihilate finners, in order to put a period to that mifery, which grows out of the inveterate wickednefs of their hearts?

At the clofe of this probationary ftate, we are told, he who is unjuft, will be unjuft ftill; and he who is filthy, will be filthy ftill. ¿ If, under all the means of goodnefs and correction—under all the motives of hope and fear—under the allurement of promifes, and terrour of threatenings, he remains perverfe, and dies in his fins, What room is there to imagine, that in a ftate, where thefe means are to be enjoyed no more, he will acquire a new temper, or feel the love of God fpringing up fpontaneoufly within him? And if his fin remains, his mifery muft continue.

This is then the fituation, in which we are placed. Made for immortality, endued with reafon and moral agency, and fully inftructed in our duty, we ftand accountable to the great Creator. Happinefs and mifery are fet before us— the terms of happinefs are ftated, with every motive to urge our compliance—the path which tends to mifery is ftrongly marked, with every warning

warning to avoid it—all neceſſary helps are offered us in the purſuit of glory—and awful guards are placed againſt our entrance on the path of deſtruction ; or, when we have madly entered, the moſt importunate calls purſue us to remand us back. What would we more ? Our choice muſt decide our fate. If we chooſe the way of death, we deſtroy ourſelves, and our mouths will be ſtopped. To us, with peculiar force, may be applied the words of Moſes to the people of Iſrael, " I call heaven and earth to record againſt you this day, that I have ſet before you life and death, bleſſing and curſing ; therefore chooſe life."

V. Our text plainly inſtructs us, that the ſaints in heaven will glorify God for the eternal puniſhment of the wicked. They ſaid, *Allelujah ; and her ſmoke roſe up for ever and* ever.

This voice of jubilation ſprings not from joy in the miſery of the wicked, abſolutely conſidered ; but from a view of the rectitude of the divine government diſplayed in their puniſhment, and a view of the important ends which it will promote. There is no malevolence in heaven ; none of the upbraidings of malice, the inſults of pride, or triumphs of revenge ; but there is a perfect approbation of the ways of God, and joy in the glorious conſequences which follow from his righteous judgments. Particularly,

1. The bleſt above glorify the holineſs, truth and juſtice of God, manifeſted in the puniſhment

of irreclaimable sinners. They say—*Praise God, for true and righteous are his judgments.*

The day of God's wrath on the children of disobedience, is called a day of the revelation of his righteous judgment. Saints and angels adore his justice in the destruction of the ungodly, as well as admire his mercy in the salvation of believers. They see it to be a righteous thing with him to recompense tribulation to the former, and rest and peace to the latter. He will then be glorified in his saints, and admired in all them who believe. *The saints will judge the world*—approve the judgment of God against a guilty world. They will say, " Great and marvellous are thy works, Lord God Almighty ; just and true are thy ways, thou King of saints. ¿ Who shall not fear thee, and glorify thy name ? for thou art holy."

2. The punishment of the wicked gives the saints occasion to admire God's grace in their own salvation. They sing—*Salvation and glory to God ; for true and righteous are his judgments.* They ascribe their salvation to God ; not to themselves. They take not the glory into their own hands, but render it to him. When they behold sinners in the **regions of** misery, and see the smoke of their torment arising, they offer the incense of praise to the Saviour, who has redeemed them by his **blood** out of every people and nation, and has **made them kings and priests unto God.** Their salvation appears more glorious, when they behold it in contrast with the misery of the guilty ;

as,

as, on the other hand, the misery of the latter is augmented, in seeing the righteous afar off in the kingdom of God, and themselves thrust out.

3. They glorify God for the great and important ends, which are answered by the punishment of the wicked.

We are not to conceive that the merciful God punishes sinners from a delight in their misery. He has declared the contrary.—*I have no pleasure in the death of the wicked, but that he turn from his way and live.* Punishment in the hands of God is always just, and always designed for a reasonable end. The judgments, which he executes on sinners in this world, are not merely because their sins deserve them, but because the wise and benevolent purposes of his government require them. And we may rationally suppose, that there will always be, in the divine government, some great ends to be promoted in this way. We are not to imagine, that when our globe shall be dispeopled, God's moral government will be finished. There are other worlds, and, for aught we know, other probationary beings. We know not how wide the intelligence of the dreadful doom of guilty men may spread through the creation of God, nor how far it may be made a warning to other moral beings. The apostacy and punishment of the angels who kept not their first state are communicated to us, and applied for our warning ; and perhaps, in distant periods of duration, the apostacy of the human race, and the punishment of those who refused the salvation offered them, may be communicated to other beings, and applied for their warning. We know not how far the general happiness may be advanced by the exemplary punishment of the impenitent part of our race. There can be no doubt, that the uses and ends of their awful doom are better known in heaven, than they can be known on earth. Saints and angels certainly see reason to glorify God for his righteous judgments on the guilty. The glorious way of salvation, and the tremendous consequences of neglecting it, are enough for us to know at present. So much we are taught. Let us be wise and improve the instruction.

END OF THE ELEVENTH SERMON.

SERMON XII.

God glorified in the Punishment of Sinners.

REVELATION 19. i, ii, iii.

And after these things, I heard a great voice of much people in heaven, saying, Allelujah, salvation, and glory, and honour, and power, unto the Lord our God, for true and righteous are his judgments; for he hath judged the great whore, which did corrupt the earth with her fornication, and hath avenged the blood of his servants at her hand. And again they said, Allelujah, and her smoke rose up for ever and ever.

THIS is a hymn of praise, sung by the church in heaven, on occasion of the downfal of that idolatrous and persecuting power, which had long corrupted the earth, and oppressed the servants of God.

In our meditations on this hymn, we have observed;

That there is much people in heaven.

That the people there are employed in praising God.

That

That one grand theme of their songs, is God's judgments in this world.

That they glorified God, not only for his judgments in this world, but also for the punishment of sinners in the future world.

A state of future punishment for the impenitent is here plainly supposed, and the eternal duration of it strongly expressed. And when the smoke of their torment arises, the saints and angels are represented as saying—*Hallelujah ; salvation and glory to the Lord our God.* We must not conceive them as rejoicing in the misery of others from malice or revenge; there are no such passions in heaven. They rejoice not in the punishment of the ungodly, considered simply as misery: But they adore the holiness, truth and justice of God displayed in their sufferings. The sight of this awful scene raises their admiration of, and gratitude for, the salvation bestowed on themselves. And as the punishment of the wicked must be supposed to answer some great purposes in God's moral government, so these purposes are better understood in heaven, than they can be here on earth.

On these thoughts, we enlarged in a former discourse. It is proper that we now attend to the practical and instructive uses of a subject so solemn and interesting.

1. It appears that the happiness of the saints in glory will suffer no interruption from a sight of those in misery, who were once dear to them

on earth. They juftify God in the punifhment of thefe, as well as of others.

In the prefent life there is a natural, and a civil connexion between faints and finners. They dwell together in the fame fociety—in the fame vicinity—and often too in the fame family. They are united in their worldly interefts, and in their natural, or contracted relations.

Children are dependent on the parent, and he, in his turn, may be dependent on them. The hufband and the wife, have a common concern in the family, and there ufually is, and always there ought to be, a ftrict union between them. The brethren of the fame houfehold, mutually related, and growing up in familiarity, ftrongly feel for each other. Neighbours and friends, by long acquaintance, free converfation, and reciprocal kindnefs, form a nearnefs little inferiour to brotherhood. In the prefent ftate, it is neceffary it fhould be fo. No man can fubfift alone. None of our defigns can be carried into effect without the concurrence of others. In the feeble ftate of infancy, the impotence of ficknefs, and the decrepitude of age, we muft foon perifh, without the fupport of thofe around us. That we may, with greater facility and promptitude, perform all neceffary offices to each other, the author of our nature has either implanted in us an affection for our relatives and dependents; or fo framed us, that we naturally acquire an affection for thofe,

who

who are cast on our care, and to whom we daily minister.

It is painful to us to behold a child, a brother, or friend in danger and distress; and we hasten to his relief. It gives great anxiety to the godly, when they see one, for whom they have an immediate care, pursuing a course which leads to misery; and they wish to reclaim him. While we live together in the present connexion and dependence, this reciprocal affection is of great utility. Without it we could not subsist. But in the heavenly world, it will be otherwise. Society subsists there; but subsists in a state of perfection. They neither marry, nor are given in marriage, but are as the angels of God. They neither hunger nor thirst any more—are no more subject to pain or danger—and no more need those kinds of service which are so necessary here. There is no more to be done for those in a state of misery; for their state is eternally fixed by God's immutable justice. There is therefore no more use for our *partial* regards to particular relatives and friends. We shall there subsist in a manner quite different from the present—not by families and separate connexions, but in one grand and glorious community, through which is diffused a universal love. Natural and partial affections are swallowed up in benevolence to all holy beings, and in supreme love to God, the most glorious of all beings. The sight then of a child, a brother, or companion, under punishment, will give no more

anguish

anguish to the saint in glory, than if the former relation had never subsisted. They are now no nearer to him than others of the human race. And he has such clear views of God's wisdom, truth, and justice, displayed in the punishment of the obstinate, that he feels a perfect approbation of it. His benevolence is not confined to those, whom once he called by the endearing name of friends— it extends to all the virtuous and good—to all whom he sees to be the objects of God's benevolence. Though he rejoices not in the misery of the wicked, considered simply as misery, yet he rejoices in the great ends for which this misery is intended; to display the glory of God, and promote the happiness of the moral creation. It gives him no disturbance to see the glory of God advanced in those who once were his relatives, more than in others. He is fully convinced that God has laid upon them no more than is right— that the constitution of his government is wise and good—that the world is judged in righteousness, and the most glorious purposes are carrying on in all the divine works. He joins in this song, *The Lord reigns—Let us rejoice and give honour to him.*

2. It appears from our subject, that God will get glory to his name from all his creatures. Even sinners, however useless they may be in their life, will be made useful in their death.

God is glorified in the irrational and inanimate parts of the creation. The heavens declare his glory; the firmament sheweth his handy work—

the

the earth is full of his riches—all his works praise him in the display of his wisdom, goodness and power. Rational creatures are to glorify him, not merely as the irrational, by the silent display of his perfections in their wonderful frame; but by contemplating him in his works—entertaining exalted thoughts of him, and pious affections to him—employing their intellectual powers in his service—proclaiming his praise with their tongues—and by imitating his character in works of righteousness and beneficence to one another. It is in this manner, that they are to glorify him.

But, ¿How great a part of the rational creation deny him this tribute of glory? Vast numbers of the angelick host have revolted from his government, and are pursuing a rebellion against it. The human race have apostatized too. And though he has sent a divine Saviour to recover them, How many refuse to return! How many live without regard to God in the world, insult his authority, and profane his name! How many neglect the great salvation, which is offered them, and trample on the precious blood, by which it was purchased! How many disbelieve, or disregard the gospel of God, spurn his invitations, mock his warnings, abuse his patience, and grieve his Spirit!

If the heathens, who are vain in their imaginations, and change the glory of God into an image made like to corruptible man, glorify him not as God; much more do they, who know his will

and

and yet defpife it, through breaking the commandment, difhonour him. The wicked lives of finners are an infult on the Divine Majefty. If they profefs to know him, yet in works they deny him. They were made to do good; but the imagination of their hearts, and the courfe of their lives is evil continually. Inftead of promoting virtue and happinefs, they are fpreading vice and mifery. It is faid in our text, concerning Babylon— *She corrupted the earth with her fornication.* Every man, who openly avows errour, and boldly practifes vice, is corrupting the earth. By one root of bitternefs many are defiled.

Sinners are now called to repent and give glory to God. If they defpife the call of God's grace, his juftice will exact glory from them in their punifhment. If they will not ferve the intereft of his kingdom by a voluntary obedience, they will be made fubfervient to it by involuntary fufferings. If they will not hear, nor lay it to heart, to give glory to his name, he will fend a curfe upon them, that the world may difcern between the righteous and the wicked.

Rational beings muft be ufeful in fome way or other. They muft anfwer fome end in God's extenfive government. If they refufe to honour him, and to promote the intereft of thofe around them, in their probationary ftate, he will, in the ftate of final retribution, fo difpofe of them, that honour will refult from them to his great and dreadful name, and important ends will be anfwered

fwered in them by his awful power. When they shall be set forth as an example suffering the vengeance of eternal fire, a voice of much people will sound through heaven—*True and righteous are thy judgments, O Lord, for thou hast judged them who did corrupt the earth.*

This thought should deeply impress every heart. Our existence is not an indifferent and trifling matter. It will certainly answer some great purpose in the grand scheme of God's government. The Creator allows us the opportunity and the means of making it forever happy. He assigns us a part to act in the world. In acting this part, we give glory to him, and contribute to the happiness of his creatures. If we rebel against his authority, we must abide the consequence. God will maintain his government, and accomplish the purposes of his wisdom. Though men disobey his laws, he will be glorious in his perfections, and appear righteous in his works.

3. How inconsolable will be the condition of sinners in the future world! They will be excluded from all relief—from all compassion.

Their punishment will appear to all virtuous beings to be entirely just; and the wisdom, righteousness, and truth of God, manifested in it, will be a subject of the songs of heaven.

Many of the troubles of the present life would be insupportable, if they were not alleviated by the compassion and succour of our friends. Their condolence and pity afford us some refreshment
under

under afflictions which they cannot remove. But this small consolation will never reach those who are confined in the regions of darkness. They are suffering under an immutable sentence, and though they call, there will be none to answer. God will shew them no favour. He is a being of infinite goodness, flow to anger—rich in mercy—waiting to be gracious—forward to forgive. But when justice shall take the place of goodness and patience, he will not pity, nor spare, nor have mercy. His anger will smoke against them, and he will separate them unto all evil.

Jesus Christ will no more appear as their intercessor.

The grace of the Redeemer brought him down from heaven to die for guilty mortals. He has suffered, the just for the unjust, that he might bring them to God. He now offers them his salvation with affectionate tenderness, and urges their acceptance of it with an importunity that would take no denial. But when the day of their probation shall expire, the overtures of his love will cease. He will shut up his tender mercies. When once he has risen and shut the door, he will no more regard their calls. Though they plead, Lord, Lord, open to us; he will answer, " I know you not, whence ye are. Depart from me, all workers of iniquity." Because he has called, and they have refused—has stretched out his hand, and they have not regarded, but have set at nought his counsels and reproofs; he will mock,

when

when their fear comes. They shall call, but he will not answer—shall seek, and shall not find him. They shall eat the fruit of their doings, and be filled with their own devices.

The saints will shew no pity. What was spoken to Jerusalem, when for her impenitence she was given over to destruction, may here be applied—*¿ Who shall have pity upon thee?—¿ Who shall bemoan thee?—¿ Or, Who shall turn aside to ask, how thou dost? Thou hast forsaken the Lord, and art gone backward. He has been weary of repenting. His hand is stretched out against thee.* Their hopeless, unpitied misery, is most affectingly represented by the Saviour, in the parable of the rich man, who died in impenitence and infidelity. *In hell he lifted up his eyes, being in torments, and saw Abraham afar off, and Lazarus,* who had in vain sought relief at his gate, *lying in the patriarch's bosom. And he cried and said, Father Abraham, have mercy on me, and send Lazarus, that he may dip the tip of his finger in water and cool my tongue, for I am tormented in this flame. But Abraham said, Son, remember, that thou, in thy life time, receivedst thy good things, and likewise Lazarus evil things; but now he is comforted, and thou art tormented. And besides all this, between us and you there is a great gulph fixed, which cannot be passed.* As obvious reasons why no mercy could be extended to him, Abraham refers him to the justice of God in his punishment, and to the immutable decree, which had made his punishment perpetual. The rich man could not have asked less,

and

and yet this little was denied. There is no room for pity, when the final sentence is passed. Abraham bade him consider, that in his life time he despised heaven, valuing and seeking only the pleasures of sense, which having enjoyed to the full, he could not think it unjust, that by the sentence of God, whose laws he had dared to violate, he was now excluded from those blest abodes, which he had utterly despised. On the other hand, Lazarus had borne the miseries of life with patience, had trusted in God with humble assurance, and had looked forward, with steady hope, to a better state; and therefore his temporary afflictions were now rewarded with everlasting consolations. And as for sending Lazarus to mitigate the severity of his torment, this was impossible, for the different states of the blessed, and the wretched, though in sight of each other, were so divided, as to admit no intercourse.

In the present world, many prayers are made, and many means are used, for the recovery of sinners; and blessings are often granted them in consequence of the fervent petitions, and kind offices of their pious friends: But in the future world, they will enjoy such advantages no more.

The godly parent now warns, exhorts, and counsels his children with affectionate concern. If he sees them still bent on their wicked course, he weeps over them, and supplicates the powerful interposition of divine grace for their recovery. The thought of their eternal destruction is too

painful

painful for him to realize. But the godly parent, in heaven, no more mourns over, or intercedes for, his children suffering for their sins. He justifies the sentence of God by which they are condemned.

Good Christians lament the perverseness, and are grieved for the madness of sinners, whose hearts are full of evil while they live, and who, with thoughtless presumption, are hastening down to the dead. But in heaven they glorify God for his righteous judgment on them, who refused the overtures of his mercy.

How wretched will be their condition, when all their sins, in full weight, fall upon them, and their presumptuous hopes sink under them—when they are cast forth from the presence of God into utter darkness, and there are none to pity them! O that they were wise, that they understood this; that they would consider their latter end!

4. How carefully ought sinners now to apply the assistances which they have, in order to their preparation for future glory. The time is coming, when there will be none to help them.

It is the duty and concern of good men, in this world, to reclaim the wicked from their destructive ways, and save their souls from death.

Ministers are to watch for souls, warning every man, and teaching every man in all wisdom, that they may present every man perfect in Christ Jesus. They are to take heed to themselves and to

their

their doctrine, that they may save themselves, and those who hear them.

Parents are to bring up their children in the nurture and admonition of the Lord, to teach them found wisdom and discretion, guard them against dangerous temptations, and restrain them when they make themselves vile. They can have no greater joy than to see their children walk in the truth, and to look forward, with strong and lively hope, to that glorious day, when they shall appear among the blessed of the Lord, and their children with them.

The aged, by their holy example, and heavenly conversation, are to teach the young to be sober-minded.

Christians are to exhort one another daily, while it is called today, lest any be hardened through the deceitfulness of sin.

These duties, though too much neglected, yet are, in some degree, performed in the Christian world. ¿ Where is the sinner, who can say, he has had none of these advantages—no publick instructions, or private counsels ?—¿ Where is the youth, who can say, he has had no parental admonitions and rebukes ?

You are now under the stated means of salvation; and there are those near you, who would rejoice to assist you in the great work of preparing for another world. There are those, who sometimes offer you their assistance. Consider, that these means can be enjoyed only in this world.

They will cease in another. None will appear to help you there. Advantages, on which your eternal happiness depends, and which can be had only now, ought to be improved with diligence and care. It is the voice of wisdom—*Hear instruction, and be wise, and refuse it not. Blessed is the man, who heareth me, watching daily at my gate, and waiting at the posts of my doors. Whoso findeth me, findeth life; but whoso sinneth against me, wrongeth his own soul.*

Ye who despise instruction and hate reproof— ye who neglect the publick institutions of God's house, or attend them in a careless and indifferent manner—ye who disobey the counsels, and contemn the warnings of parents, and break loose from the kind restraints, which they lay upon you—ye who give indulgence to every evil inclination, and treat religion as a matter of no concern—ye who resolve that you will rejoice in your youth, and that your hearts shall cheer you in the days of health, that you will walk in the way of your own heart, and the sight of your own eyes— know ye, that for all these things, God will bring you into judgment. ¿ Can your heart endure, or your hands be strong, when God shall deal with you? He has spoken it, and will do it. And you will mourn at the last, when your flesh, and your body are consumed, and will say, *¿ How have we hated instruction, and our hearts despised reproof? We have not obeyed the voice of our teachers, nor inclined our ears to them, who instructed us. We*

were

were in almost all evil in the midst of the congregation and assembly.

5. We see the madness of sinners, who, for a transient pleasure, expose themselves to permanent misery.

The wise man looks forward to futurity. He considers what will make him happy on the whole. It is not the enjoyment of today, or tomorrow, of this year, or this life only; it is the happiness of his whole existence, which determines his conduct. He will not pursue a present pleasure, at the hazard of incurring future misery, greater in degree, and longer in duration. For misery, though future now, will be real when it comes. How contrary to this dictate of wisdom is the conduct of wicked men! Some present interest or gratification is the motive which draws them into iniquity; and yet they know full well, that the advantage is momentary, and the pleasure transient; but the consequence of sin, indulged through life, is permanent as their existence, and more dreadful than their imagination can paint. What infatuation is here! Ye men of reason, be astonished at this!

Esau stands marked in scripture, as an example of folly and profaneness. He for one morsel of meat sold his birthright. The indulgence was a single meal—The loss was his birthright. The birthright, once alienated, was gone forever, and the blessing with it, and could never be regained. Afterward, when he would have inherited

ited the blessing, he was rejected, though he sought it carefully with tears. Take heed, lest there be among you any profane person like him.

6. We see the peculiar guilt and danger of those sinners, who seduce and corrupt others. The people in heaven glorify God for his righteous judgments on that idolatrous church, which had corrupted the earth with her fornication.

Zealots in a false religion will be condemned with distinguished severity; for the greater the zeal, the more extensive the mischief.

It is vain to imagine, that the holy God will approve and accept all, who, as some express it, are sincere in their way; i. e. zealous and engaged in the religion which they have adopted, whether true or false. ¿ Who more zealous in their way, than that corrupt body, which, in the text, is characterised by an infamous name?—¿ Who have ever taken more pains, used more arts, and applied more force, to spread their doctrines in the world? And yet we find, that their zeal and engagedness are urged, not as an excuse for, but as an aggravation of, their crimes—not as a reason for a reward, or for the extenuation of their punishment, but as a reason why they should be punished with greater severity. They had corrupted the earth. And when their smoke arose, the people in heaven sang, Allelujah. It is mentioned in scripture, as a mark of consummate wickedness, when men not only do evil, but have pleasure in them who do it. The woes denounced

by

by the Saviour againſt the Phariſees, are chiefly grounded on that falſe zeal, by which they propagated their corrupt opinions, and obſtructed the progreſs of truth.—" Woe unto you, for ye ſhut up the kingdom of heaven againſt men—ye neither go in yourſelves, nor ſuffer thoſe, who are entering, to go in—Woe unto you, for ye compaſs ſea and land to make one proſelyte; and when he is made, ye make him twofold more the child of hell than yourſelves."

How dangerous is it then to corrupt the eſſential principles of religion! God has taught us, what religion is. His goſpel is plain. If we err from the truth, it is through the corruption of the heart. Think not that miſtakes will excuſe you, when the miſtakes themſelves proceed from the love of ſin, not from the want of light. They who fall into ſtrong deluſion to believe a lie, becauſe they love not the truth, but have pleaſure in unrighteouſneſs, will receive a diſtinguiſhed condemnation.

How dangerous is it to deceive and ſeduce others! To become partakers of their ſins! How careful ought we to be, who are teachers of religion, to underſtand for ourſelves, and declare to you, the whole counſel of God! How cautious ſhould the parent be, that he give to his children only good doctrine—ſound wiſdom—not the inſtructions which cauſe to err from the words of knowledge! How watchful ſhould every Chriſtian be, that he ſeduce none into errour or vice—that

by

by no evil communication he corrupt good manners!

Finally, How glorious is that salvation, which the gospel reveals!

It is a deliverance from that awful state, which we have been contemplating. It is a great salvation, purchased at an infinite price. It is an eternal salvation—a salvation which saints and angels celebrate in perpetual songs. Since Christ has died to procure it for us, let us be solicitous to obtain a share in it. By a neglect of it, our future misery will be mightily augmented. Imagine not that your attention to such an object may safely be suspended. When the happiness, on the one hand, is so vast; and the danger, on the other, so amazing, every day's neglect is presumption and madness—every day's neglect adds guilt to guilt, and danger to danger.

Come now, every soul who has heard the warning of God this day—come to an immediate resolution, that you will renounce the guilty path, which leads down to the chambers of death; and with diligence and perseverance will strive to enter in at the strait gate, lest the master of the house soon arise and shut to the door, and ye be excluded in eternal darkness and horrour. Now is the accepted time, and day of salvation. Know, in this your day, the things which belong to your peace. Delay not, lest they soon be hidden from your eyes.

Now

Now our Lord Jesus Christ himself, and God, even our Father, who hath loved us, and sent us the word of salvation, give us everlasting consolation, and good hope through grace—establish our hearts in every good word and work, and grant us to obtain the salvation, which is of Christ, with exceeding joy.

END OF THE TWELFTH SERMON.

SERMON XIII.

Jesus rising early for secret Prayer.

MARK 1, XXXV.

And in the morning, rising up a great while before day, he went out, and departed into a solitary place, and there prayed.

THE morning here mentioned followed a Jewish sabbath, on which Jesus had been very diligently employed in the duties of his publick ministry. It is said, verse 21st, that Jesus, with some of his disciples, whom he had lately called to attend him, *went into Capernaum; and straightway, on the sabbath day, he entered into the synagogue, and taught.* He carefully observed all divine institutions. It was his custom to repair to the synagogue on the sabbath, and there instruct the people, who were assembled for divine worship. His example reproves the carelesness of those, who forsake the assembling of themselves together; and instead of entering into the house of God, do their own ways, and find their own pleasure, on his holy day.

Jesus, seeing in the synagogue a man possessed with an unclean spirit, immediately healed him, to the astonishment of all who were present.

He

He has taught us, that we may do good on the fabbath day. Though we are to ceafe from the common labours of life, yet we are allowed to perform works of mercy to our fellow mortals.

This miracle, fo great in its nature, and performed in fo publick a manner, was immediately fpread around through all the region. The people, who attended the fynagogue worfhip, carried the intelligence of this furprifing work, when they returned to their refpective homes. *And at even, when the fun was fet, they brought unto him all who were difeafed,* **and them** *who were poffeffed with devils. And all the city was gathered together at the door of the houfe where he was.* The Jews thought it not lawful to bring their fick to be healed on the fabbath; but when the fun was fet, and the fabbath was ended, they brought to him their fick from all parts of the city, and he healed them.

After fpending the evening in this important work, he retired to reft. But he allowed himfelf only a fhort repofe. *In the morning, rifing up a great while before day, he departed to a folitary place, and there prayed.*

You will remark,

I. How diligent the Saviour was in the improvement of his time.

Many great and important works had he to do, and he would not loofe the feafon of doing them.

As he took part of our flefh and blood, and was compaffed with our infirmities, he needed reft and refrefhment as well as we. But he fpent

no

no more time in sleep by night, than was consistent with his business by day. When his work called with urgency, he shortened the hours of his repose. He says, *I must work the works of him who sent me, while it is day; the night cometh, when no man can work.*

But, ¿What was the work, which called him so early from his bed, and so constantly employed his wakeful hours?—¿Was it the acquisition of wealth, honour or dominion?—¿Was it the destruction, or subjugation of hostile nations? ¿Was it settling the form and establishing the foundation of a temporal kingdom?—These things were remote from his thoughts. He had neither houses, nor lands, nor any kind of worldly property; nor sought he any. More destitute than the birds of the wood, and the foxes of the mountain, he had not where to lay his head. So distant was he from all ambitious views, that when the people, struck with admiration of his power, would have taken him by force and made him their king, he refused the offer, and hid himself from their search. ¿What work was it then, which so mightily urged his diligence?—It was the salvation of fallen men. The present occasion seemed exceedingly favourable to this great design. There was a most encouraging appearance, which he would by all means improve. His preaching and miracles, on the preceding day, had spread the fame of his wisdom and power, and awakened a general inquiry after him. When

he

he arose and went out, his disciples followed him, and as soon as they had found him, they said to him—*All men seek for thee.* He answered—*Let us go into the next towns, that I may preach there also; for to this end came I forth. And he preached in the synagogues throughout all* **Galilee.** The circumstances of mankind called for his instructions. The present attentive disposition of the people promised an opportunity to do them much good. The time allotted for his ministry was but short; no more than three or four years. He therefore resolved to fill up his time with diligence, and to improve with particular attention, a season so inviting as the present. He would not waste in useless slumber the morning of a day, which was opening with so fine a prospect.

¿ Shall not his example awaken us from our slumbers, and call up all our powers to diligence and activity in the work of our own salvation? ¿ When we see him rising so early, and labouring so diligently in our cause, Shall we sink away into indolence? He judged the time precious, which might be employed to the benefit of mankind: ¿ Shall we waste our time in vanity and vice?

He taught on the sabbath, that men might learn the truths, which concern their salvation: How inexcusable then is our neglect of the appointed means of religious instruction! He improved those favourable opportunities, when men appeared most serious, inquisitive and thoughtful: How attentive then should we be to those soft and tender seasons, when our own hearts are sensibly impressed with the importance of religion!

By the zeal and activity of the Redeemer in the work of men's salvation, ¿ How many stand reproved and condemned? In their worldly designs they are warmly engaged; but on the one thing needful they scarcely bestow a thought. They rise up early, and sit up late, and eat the bread of carefulness, that they may obtain the meat which perishes; but for that meat which endures to eternal life they discover little concern. How preposterous is their conduct! How contrary to the example of Jesus Christ! His labours were directed, not to make us rich in this world; but rich in knowledge, faith, and good works. If we pursue the interests of this world, in the neglect of the greater interest of the future, we contradict the will of our Redeemer, declared, not only by his doctrines, but more emphatically by his works and sufferings.

There are certain seasons, which demand uncommon diligence. Seed time and harvest are the most busy and important parts of the year. On these principally depends the life of man. *He who will not plough by reason of the cold, shall beg in harvest, and have nothing. He who sleeps in harvest, is a son that causeth shame.* We all condemn the man, who, in these seasons, will yield to sloth, or give himself to pleasure. But let us remember, that our whole life is seed time. And according

cording to our sowing will be our harvest. He who soweth to the flesh, shall of the flesh reap corruption; and he who soweth to the spirit, shall of the spirit reap life everlasting. The seed time allowed us is short and uncertain. The season, once past, cannot be recalled. What our hands find to do, let us do it with our might.

Worldly diligence, however commendable, must never be allowed to exclude the concerns of futurity. These demand our attention every day, amidst the most urgent calls of our secular business. If in our immoderate labour and carefulness for the world, we deny ourselves leisure, or deprive ourselves of capacity, for the daily exercises of piety, and for an attendance on the publick institutions of religion, we invert the order of things, and make our greater concerns give way to the smaller.

The Christian is to fill up his time in a useful manner. Worldly business justly claims its proper place; but claims no more. It must ever leave room for the vaster concerns of immortality. Whatever thought we may take for the body, we must seek first the kingdom of God.

We may remark,

II. That no crowd of company, or calls of business, could divert Jesus from his daily, stated devotions. He rose up before day, and retired to a solitary place for prayer.

While Christ dwelt on earth, his thoughts were much in heaven. He maintained a constant intercourse

tercourse with the world above; and God heard him always. As a man he was, like others, dependent on God. As a man of sorrow and affliction, he had more occasion than others for that relief which comes by prayer. The Apostle says, that *Christ, in the days of his flesh, offered up prayers and supplications, with strong crying and tears, unto him who was able to save him from death; and was heard in that he feared. And though he was a son, yet he learned obedience by the things which he suffered.*

One end of his appearing in the flesh, was, that he might exhibit to mortals a complete example of that religion which is adapted to their nature and condition. He was made in all things like unto us, that he might in all things shew us what we ought to be, and how we ought to walk. He became a man, that he might teach men how to glorify God; and he was placed in a state of affliction, that he might teach the afflicted how to draw consolation from the fountain of mercy.

By withdrawing with his disciples from the multitude for social devotion, he has recommended family prayer. By retiring to solitude for his own personal devotion, he has recommended secret prayer. On some occasions, he spent whole nights in prayer to God; on others, he retired often, in a short time, to repeat the same petitions. In our text it is said, that *he rose up a great while before day, and departed to a solitary place, and prayed.*

The

The circumstances of his retirement, on this particular morning, shew that secret prayer was a stated morning exercise; an exercise which he was careful never to omit. It does not appear, that he always rose so early for prayer; but his rising so early this morning, shews that he made morning prayer his daily practice.

The transactions of the preceding day had drawn together a vast concourse around the house where he lodged. The evening he had spent in healing the sick, who had been brought to him in great numbers. When he retired to rest, the multitude were waiting in the neighbourhood to see him in the morning. The disciples observe to him, that all men were seeking him. He knew, that, by morning light, he should again be thronged by the admiring multitude, whose close attendance would prevent his retirement. Lest, therefore, he should find himself under a necessity of omitting the secret devotions of the morning, he rose earlier than usual, and before the people could have time to collect. Had secret prayer been only an occasional, not a daily exercise, he would not have taken this precaution to prevent the omission of it. If he had thought proper to dispense with it at any time, he would doubtless have excused himself from it at such a time as this, when he could not attend it without the self-denial of rising long before day, and the labour of retiring to a solitary place.

His example then clearly inſtructs us, that ſecret converſe with God, is a duty which we ſhould daily attend, and from which we ſhould not be eaſily diverted. Jeſus could find a time and place for retirement, even when the duties of his miniſtry were moſt urgent, and when the multitude were impatiently waiting to hear him. That he might not omit his retirement, nor diſappoint his hearers, he roſe the earlier. ¿ Shall we then excuſe ourſelves from ſecret prayer, or run it over with precipitancy and indevotion, becauſe our worldly affairs ſolicit our attention, or company is waiting around us?—¿ Can we not ſuſpend our ſecular cares, or our ordinary pleaſures and amuſements, long enough to converſe with God, and implore his favour and bleſſing? How different is our ſpirit from the mind which was in Chriſt! I will not ſay, there is no occaſion which can juſtify the omiſſion of a formal retirement. But this I may ſay; a man, whoſe heart is much with God, will ſeldom find ſuch an occaſion. An indevout heart creates occaſions for the omiſſion, much oftener than real occaſions render the omiſſion neceſſary. The ſlothful man ſays, *There is a lion in the way.* Objections eaſily ariſe againſt a duty, which we have no heart to perform. But when the heart is warmly engaged, difficulties are not felt, or are eaſily ſurmounted.

Secret prayer is a uſeful and important exerciſe. It is by *this*, that we kindle and keep alive the flame of piety. *While I was muſing,* ſays David,

vid, *the fire burned; my heart waxed hot; I spake with my tongue. Hear my prayer, O Lord, and give ear to my cry.* It is by *this* that we place God always before us, and view him always as present with us. *This* leads us to contemplate him in all our ways, to regard his goodness in all our enjoyments, and to feel his justice in all our afflictions. *This* inspires us with resolution to duty, and with fortitude in danger. It elevates the soul above the influence of earthly things, and, in the troubles of life, it opens a thousand springs of consolation and joy. To humble and hoping Christians, how refreshing must it be, to retire alone, and converse familiarly with their God—to tell him all their wants and all their sorrows—to confess before him their temptations and their sins, and receive the tokens of his forgiving love—to supplicate the supports of his arm under the pressure of their burdens, and the assistance of his grace, under a sense of their weakness! And if they can find, that they have really been with God—have come even to his seat—have risen to an unusual elevation above the world—they will say, It is good to be there. ¿ Will the man, who has repeatedly experienced the pleasure and advantage of communion with God, need other motives to the duty? Or, ¿Will he seek excuses for the omission of it?—From experience, he will say, " It is good for me to draw near unto God. I have put my trust in him, that I may declare all his works."

That we may enjoy the benefit and delight of heavenly communion, we must make it a *stated* exercise. If we yield to small diversions, we shall soon find them multiplying, until they entirely draw us away from God. And they who are far from him, will perish.

The prudent Christian easily finds opportunity for retirement. He disposes his affairs with discretion, lives by rule, arranges his business in due order, postpones his temporal concerns to his eternal interest, considers religion as his high calling, and involves himself in no such multiplicity of earthly cares, as shall be inconsistent with a regular attention to this great work, this one thing needful. By a wise adjustment of his affairs, and a diligent improvement of his time, he finds opportunity for the discharge both of his spiritual, and his secular duties, and prevents their interference. He can attend on the duties of devotion, with as much fervour and constancy, as if he had retired from the world to a cloister. He can pursue his worldly calling with as much industry and success, as if he had shut up his closet door and thrown by his Bible. There will be no inconsistency between the duties which relate to this world, and those which relate to another, as long as we assign them their proper places, and keep our hearts in a proper frame. If they interfere with, and crowd upon, one another, it is because they are jostled out of order.

We

We may remark,

III. What care our Lord took to find a place of solitude for his prayers, that he might neither meet with disturbance, nor seem ostentatious. He rose while it was yet dark, and retired, unseen by the multitude, to a solitary place.

Agreeable to this example, is the precept which he gave to his disciples—*When thou prayest, thou shalt not be as the hypocrites; for they love to pray standing in the synagogues, and in the corners of the streets, that they may be seen of men. But thou, when thou prayest, enter into thy closet; and, when thou hast shut thy door, pray to thy Father, who is in secret; and thy Father, who seeth in secret, shall reward thee openly.*

1. One reason why we should retire to a secret place for solitary prayer, is, that we may avoid the appearance of ostentation.

All our religion must be without hypocrisy. Whatever we do, we must do it heartily, as to God, and not to man. A supreme regard to the applause of the world, mars the virtue of our best actions.

There are some duties, which, in their nature, are open and publick. In these we must carefully attend to the workings of our hearts, and guard against the influence of vain and unworthy motives. We are not to neglect the duties from a false and affected humility, as if we had better not do them, than be seen in them. We are to perform them, though we are seen of men; but not to perform them for *the fake* of being seen. There are other duties which are to be performed in a secret manner, and in which we must not only suppress the unworthy *aim* to be seen; but, as far as circumstances allow, must avoid *being seen*. Christ condemns the hypocrisy of those, who, when they fasted, disfigured their faces; when they gave alms, sounded a trumpet; and when they prayed by themselves, chose the corners of the streets and other conspicuous places, that they might receive praise from men. Of the same hypocrisy are they guilty, who, retiring to fields, or groves, or other solitary places, there pray with an elevated voice, that they may be heard at a distance, and deemed uncommonly fervent and devout. *Secrecy* is a circumstance expressly enjoined. And to pray with loud vociferations in a field or wood, is as inconsistent with secrecy, and with sincerity, as to pray in the corner of a street. A needless ostentation of our piety and devotion is hypocrisy, in whatever manner this ostentation is made.

2. Another reason for secrecy in our personal or solitary prayers, is, that we may be undisturbed.

Too easily are our pious thoughts diverted by objects, which present themselves in our way. The noise and tumult of the world will interrupt our devoutest frames. Even in retirement the spirit of devotion will often languish; and impertinent thoughts will insensibly steal in upon us. Prudence will therefore direct us, as far as possible,

possible, to shun external diversions. When we shut the door of our closet against the intrusion of worldly objects, we must shut the door of our hearts against the entrance of worldly thoughts. We may often be surprised with them before we are aware; but we must not invite them. On the contrary, as soon as we discover them, we must banish them to a distance, and call in devout meditations to fill our minds. The more vacant the soul is of pious and heavenly affections, the more room is there for evil thoughts to enter. When the house is empty and swept, unclean spirits come in and dwell there. To shut the door of the closet, is the means of preventing disturbance from abroad. But in vain is this door shut, if the door of the soul is thrown wide open for every irregular passion and earthly care to rush in and occupy the place. ¿ Who is he that engageth his heart to approach unto God? Him God will cause to draw near to himself.

3. A farther reason for secrecy and solitude, is, that our minds may enjoy greater freedom in communion with God.

In our social prayers, the special and peculiar cases of each worshipper cannot always be distinctly and fully expressed. He who speaks in behalf of others, accommodates the matter and manner of his prayer to the capacities and circumstances of his fellow worshippers in general. They who join with him, employ their minds in adopting and appropriating his petitions. Every Christian

ian finds in himself wants and desires, which it is not possible, nor indeed proper, that others should know; and which, if they knew them, they could not so well express, as he may himself from the feelings of his own heart. Be sure, there are many things, in the case of every Christian, which, though proper to be laid before God, could not, with propriety and common edification, be introduced into a publick prayer.

But in the closet we are under no restraints of this kind. There we may open our bosoms, utter all our desires, and pour out our whole souls. There we may confess those secret sins, lament those secret infirmities, and mourn those secret temptations which we never have disclosed, and choose not to disclose, to the most intimate friend on earth. There we need not be confined to method or order, nor be solicitous in the choice of our expressions. We may address the throne of God on matters which lie heaviest on our hearts, and in language which our feelings dictate. We may there speak in desires and groans, which cannot be uttered: *And he who searcheth the heart, knoweth what is the mind of the spirit.* He who possesses our reins, knows our thoughts afar off. He who is present with our spirits, knows our feelings and desires, before they are expressed in words. While we are speaking, he hears; before we call, he answers. The forward motions of his love, David joyfully experienced.— *I said, I will confess my transgressions unto thee; and thou forgavest the iniquity of my sin.* For this shall every

every one that is godly pray to thee in a time, when thou mayeſt be found.

This example of our gracious Redeemer may be applied for the reproof of the irreligious, and the encouragement of the godly.

They who wholly neglect, or often intermit, the duty of ſecret prayer, are reproved by this example. Chriſt made it ſo much his conſtant exerciſe, that, rather than once omit it, he would riſe before day, in a morning too which followed a laborious evening. Awakened and encouraged by this example, let us daily draw near to God. Let us never yield to trifling diverſions, nor ſuffer the cares of the world to extinguiſh the ſpirit of devotion.

They who plead the want of leiſure, or the want of place, for retirement, ſhould conſider, that when labours crowded, Jeſus found leiſure by riſing the earlier, and when company thronged, he found a ſolitary place, by departing the farther.

Let thoſe, who neglect the care of their ſouls, remember how laborious Jeſus was in the work of men's ſalvation. ¿ Was that a trifling object for which he was ſo ardently engaged ?—Or, ¿ Can you be ſafe in neglecting a work in which he was ſo aſſiduouſly employed ?

Great was that ſalvation which the Son of God came to procure for ſinful men. Great were his labours, and greater his ſufferings, in this deſign. Great was the price which he paid for our re-
dempticn.

demption. ¿ How shall we escape, if we neglect this great salvation?

What mighty encouragement have we to seek it! The Saviour, who was so laborious in our cause, will approve and aid our labours. He, who was so much in prayer for men while he was on earth, will regard our humble prayers now he is in heaven. He is able to save to the uttermost them who come to God by him, seeing he ever lives to make intercession. He has departed from this world, and ascended into heaven, to appear in the presence of God for us. Let all men seek after him. They who seek shall find. Them who come to him, he will in no wise cast out. He has commanded us to seek him; and he has not said to us, Seek ye me in vain.

END OF THE THIRTEENTH SERMON.

SERMON XIV.

Family Prayer.

EPHESIANS 6, xviii.

Praying always with all prayer and supplication in the spirit, and watching thereunto with all perseverance.

OUR text might naturally lead us to consider the duty of prayer at large: But what I have more especially in view, is the duty of *family prayer*. This is one kind of prayer, and therefore one thing intended by the Apostle, when he directs us to pray *always* with *all* prayer.

If family prayer was practised by pious men, under the old testament, and in the time of our Saviour and his Apostles, as I shall shew that it was; and if the expression, *pray always*, is generally used to signify *daily* prayer, as I think will appear in its proper place, then we must suppose, that in this exhortation, family worship is included, and principally designed.

I shall therefore,

I. Shew our obligation to family prayer.

II. Inquire what reasons there are for stated morning and evening prayer.

III. Represent

III. Represent the manner in which family worship ought to be performed.

1. I shall shew our obligation to family prayer.

The scripture, in giving us rules of conduct, has not descended to every minute case, nor stated the precise limits of duty in every possible circumstance; for had it done so, it would have been too voluminous for common use. All that we can expect from it, is, that it should lay down such general rules, as common reason, with an honest heart, may easily apply to all particular cases; and should illustrate these rules by such familiar examples, as will, on all occasions, direct us to a just application of them. And this is what it has done. It has, for instance, explained and inculcated the duties of justice and charity; but has left it to human reason to apply the general precepts to particular cases. So it has urged the duty of prayer, pointed out many of the occasions of it, and shewn the temper with which it should be performed. But it has not distinctly specified all the possible occasions or matters of prayer. To have done this, would have been not only endless, but needless, as wisdom, accompanied with a devout heart, will be sufficient to direct. It has inculcated prayer in general, and distinctly recommended *secret* and *social* prayer, as well as enjoined us to pray *always* with *all* prayer; and family prayer is so evidently included in the general precepts, and comprehended within the general reasons of *social* prayer, that no devout and
serious

serious heart can doubt, but this is as much intended as any kind of prayer; and he who attempts to difprove his obligation to it, muft, at the fame time, deny his obligation to pray at all. And he who denies this, muft not only renounce Revelation, but difcard natural religion, and even the government of Providence.

The obligation to focial prayer is fo plain, and fo generally acknowledged, that I fhall here take it to be conceded.

If this is a duty, ¿ Who are the perfons to affociate for the performance of it ? Certainly they who are in a capacity to meet together—they who are connected by common intereft—they who fhare in the fame wants and the fame favours— they who are united in affection, and can make each other's cafes their own.—¿ Who then are under fo ftrong obligations to this duty, as the *members of a family* ? They dwell in the fame houfe— they naturally care for each other—their afflictions and mercies are in common—if one member fuffers, the reft fuffer with him—if one be honoured, all rejoice. A family then is fuch a fociety, as is under the firft obligation to focial worfhip. If you can find any precept in the Bible, which enjoins focial worfhip, you need look no farther: You have found one for family worfhip.

You will not deny, that it is your duty, as the mafter of a family, to bring up your children and domefticks in the nurture and admonition of the Lord.

Lord. But, ¿ Can you do this without the maintenance of **family** worship?—¿ Will the younger members of your houſehold act under a ſenſe of God and religion, when they ſee you regardleſs of him, and of the honour which you owe him?

To impreſs on tender minds devout and pious ſentiments, nothing can be better adapted, than family worſhip; in which they daily hear a **God** acknowledged, his perfections adored, ſin and guilt confeſſed, pardon and grace entreated, their dependence recognized, and every needed bleſſing implored.

If prayer belongs to religion you are to inſtruct **your children in** this, as well as other parts of religion. And, ¿ Is not example the moſt familiar **and ſucceſsful method of** communicating to the young, religious inſtruction?—¿ Without this, will other means avail? Prayer was one thing, in which Jeſus and John inſtructed their diſciples: And, ¿ Is there not the ſame reaſon why you ſhould inſtruct **your children** in prayer? And, ¿ How can you ſo eaſily teach them to pray, ſupply them with matter **for** prayer, and impreſs their minds with a ſenſe of its importance, as by requiring their daily attendance, when you addreſs the common Father, in your own and **their** behalf?

In moſt families there are ſome, who have not capacity diſtinctly to apprehend, and properly to expreſs their own wants. Theſe need the aſſiſtance of others. Now, as children can underſtand

a language,

a language, before they can fpeak it with proprie‑
ty; fo they can join in a prayer, before they can
frame one for themfelves. If then it is your du‑
ty to affift your younger domefticks in prayer, it
is your duty to lead them in fuch petitions, as
you would offer to God for them, and wifh them
to offer for themfelves.

¿ Does not family worfhip appear to you rea‑
fonable? I am fure, it cannot appear otherwife.
But you will afk, perhaps, for fome commands.
Thefe are not wanting. There are examples,
which have the force of commands: And there
are commands, too, fome more implicit, and oth‑
ers full and exprefs.

We will firft attend to the examples, which have
the force of commands.

¿ What is a command? It is any fignification
of the divine will concerning our conduct. God,
by approving a thing which is done, fhews it to
be his will, that it fhould be done. By approv‑
ing the examples of pious men in maintaining
family religion, he has given thefe examples, with
refpect to us, all the authority of precepts; for
he has fhewn it to be his will, that we fhould do
the fame.

The firft example, to which I would refer you,
is that of Abraham. He, at the command of God,
left his native country, his kindred, and his fa‑
ther's houfe, on account of the idolatry and irre‑
ligion which prevailed there, and came with his
family into the land of Canaan, for the fake of
enjoying

enjoying the pure worship of the one true God. In his pilgrimage he made various removes; but wherever he chose a residence, we find that he immediately built an altar to the Lord, and there called on his name. How highly God approved his piety in maintaining religion in his family, you learn from the commendation given of him in the xviiith chapter of Genesis:—*I know Abraham, that he will command his children, and his houshold after him, and they shall keep the way of the Lord, to do justice and judgment, that the Lord may bring upon Abraham that which he hath spoken of him.*

The example of Joshua, in the xxivth chapter of his history, is pertinent to our purpose. He says to the people of Israel—*Fear the Lord and serve him, and put away the strange gods, which your fathers served, on the other side of the flood,* meaning Abraham's idolatrous ancestors, *and in Egypt,* where their ancestors had been corrupted, *and serve ye the Lord. And if it seem evil to you to serve the Lord, choose ye, this day, whom ye will serve: But as for me and my house, we will serve the Lord.* To *serve* the Lord, in the language of the old testament, usually signifies, to *worship* him. This must be the meaning of the phrase in this place, because it stands opposed to the worship of *strange gods.* But, ¿How could Joshua resolve for his family, as well as for himself, that they should worship the Lord? Most certainly he maintained stated forms of social worship in his house, and required their attendance. In this manner you may

may make and execute the same resolution. When he commands the *people* to fear the Lord and serve him, doubtless he meant, that they should serve him in the same manner, in which he served him himself. If Joshua then spake under divine direction, here is an express command, binding all heads of families to maintain the worship of God in their houses.

The next example, which I shall mention, is that of Job, chapter 1st. When his children, according to the family custom, were holding a feast on each one's birth day, *he sent and sanctified them, and rose up early in the morning, and offered sacrifice according to the number of them all; for he said, It may be that my sons have sinned, and cursed God in their heart.* Sacrifice, which was accompanied with prayer, often signifies divine worship in general. Job *sent and sanctified his children.* He called upon them to prepare for, and join in, the religious solemnity, which he was about to perform. *He* offered sacrifice *according to the number of them all.* He presided in the solemnity, and addressed the Deity in a manner adapted to the several cases of his children. It is added, *Thus did Job continually*—every day of the feast, or at every festival solemnity.

This example, which is recorded as an instance of Job's piety and uprightness, is a virtual command to all heads of families, to worship God in their houses continually. You will say, perhaps, " Job's children were now settled in distinct families, and therefore this is rather an instance of *occasional*, than an example of *stated* family worship." But consider—Job and his sons lived in a vicinity; in those early times the father officiated as a priest among his children; and sacrifices were open acts of religion accompanied with prayer. ¿ Now if Job, after his children were removed to their respective houses, still embraced every opportunity, when they were occasionally together, to lead and engage them in social worship, Can it be thought, that there was no such thing as family devotion, while his children were about him, in his own house, and under his immediate care? In this view, the example comes with additional force.

We have also the example of David, 2 Samuel, vi. The king had brought the ark of God and set it in its place, had blessed the people in the name of the Lord, and distributed among them his royal bounty. And when these things were done, *all the people departed, every man to his house; then David returned to bless his household*—to bless them, as he had before blessed the people. To *bless* another in the name of the Lord, is to *pray* for a blessing upon him. Thus Aaron and his sons are directed to *bless the people, saying, The Lord bless thee, and keep thee, and make his face to shine upon thee*. David's *blessing* his household, must then mean his praying for the blessing of God to attend them. And that this was an act of social worship, at which his family were present, is evident

dent from the circumstance of his returning to bless them. Had it been only a secret prayer for them, it might as well have been made elsewhere, as at home.

Our blessed Saviour, whose life was filled up with religious services, often **took his disciples** apart for prayer, and other acts of worship. We read of his *going up with them into a mountain to pray;* and of his being *alone praying, and his disciples with him.* He was *alone* in relation to the *multitude,* whom he had just before dismissed; but in the company of his disciples, who were his family. They were *with him,* while he prayed.

You remember **the high** commendation given of the centurion **Cornelius, in the** xth chapter of the Acts. *He was a devout man, and one who feared God with all his house—and prayed to God alway;* or *daily,* at the stated hours of prayer, which were morning and evening. ¿Can it be thought that this devout Gentile had no prayers in his house? Or, ¿That the attendance of his domesticks, at the hours of prayer, was not required?—¿How then could he be said to pray *alway,* and to fear God *with all his house?* The happy consequence of his family devotion, you well know. God heard his prayers, directed him, in a vision, to send for Peter, who, at the same time, was divinely instructed to go with the centurion's messengers, and tell him words, by which he and all his house should be saved. The Apostle went and preached to them. They believed, were baptized

tized and received the Holy Ghost. Salvation, you see, came to his house, in consequence of that devout spirit, by which he worshipped God, gave alms, and prayed alway.

In the apostolick times, frequent mention is made of churches in particular houses. *To such an one and the church in his house*, is a common salutation. On the other hand, we meet with salutations, *from such an one and the church in his house.* This phrase cannot import, that all the Christians, in such a city or place, assembled in that house for worship; for then the salutation to, or from, such a person and the church in his house, would be a salutation to, or from, all the Christians in that city where the house was; and the Apostle would not be so particular, as he usually is, in mentioning salutations to, and from, families and persons, in the same city. The meaning therefore must be, *Salute such an one, and his Christian family.* Now, ¿ In what sense is a family called a church ? A church, you know, is a society of Christians united for the worship of God. A family then can in no other sense be called a church, than as the members of it agree in acts of social worship, and thus form the resemblance of a church. Family worship, you see, was practised by the primitive Christians, and approved by the Apostles. Surely we need not more examples.

¿ Do you call for express precepts ?—Our text is one. Pray *always* with *all* prayer. The word *always,*

always, applied to prayer, is an allusion to the morning and evening sacrifice, which was called, *the continual sacrifice*, and therefore plainly directs us to *morning* and *evening* prayer; **as I shall have** occasion to shew under the next head. And *all prayer* must include family prayer. Indeed if no such thing as family worship had ever been known, and the Apostle had been about to introduce a kind of worship entirely new, he would probably have been more explicit. **But as it was then,** and long had been known and practised **in religious families**; had been a usage among the patriarchs and the Jews, and was continued among Christians, it must necessarily be included in this universal injunction.

The Lord's prayer is an express command for daily family prayer. It is introduced in the form of a precept. *After this manner pray ye.* That social prayer is intended, cannot be doubted, for the form runs wholly in the plural number. In the preceding verses, our Lord gives directions for *solitary* prayer. In treating of this, he uses the singular number. *When* thou *prayest enter into* thy *closet, shut* thy *door, and pray to* thy *Father in secret.* He then passes to *social* prayer, and, as his subject naturally led him, he changes the number. *But when ye pray, use not vain repetitions—after this manner pray ye,* Our *Father who art in heaven.* Not only the change of number, but the disallowance of *repetitions* and *much speaking,* shews that social prayer is the subject; for

these,

these, though improper in joint prayer, for very obvious reasons, may be admitted in solitary prayer, where we may breathe the feelings of the heart with less regard to order, time or diction, than when we are speaking in behalf of others. Our Saviour continued *all night* in *solitary* prayer. He prayed *three times*, saying the *same words*. I would observe farther: This form is intended to direct us in *daily*, as well as social prayer; as appears from the fourth petition, *Give us this day, our* daily *bread*. Family prayer must here be principally intended; for a family is the only society that can meet for *daily* prayer.

You will also find an express command in the ivth chapter of the epistle to the Colossians. The Apostle is here, and in the preceding chapter, treating of domestick and relative duties, as the duties between husbands and wives, parents and children, masters and servants; and to *these* he immediately subjoins a precept concerning prayer. *Continue instant in prayer, and watch in the same with thanksgiving.* As the duties incumbent on families are his subject, it is natural to suppose that family prayer is here intended.

I shall mention but one authority more, which is that of the Apostle Peter in the iiid chapter of his 1st Epistle. He there in the first place points out to wives their duty to their husbands, such as obedience, chastity, modesty and peaceableness. He next shews the duty of husbands to their wives,

wives, as dwelling with them, giving them honour, and treating them with kindnefs. In a word, he directs them to regard each other, *as being heirs together of the grace of life.* And the general reafon which he affigns, is this, *that their prayers be not hindered.* You will here obferve, that the neceffity of a fuitable performance of the duty of prayer, is made an argument for other domeftick duties. An argument ufed to prove the obligation, or urge the practice of any duty, is always fuppofed to be more plain, if poffible, than the duty recommended. When therefore the Apoftle, from the danger of the interruption of their prayers, urges the wife to be fubject to her hufband, and him to give honour to her, he fuppofes it to be more obvious, that they fhould live together in focial prayer, than that fhe fhould be obedient to him, or that he fhould give honour to her.

I will only remark farther, that in this paffage the Apoftle confiders joint prayer as incumbent on fmall families, fuch as confift only of the hufband and wife. He urges a fuitable treatment of each other in the conjugal relation, that their prayers may not be interrupted. Let this be confidered by thofe, who have newly entered into a family ftate.

I have the more largely ftated the arguments for this duty, becaufe fome have pretended, that there is no warrant for it in the word of God. Such infinuations are as groundlefs, as they are dangerous.

dangerous. The very perfons who make them, will, under certain circumftances, fhew that they do not believe them. If they fhould hear of fome officer in the church, or of fome Chriftian profeffor, who neglected family worfhip, they would not fail to cenfure and reproach him. But, ¿ Is this **a duty incumbent** only on certain characters? **In a time of** family diftrefs, they will defire that prayer may be made in their houfes. But, ¿ Are they dependent on God only when they are fick, or when one lies dead by their wall? Live under a fenfe of your **continual dependence,** and you will pray always with **all prayer.**

Let heads of families ftand within their houfes, as priefts **of God,** offering the facrifice of prayer and praife continually. Let the younger members give a ferious attendance, realizing the divine **prefence, and approaching** it with godly fear. Let your houfes become as churches of God; and the churches **will become** more glorious. Let **them be the places,** where prayer is wont to be made, where God's word is read, and where fuitable inftructions are given, and the fervices of the fanctuary will be more edifying. Happy is the family, which, with united hearts, ferve God and pray always—happy the man, who is the head of fuch a family—happy the members of a houfe, which is bleffed becaufe of the ark of God—happy the church, which confifts of fuch families.

families. Such a church is one greater family, whose members are pursuing one common design; and the families are so many smaller churches, all builded together for an habitation of God, through the Spirit, and growing unto an holy temple in the Lord.

END OF THE FOURTEENTH SERMON.

SERMON XV.

Family Prayer.

EPHESIANS 6, xviii.

Praying always with all prayer and supplication in the spirit, and watching thereunto with all perseverance.

IN our former discourse, on this text, we considered our obligations to maintain the worship of God in our houses.

We will now, as was proposed,

II. Inquire, whether there is any thing in reason, or scripture, leading us to fix on morning and evening, as the stated seasons of family worship.

1. Our prayers, certainly ought to be *frequent* and *constant*.

So much, at least, must be intended by our Apostle, when he directs us to pray *always*. Whatever reasons oblige us to pray at all, bind us to pray often.

We are continually dependent on God, and indebted to him. We daily feel new wants, or the return of former ones, and receive fresh favours, or the repetition of past ones. We often commit

offences

offences against God, and contract new guilt. If then it becomes us *at all*, it becomes us *often* to repair to the throne of grace with earnest petitions for the blessings which we need, and thankful praises for those which we have received; with humble confession of conscious guilt, and penitent supplication of God's gracious pardon.

If prayer is useful, *frequency* in it will make it more useful. One use of prayer is to cherish and strengthen our serious sentiments and resolutions, which, through the infirmity of the flesh and the influence of worldly objects, are too apt to languish and decay. It is by frequent communion with God, that our souls, which so naturally cleave to the dust, are raised above the world, enlivened in duty, and made to feel the power, and taste the pleasure of religion. If our converse with him should be but seldom, our holy affections and purposes, in the long intervals, would die away; and this deceitful world would get such strong possession of our hearts, that the rare exercises of devotion would be too feeble to dispossess it, or turn our hearts to better objects.

Family worship, if but seldom attended, will be of little use to the younger members of our houses. The frequent, unnecessary omissions of it, indicate such an indifference in us, that our children will easily be led to view it as a matter of trifling consequence. If we pray in our families only on the sabbath, or in a time of family affliction, taught by our example, they will naturally

ally give the bufinefs of the world a preference to the duties of piety, and to the care of their fouls. If now and then we fuggeft to them a different thought, it will but feebly imprefs their minds, while they fee it fo plainly contradicted by our daily conduct.

Frequency in prayer is as exprefsly, and almoft as often, inculcated in fcripture, as prayer itfelf. We are to pray *always with all prayer*—to pray *without ceafing*—to *continue inftant in prayer*—to *watch thereunto with all perfeverance*—to *pray always and not faint*—in *every thing to make known our requefts.* ¿ What lefs can thefe expreffions import, than fuch frequency in devotion as to keep alive a devout, fpiritual and heavenly temper?

2. If we are to pray frequently, then there muft be fome *ftated* feafons of prayer; for otherwife it cannot be attended with decency and order.

As it is neceffary that certain days fhould be ftated, by divine appointment, or by mutual agreement, for *publick worfhip*, that the whole church may come together into one place, and at the fame time; fo it is neceffary, that certain hours of the day fhould be ftated for *family* worfhip, that all the members may with one mind, and one mouth, glorify God. Accordingly we find in fcripture, that there were periodical times, called the *hours of prayer*, which pious men ufed conftantly to obferve. Peter and John went up into the temple *at the hour of prayer, being the ninth hour.* ¿ What lefs can we underftand by the directions,

rections, to *pray always*, and *without ceasing*, than that we should have some *fixed* and *stated* seasons of prayer? When we pray at all proper seasons, and keep alive the spirit of piety, then we may be said to pray *always*. Prayer has a just proportion of our time and attention.

3. It is evident, that prayer ought to be a daily exercise.

Our Saviour instructs us to pray after this manner—*Our Father, who art in heaven, give us this day our daily bread*. The Psalmist says, *every day will I praise thee*—*I will* daily *perform my vows*—*I cry unto thee* daily—*I have called* daily *upon thee, and stretched out mine hand unto thee*. It is the voice of wisdom—*Blessed is the man who heareth me, watching* daily *at my gates, waiting at the posts of my doors*. The primitive Christians *continued* daily *with one accord in the temple*. They daily attended the stated hours of prayer.

4. If prayer is to be made *daily* and *statedly*, then there is a special propriety in fixing on *morning* and *evening* for the performance of it. Reason itself points out these, as suitable hours for family worship.

In the morning, when we arise from our beds, and are returning to the labours of our calling, how just and reasonable it is, that our thoughts should be with God; that we should acknowledge his care, who has made us to dwell in safety, and at the same time should commit ourselves to him, imploring the protection of his providence, the

restraints

restraints of his grace, the guidance of his counsel, and his blessing on the works of our hands!

In the evening, when we have finished the work of the day, how decent and proper it is, that we should gratefully **recollect** the benefits which we have received, penitently confess the evils which **we have done, and commit** ourselves to that Almighty Keeper who never slumbers nor sleeps; and thus lay ourselves down in peace!

At these hours our **minds are more** free from worldly cares, and our families **more at liberty** from worldly occupations, than at other seasons. We can therefore more readily unite in the worship of God, and more easily attend upon it without distraction.

And as reason, so scripture points out these for the stated hours of prayer. The prophet says, *With my soul I have desired thee in the night, and with my spirit within me I will seek thee* early. This was the practice of the devout Psalmist, and he commends it as a good and useful practice for others. *It is a good thing to give thanks to the Lord, to sing praises to thy name, O Most High, to shew forth thy loving kindness* in the morning, *and thy faithfulness* every night. He is speaking, not of *secret*, but of *social* prayer. By the former we may offer our praises and petitions to God; but it is by the latter only that we *shew forth*, and *declare* his loving kindness and faithfulness. This, he says, ought to be done, in the *morning* and in the *evening*; not only on special occasions, but

constantly

constantly every night. And he must have particular regard to *family* worship, for families are the only societies, which can *every* morning and night associate for divine worship.

We find that devout men, under some peculiar circumstances, observed other hours of solitary or private prayer. Daniel, in his captivity, prayed *three times* a day. David says, *morning, noon*, and *night*, will I pray. And again, *Seven times a day will I praise* thee. But the more common hours of prayer, especially of *social* prayer, mentioned in scripture, are *morning* and *evening*.

Job rose up *early in the morning and offered sacrifice* for his family. David says, *My voice shalt thou hear in the* morning, *O Lord ; in the* morning *will I direct my prayer unto thee. I will sing aloud of thy mercy in the* morning. *I prevented the dawning of the* morning, *and cried*. Heman says, *In the* morning *my prayer shall prevent thee*.

We have many examples of evening prayer. David, having spent the day in publick devotions, *returned* home to *bless his household. Let my prayer*, says he, *be set forth as incense, and the lifting up of my hands as the* evening *sacrifice. Commune with your own heart* on your bed—*offer the sacrifices of righteousness*.—*I will lay me down and sleep, for thou, Lord, makest me to dwell in safety.*

It was the duty of the Levites to stand *every morning* to thank and praise God, and likewise at *evening*. When David had replaced the ark, he left before it some of the priests, to minister continually,

tinually, as *every day's* work required, and to offer burnt offerings to the Lord *continually, morning and evening,* and to do according to all that is written *in the law of the Lord.* The law of Moses instituted a particular sacrifice to be offered *daily,* half in the *morning,* and half in the *evening.* This was called the *continual* sacrifice. And as this was accompanied with prayer, here is an express institution of *morning* and *evening* prayer.

This sacrifice, after the temple was built, was offered there—and there, such as dwelt near, usually attended at the hour of sacrifice. To this institution our Lord alludes in the parable of the pharisee and publican, *who went up to the temple to pray.* When Zacharias entered into the temple to burn incense, the whole multitude of the people were without, *praying at the time of incense.* They who, by reason of distance, or other circumstances, could not attend at the temple, used to pray, at the hour of sacrifice, *with their faces toward the temple.* Jonah, when he was cast out of God's presence, resolved, that *he would look again toward God's holy temple.* Solomon, in his dedication prayer, says, " If thy people be carried away captive, and in the land of their captivity return unto thee, *and pray toward this house,* then hear thou and forgive." Daniel prayed *at the time of the evening sacrifice,* and *with his face toward Jerusalem.*

After the abolition of the legal sacrifices, the Apostles and primitive Christians still observed

these

these stated hours of morning and evening prayer. Luke tell us, that after Christ's ascension, " they were *continually*, and *daily*, in the temple, praising and blessing God." They resorted thither at the *third* and *ninth* hours. To these stated hours the Apostle evidently alludes, when he directs us to pray *always*—to pray *without ceasing*—to offer the sacrifice of praise *continually*. And thus we are to understand, what is said of Anna the prophetess, that *she deparied not from the temple, but served* God *with prayers night and day.*

Thus from the institution of the morning and evening sacrifice, which was accompanied with prayer; from the practice of pious men under the old testament, and of the Apostles and early Christians under the new; from the frequent directions to pray *always*, which plainly allude to the continual sacrifice, and from the express words of the Psalmist, who recommends it, as a good thing, to shew forth God's loving kindness in the morning, and his faithfulness every night, it fully appears to be the indispensable duty of every Christian family to maintain the stated worship of God, and to attend upon it, ordinarily, every morning and evening.

I proceed now to shew,

III. In what manner our family worship ought to be performed.

1. In this, as in all other religious exercises, there must be an *attention* and *engagedness* of mind,

We are directed to *pray in the spirit*—to *watch unto prayer*—to *lift up our hearts,* **with our hands,** *unto God in the heavens.* It is the *inwrought* and *fervent* prayer, which avails much. If while we draw near to God with our mouths, our hearts are far from him, we worship **him in vain.** Our prayers must be the expressions of real, heartfelt desires, not the tinkling of an unmeaning cymbal. **God** hears the *desire* **of** the **humble.** Without the concurrence of the heart, bodily exercise profits little. We must draw near to the throne of grace, with a serious, collected and **devout spirit.** This is alike the duty of him who leads, and **of** them who join in prayer; **for unless** these adopt the petitions which are made, **and, with the words of the speaker,** send up their **own hearts to God, with no propriety can** they be said to join with him in prayer.

2. There is an external *decency* and *solemnity,* which ought always to **be regarded** in our family devotions.

The person, **who conducts** them, is to consult not merely **his own,** but the common edification. His manner should be grave, his expressions pertinent, his utterance deliberate, that others may understand the nature, and **feel the weight** of what he offers; and that, "seeing him affected with a sense of what he is doing, proportionally to its importance, they may catch the flame of his devotion, and feel their own hearts burn with the same pious ardour."

3. Some

3. Some *preparation* is ordinarily expedient, that, dispossessing our minds of worldly thoughts and cares, we may attend upon God without distraction.

Job *sent and sanctified his children*—called upon them to prepare for the family sacrifice. The prophet inquires, *¿ Who is he that engageth his heart to approach unto* God ? The heart must be engaged, that the approach may be acceptable. For those who attended the passover without opportunity for the legal purification, Hezekiah prayed, saying, " The good Lord pardon every one, who *prepareth his heart* to seek God, though he be not cleansed according to the purification of the sanctuary." On a like occasion Josiah commanded the Levites to *prepare* and *sanctify* themselves, and their brethren. These examples teach us, that some preparation is requisite for a suitable performance of social worship. The practice of reading a portion of scripture, previous to family prayer, is very commendable, and highly useful. It not only disposes the mind for devotion, but begets a reverence for the word of God. The master of a household should require his domesticks to give a serious and orderly attendance, and should choose those seasons, which will best admit of it, and most easily comport with it.

4. Family worship should be maintained *steadily, without unnecessary omissions.*

It is the Apostle's direction to families, that they *continue* in prayer, and *watch* in the same

P 3   with

with thankfgiving. The morning and evening facrifice was offered *continually*. The Apoftles were *daily*, with one accord, in the temple. There is ordinarily the fame reafon for prayer and praife, *every* day, as *any* day; for we *daily* need, and *daily* receive new favours from God. Our Saviour has taught us to pray, Give us *this day* our *daily* bread. We muft not admit little trifling excufes for the omiffion of this duty. Too great an indifference to this important exercife appears in thofe, who are frequently abroad themfelves, and allow their children alfo to be abroad, at fuch unfeafonable hours, that it muft either be often neglected, or performed at a time, when few of the family are prefent, and none of them in a fuitable frame and preparation to attend it.

5. The *matter* of our addreffes fhould be taken from the *common concerns*, and the *manner* of them adapted to the *common capacities* of the family.

Job offered burnt offerings for his children *according to the number of them all*. He accommodated his prayers to the ftate of his houfehold; and fo ought every parent.

There are many wants, and many mercies, which are common to all. Thefe are always proper matter of our joint devotions. Some members may be under peculiar circumftances of joy or forrow. If one member fuffers, all are to fuffer with him. If one be honoured, all fhould rejoice. The ftate of each member, fo far as it is

a common

a common concern, and worthy of so serious notice, ought to be introduced into our family worship.

In most families, there are some, whose minds are tender, and whose capacities are but small: He therefore who speaks in prayer, should utter with the tongue, things easy to be understood; and while he prays in the spirit, he should pray with the understanding also; else, ¿ How will they who occupy the room of the unlearned, say, Amen, at his petitions and giving of thanks, seeing they understand not what he says?

6. In our daily worship, *tediousness* should be avoided.

"For want of prudence in this matter, it is possible, some young persons, in religious families, have been led to disrelish religion, more than they would otherwise have done." Youthful minds cannot long be fixed in close attention, without pain and weariness. When the service becomes burdensome, it is no longer edifying. If family worship is customarily drawn out to undue length, the young, instead of attending on it with pleasure, will seek occasions to shun it. Our Saviour cautions us not to imitate those, who use vain repetitions, and think they shall be heard for their much speaking. In our closets, we may give full vent to the fervour of our own devotion: But in our family prayers, to which Christ's instructions especially relate, we should consult the devotion of our fellow worshippers. And the model, which he has given us, shews, that

that these should be compendious, plain and familiar.

7. Every master of a family should be careful that the manner of his life corresponds with his devotions.

He should maintain the worship of God, not as a substitute for holiness of life, but as a mean of promoting it. And in this light he should teach his children to regard it. If, while he is strict in his prayers, he is loose in his morals, or if, while he requires their attendance on the forms of devotion, he indulges them in the practice of iniquity, he represents religion as a self-contradiction, and teaches them to view it with utter contempt. When Jacob was about to erect an altar to God at Bethel, where God had ordered him to dwell, he said to his *household*, and to *all who were with him, Put away the strange gods which are among you, and be clean, and change your garments, and let us arise, and go up to Bethel, and I will make there an altar unto God.* The Apostle Peter urges husbands and wives to a virtuous behaviour in that relation, *that their prayers be not hindered.* He teaches them, that they cannot pray together to their own, and the family's edification, unless *they live together, as heirs of the grace of life.* David contented not himself with blessing his household, but resolved, that he would *behave himself wisely in a perfect way—that he would walk within his house with a perfect heart—and that he would not countenance* in his family *a wicked person.*

I shall

I shall now close this discourse with two remarks.

1. Union between the heads of a family appears to be a matter of great importance.

The maintenance of social worship, and the transmission of religion, by a pious education of children, is evidently one end for which families are formed. Where prayer is hindered, one great design of the domestick relation is defeated. Social worship can be acceptable only when it is offered with humility, meeknefs and love. Fellow worshippers must be like minded one toward another, lift up holy hands without wrath, and forgive, if they have aught against one another, or against any man. Wrath, clamour and contention, are palpably contrary to the spirit of prayer. ¿If the heads of a family, who ought to be one spirit, as well as one flesh, live in eternal brawls, wrangles and contradictions, What is their house but a Babel?—¿Amidst such a tumultuous scene, Can the members unite their hearts and voices in the daily worship of their Creator? Or, ¿Will God regard their offering, or accept it with good will at their hands? God is not the author of confusion, but of peace. Let all things be done decently and in order.

2. If social worship, and the religious education of children, are duties incumbent on all heads of families, then there ought to be a knowledge of the nature, a belief of the principles, and a regard to the duties of religion, in all who enter into the married state. The ignorant, the unprincipled,

the profane, when they unite to become the heads of a houshold, are often the guilty instruments of bringing forward a family for ruin. Let none think themselves qualified for so important a trust, until they have acquired such a knowledge of religion, and possess such a sense of its importance, as to be able and disposed to maintain those duties of piety, government and instruction, which are expressly enjoined on all who are placed in that station. ¿ What, then, you will ask, Are none but the *godly* allowed to marry? Know, my pert young friend, none who marry are allowed to be ungodly. Remember, religion is of importance to you now in your single capacity; and its importance will be vastly increased, when you become the head of a family; for then you will stand in a connexion with others, whose virtue and happiness will much depend on your conduct.

And you, my brethren, who have children growing up under your care, realize your obligation to bring them forward on the stage of life, furnished with such religious knowledge and sentiments, that when they, in their turn, shall become heads of families, they may transmit religion to another generation. For this purpose, you must maintain the worship of God in your houses, in the manner which has been recommended. Perhaps there are some who study evasions and excuses, and determine to continue in their neglect. But after all you can say, I dare appeal to your conscience, whether there is not such evidence

dence of the indispensable obligation of this duty, as would be more than enough to satisfy you in any case, where your mind stood previously indifferent. I dare appeal to your conscience, whether you are restrained from praying in your family, by a persuasion that it is an unscriptural and unwarrantable practice; or by an apprehension that it will bring guilt on your soul, and misery on your family. I dare appeal to your conscience, whether your neglect of family worship is not owing more to a spirit of indifference, than to any real scruples in the matter. Bring the question home, for once, to your conscience, ¿ Whether you did not first omit it through disinclination, and then seek reasons to justify the omission? It was not a sense of duty that dictated the neglect; but previous neglect that suggested your evasions of the duty. However easy it may be, in the days of prosperity, to reconcile your minds to a prayerless life, yet in the day of family adversity, when your children are by death torn from your embraces, or when you feel yourselves under his arrest, the reflection on such a life will pierce you through and through. Encouraged by God's gracious promises in favour of the godly and their houses, and awed by the threatenings of his wrath against the families which call not on his name, adopt the resolution of the pious captain of Israel. *As for me, and my house, we will serve the Lord.*

END OF THE FIFTEENTH SERMON.

SERMON XVI.

A Christian Family helping their Minister.

ROMANS 16. iii, iv, v.

Greet Priscilla and Aquila, my helpers in Christ Jesus; who for my sake have laid down their own necks; unto whom not only I give thanks, but also all the churches of the Gentiles. Likewise greet the church that is in their house.

AQUILA, and his wife Priscilla, the two persons whom Paul here salutes, are several times named in his epistles, and always mentioned with particular marks of friendship and esteem. His first acquaintance with them, was at Corinth. It is said in the 18th chapter of the Acts, *Paul came to Corinth, and found a certain Jew named Aquila, born in Pontus, lately come from Italy, with his wife Priscilla, because that Claudius had commanded all Jews to depart from Rome.* Aquila was by nation a Jew; the place of his birth was Pontus, a province in lesser Asia, where great numbers of Jews inhabited; and he had lately made his residence in Rome. But a company of thieves, in Judea, having fallen on one Stephanas, a servant of the emperour, robbed his baggage, and slain the soldiers who guarded it, an edict was passed, requiring all Jews to leave that city. In consequence of this edict, Aquila, with his wife, came to Corinth, and there wrought in his occupation, which was that of a *tent maker*.

He is said, by the ancients, to have been a man of great learning. St. Jerom makes mention of him and of his writings. He says, the books of the prophets were, by this learned Jew, translated from the Hebrew into the Greek language, for the benefit of the Greeks. From this translation, which was extant in his time, he makes frequent quotations.

Paul, coming from Athens to Corinth, meets with Aquila, takes lodging in his house, and abides there for some time, working with him in his occupation, as he had leisure; but preaching every sabbath, in the synagogue, to Jews and Greeks, who resorted thither to hear him. It was probably at this time, that Aquila and his wife first gained the knowledge and professed the faith of the gospel. As they enjoyed Paul's company for some time in their own house, as well as heard him preach statedly in the synagogue, they doubtless became well instructed in the nature and evidence of the Christian religion. Accordingly we find, that they were able to expound to Apollos the way of God more perfectly, than he had before understood it.

Paul's refidence with them laid a foundation for a clofe and intimate friendfhip, which we find remaining until the time of his death. In his fecond epiftle to Timothy, which he wrote in his laft bonds, when he was ready to be offered, he remembers them in his falutations.

How worthy they were of his affection and efteem, we learn from the character given of them in the words which we have chofen for our text. With united attention they had helped Paul in his labours for Chrift. With the hazard of their own lives they had preferved *his* for the fervice of the churches. And while they promoted the general intereft of religion, they were careful to maintain it in their own family. They had a church in their houfe.

The contemplation of the character and example of thefe pious perfons, will bring home to us fome inftructions in our own duty.

I. This godly couple appear to have been happily united in all their concerns, and efpecially in the great concerns of religion.

On all occafions they are both mentioned together; neither of them is once named without the other. They were one flefh, and one fpirit. They appear as patterns of conjugal union. They dwelt together in days of tranquillity, and jointly fhared in the calamities of banifhment. With united hands they laboured in the occupation by which their houfehold was fupported. Whereever one went or refided, the other attended;

whatever

whatever bufinefs employed one, the other affifted; and in *their* falutations to the churches, both unite. When Paul falutes one, he falutes the other; he fpeaks of both as his helpers in Chrift; he acknowledges both, as having laid down their necks for him; and he commends both as prefiding in their houfe, and rendering it a church of Chrift. Aquila had fuch underftanding in the things of religion, that he was able to inftruct Apollos, a man mighty in the fcriptures of the old teftament. And Prifcilla had made fuch proficiency in Chriftian knowledge, that fhe was able to affift him in expounding the way of the Lord.

Thus cemented by love, fharing together in all changes of condition, uniting in the labours of life, and cooperating in the duties of religion, they muft have enjoyed all the felicities, which can fpring from the conjugal relation.

As this is one of the moft important relations in life, to the parties themfelves, to fociety, and to pofterity, they who fuftain it, ought, above all things, to ftudy mutual peace. This will render the relation a blefling; without this it will become a vexation and a curfe.

The Chriftian pair, confidering themfelves as having one common intereft, and feeling themfelves animated by one foul, will readily participate in each other's labours and forrows, and will cheerfully communicate to each other their own pleafures and joys. The rougher paths of life

life they will tread hand in hand, and, by reciprocal fmiles of content, will beguile the tirefome walk. The pains of life they will lighten by bearing each other's burdens, and heighten every enjoyment by fharing it in common. In the education and government of the family, they will ſtrengthen each other's hands; and, inſtead of contending for an idle fuperiority, will combine their influence for the good of the houfehold. Little differences of opinion will be compofed by mutual condefcenfion. Accidental miſtakes and trivial faults will be overlooked, or viewed with the eye of candour. More ferious errours will be mentioned with tendernefs, and correcked with meeknefs. Real virtues and worthy actions will meet the cheering fmiles of approbation; and worthy defigns will be encouraged by a prompt, unfolicited concurrence. Unavoidable infirmities will be viewed with the comforting eye of pity, not with the infulting eye of difdain. Real failings will not be matter of keen reproach, but of kind expoſtulation. Under trifling inconveniences they will not teafe and vex each other by eternal complaints; nor under fevere misfortunes will they imbitter each other's fpirits by mutual upbraidings. But on the contrary, by examples of patience, cheerfulnefs and heavenly mindednefs, they will elevate their own and each other's minds above the fmaller, and fortify them to bear the greater troubles of this changing world.

In

In the important concerns of religion, they will walk, as being heirs together of the grace of life, that their daily prayers be not hindered, their virtuous refolutions weakened, nor their good works obftructed. While he leads in the devotion of the family, fhe will encourage him by her perfonal attendance, by calling the attendance of her houfehold, and by fuch a prudent difpofition of her domeftick affairs, as may give feafonable opportunity for the folemnity. When he adminifters inftruction or reproof to thofe under their care, fhe will prudently fecond it ; or, if fhe thinks it mifapplied or illtimed, fhe will not defeat his honeft intention, by open, petulent contradiction ; but rather, by private advice, prevent future miftakes. In their fpiritual walk, they will be fellow helpers to the kingdom of God, animating each other by mutual counfel and example, and confidering each other to provoke unto love and good works.

Such a conduct in the domeftick relation is recommended by the example of this amiable pair, and enjoined by the precepts of the gofpel of Chrift.

Paul, in his epiftles to the Ephefians and Coloffians, directs, that this relation be diftinguifhed by mutual affection, tendernefs, fidelity and fubmiffion ; and that every thing which is bitter, be far removed from it—that the love, on the one hand, be like that which Chrift fhewed to the church ; and the fubmiffion, on the other, like that

that which the church owes to him. The instructions of the Apostle Peter, on this subject, are to the same purpose. Their conversation must be chaste and pure; their adorning, a meek and quiet spirit; their language and manners, expressive of mutual honour and esteem; and all their conduct, such as tends to engage affection, encourage a virtuous life, and assist in the necessary preparation for the world of glory.

A family, educated under the care of heads thus united in all the duties of the secular, domestick and religious life, will, by the smiles of heaven, grow up in knowledge and piety, and, like the household of Aquila, become a little church of Jesus Christ.

II. The next thing observable in the character of these persons, is, that the Apostle calls them *his helpers in Christ Jesus.*

Convinced of the truth, and feeling the importance of the gospel, they wished its prevalence and success among their perishing fellow mortals. When they looked around on the ignorant Gentiles and deluded Jews, they pitied their deplorable state, rejoiced that the gospel was proclaimed, and desired its universal spread. As Paul was sent to preach the way of salvation, so out of love, not merely to him, but to mankind in general, they became his helpers in Christ Jesus.

There are various ways, in which private Christians may help their minister, and in which these

godly

godly perfons may be fuppofed to have helped the Apoftle, in the work of Chrift.

1. They helped him by their *hofpitality*.

For a confiderable part of the time that he preached in Corinth, he abode in their houfe.

Banifhed from Rome, they had but lately come hither. Their prefent condition could not be the moft eafy and plentiful. In the opulent city of Corinth, there were doubtlefs many more wealthy than they; but none fo ready to open their doors to an Apoftle of Jefus, who came to bring the gofpel of falvation. By induftry in their calling, they had acquired not only a competence for themfelves, but ability to contribute fomething to the caufe of religion. Paul, however, that he might not be burdenfome to his liberal friends, laboured with them in their occupation. Though he claimed a right to live of the gofpel, he ufed not this right in Corinth, left the fuccefs of his preaching fhould be obftructed. He fays to the Corinthians—*Now ye are full, ye are rich, ye have reigned as kings—but we are weak and defpifed; we hunger and thirft, and are naked, having no certain dwelling place; and we labour, working with our hands—I have kept myfelf from being burdenfome to you, and fo will I keep myfelf.*

Every Chriftian is bound to make his worldly fubftance, in fome way or other, fubfervient to the intereft of religion. The minifter is to preach the gofpel, not for filthy lucre, but of a ready mind. But, then, they who are taught in the word,

word, muſt communicate to him who teacheth, in ſuch meaſure, that he may wait on his teaching, and attend to it without diſtraction.

2. This Chriſtian pair helped the Apoſtle by a *faithful attendance* on his miniſtry.

Paul reaſoned in the ſynagogue every ſabbath, perſuading the Jews and Greeks ; and doubtleſs theſe pious perſons, who entertained the preacher in their houſe, accompanied him to the ſynagogue.

Heads of families, by an exemplary attendance on the preaching of the word, greatly aſſiſt their miniſter. There is no way in which they can more effectually ſecond his labours. They thus ſhew to their children, to youth in general, and to all around them, that they eſteem the goſpel divinely excellent, and infinitely important—that they regard the preaching of it, as an inſtitution of God, and honour the preachers of it, as the meſſengers of Jeſus Chriſt. Their attendance invites others to accompany them, animates their miniſter, gives an elevation to his ſpirits, and an ardour to his zeal. It raiſes his hopes of ſucceſs among his people, and particularly among the youth.

But if, on the contrary, they treat the preaching of the word with cold indifference, and contemptuous neglect, ſeldom attending on it, except when the ſeaſon is remarkably inviting, or the occaſion gives an expectation of ſomething new ; far from helping, they rather hinder their miniſter. He can hardly forbear to ſay to them,
" I would,

"I would, that ye were cold or hot." Their declared indifference to the miniſtry, leads others, eſpecially the young, to view it as a uſeleſs invention, and to regard it rather as matter of amuſement, than a mean of ſalvation.

My brethren, if you expect from your miniſter no help to *your own* ſouls—if *your* Chriſtian attainments raiſe you above ſuch means of edification, as his preaching; yet you will permit him to aſk your attendance, that you may be *his helpers* in Chriſt Jeſus—that you may contribute to the efficacy of his preaching among your *children*. He will thank you for this favour; for he would by all means ſave ſome. He ardently deſires that Chriſt may be formed in the youth, and that they may grow up in all things into him, who is the head. They are not yet ſuperiour to religious inſtruction. You will help them, when you help your miniſter, by your conſtant attendance at the ſanctuary.

But then let your attendance be grave and devout; and on what you hear, let your remarks be candid and ſerious. Ludicrous or captious animadverſions, defeat the proper influence of the word on youthful minds. What is pertinent to your caſe, take home to yourſelves, and aſſiſt your youths in applying what is pertinent to theirs. Retain and improve what is good. If you meet with any thing, which appears otherwiſe, let prudence point out the proper time and place to mention it.

3. Theſe

3. These persons helped Paul by their *conversation* and *example*.

From a particular instance, mentioned in the xviiith chapter of the Acts, we learn, how assiduous they were, by their private conversation, to promote the interest of the gospel. When Paul went from Corinth to Jerusalem, they accompanied him as far as Ephesus. Here they met with Apollos, who was an eloquent and zealous man, and mighty in the scriptures of the old testament, and had been instructed in the way of the Lord; but being a Jew, and having lived in Alexandria, he had not yet gained a complete knowledge of the gospel. Aquila and his wife heard Apollos speak in the Jewish synagogue, and teach the things of the Lord. But finding, that he needed farther information, they took him and expounded to him the way of the Lord more perfectly. After this Apollos helped those much, who through grace had believed. Their attention, in this case, shews their pious concern to be useful by private instruction.

My Christian friends, you may greatly help your minister, by inculcating on your families the truths which you hear from him—by adding your own to his reproofs and exhortations—by seasonable admonitions to the young members of other families—and often, too, by your advice to him, as well as by applying for his advice in your spiritual concerns. Apollos, after he began to teach the things of the Lord, was more perfectly instructed

structed in those things, by conversation with private Christians.

You may be especially helpful by your holy example. This, as far as it is seen, will be a standing exhortation to virtue, and reproof to vice. Let your light so shine, that all around you may see your good works, and glorify God.

4. They were doubtless helpful by their *prayers*.

Paul greatly valued the prayers of Christians; and, from a persuasion of his continual remembrance in them, was mightily encouraged in his work. He says to the Corinthians, "God has delivered us from death, and we trust he will yet deliver us, you also helping together by prayer for us."—He entreats the brethren, for the Lord Jesus's sake, and for the love of the Spirit, that they would "strive together with him in their prayers to God for him, that he might be delivered from them, who believe not; that his own service might be accepted of the saints; that utterance might be given him; and that he might speak the word, as he ought to speak." If the fervent prayers of the righteous avail much, they may, by their prayers, exceedingly help their minister in his work; and while they help him, they may help their own souls, too, and the souls of many around them.

5. The Apostle particularly remarks, that these persons, *for his life, had laid down their own necks, for which service, not only he, but all the churches of the Gentiles, gave them thanks.*

He here refers to some case, in which they had rescued

rescued his life with the hazard of their own. What the particular case was, we are not informed; but it was then in the churches a matter of publick notoriety, and general gratitude and praise.

Their motive, in this case, was not a partial affection for Paul, but a regard to the general interest of religion. This Apostle, in preaching the gospel, shewed the same benevolence. He says to the Philippians—*If I be offered on the sacrifice and service of your faith, I joy and rejoice with you all.* And to the elders of Ephesus—*In every city bonds and afflictions abide me; but none of these things move me, neither count I my life dear to myself, so that I may finish my course with joy, and the ministry, which I have received of the Lord Jesus, to testify the gospel of the grace of God.* The Apostle John says—*We ought to lay down our lives for the brethren.* His meaning cannot be, that one man is simply bound to die for another. This would be carrying the rule of benevolence beyond the limits which Christ has stated. " Love thy neighbour, *as thyself.*" The precept, understood in so absolute a sense, would come to nothing. For if I am bound to take on myself my brother's danger, then he is bound immediately to take it back. But his intention must be, that in some extraordinary cases, especially in cases where the life and happiness of numbers are depending, we ought to interpose for the preservation of our brethren, though it be with great danger to ourselves. On a principle of general benevolence,

the

the Apostle sought not *his own* profit, but the profit of *many*, that they might be *saved*. He supposes it possible, that for a *good* man, a man of extensive beneficence and usefulness, in distinction from a man who is *merely righteous*, some would dare to die; because with his life the happiness of numbers is connected. What the Apostle so highly commends in Aquila and his wife, was their general benevolence; their concern for the interest of the churches, and their zeal for the extensive spread of the gospel among the Gentiles. The spirit which appeared in them, ought to operate in all Christians, and such a spirit, operating in Christian professors, would greatly facilitate and increase the success of ministers.

III. There is one thing more to be observed in the character of these persons. *They had a church in their house.* Their family resembled a church.

The honourable appellation, which the Apostle bestows on their household, suggests what a kind of family theirs was, and what every family ought to be.

To justify the application of such a name, a family must be under wholesome discipline and prudent government. There must be in it order and regularity. Each member must know his own station, and observe his proper place. The heads must preside with wisdom and dignity; and the subordinate members must obey with cheerfulness, and submit with reverence. Stated worship must be maintained, the scriptures read, instructions communicated, reproofs administered,

love

love diffused through all the branches, and peace unite them in one body. Such is the proper state of a church, and such the state of a family which resembles a church. Such then was the household of Aquila, which the Apostle salutes by this honourable name.

A house, in which there is no peace or order; no social worship or religious instruction; but every one walks in his own way, and pursues his own inclination; the heads contend with each other, and the children despise both; the former treat religion with neglect, and the latter grow up in ignorance and vice; such a house is not a church, but a Babel.

We, then, who have the care of families, ought to make them churches. For this end we must dedicate our children to God, and bring them up in his fear, instruct them in the doctrines of the gospel, govern them with wisdom, lead them in prayer, encourage their attendance on the ordinances of the sanctuary, and inculcate on them the necessity of a heart devoted to God.

The Apostle's commendation of the example under consideration, is a severe reproof on those, who call not on God's name, nor train up their children in the way in which they should walk.

The growth and prosperity of the church of Christ, depend much on family religion. As this is attended or neglected, that will increase or decline.

Greater societies are formed from smaller; churches grow out of families; and the spirit and complexion

complexion of the latter will be transfused through the former.

When family religion sinks into disuse and discredit, publick worship will be more and more neglected, ordinances will be despised, the sabbath profaned, or but carelessly observed, and the number, or, at least, the proportion of open professors, will diminish more and more.

But when families become little churches, real societies of religion; when prayer is maintained, instruction communicated, government exercised, and order preserved, according to the commands of Christ, then will the young, under these benign influences, spring up as among the grass, and as willows by the water courses, and will yield the pleasant fruits of righteousness, as plants which God has nourished. They will come and join themselves to the Lord in a perpetual covenant. They will encourage one another, and say, Come, let us turn to the Lord, let us go up to his house, and he will teach us of his ways, and we will walk in his paths. The church here below, thus growing out of godly families, will bear a beautiful resemblance to the church above. And the saints, translated to the superiour world, will find themselves in the midst of that society, for which they were preparing on earth. The church will then be properly the gate of heaven, and easy will be the passage through this gate into the city of God.

END OF THE SIXTEENTH SERMON.

SERMON XVII.

Children, in the Temple, praising the Redeemer.

MATTHEW 21. xv, xvi.

And when the chief priests and scribes saw the wonderful things that he did, and the children crying in the temple, and saying, Hosanna to the Son of David; they were sore displeased, and said unto him, ¿ Hearest thou what these say? And Jesus saith unto them, Yea; ¿ Have ye never read, Out of the mouth of babes and sucklings thou hast perfected praise?

THE prophet Zechariah foretold, that the King of Sion would come to her, meek and lowly, sitting on an ass, on a colt, the foal of an ass. In this manner, the evangelist tells us, Jesus once made his publick entry into Jerusalem. "In the eastern countries, riding on horses was anciently reckoned the greatest ostentation of magnificence. It was therefore becoming the meekness of the lowly Jesus, that, in his entry into the capital city, he chose to ride on an ass. At the same time,

time, there was nothing mean or ridiculous in it, asses being the beasts, which the easterns commonly made use of in riding." The particular reason of his riding into the city, might be the throng, which now, at the time of the passover, attended him, and which would have much incommoded him, had he walked on foot, as usual. Besides; as he was about to perform some mighty works in the city, he might choose, on this occasion, to be distinguished from the multitude. However, to avoid unnecessary ostentation, he rode in the humble manner abovementioned.

It was become a prevailing opinion, that he was the Messiah, and would soon take the government into his hands. Many, probably, expected that he would do it at this passover. Some therefore spread their garments in the way, and others cut down the boughs of trees, and strewed them along the road: A kind of honour, which was sometimes paid to kings when they entered into populous cities. When the front of the procession, which attended Jesus, had reached the descent of the mount of Olives, where the royal city rose to view, they were met by a multitude coming from the city, to join them, with palm branches in their hands. As soon as these from the city met the procession, they exclaimed—*Hosanna, blessed is the King of Israel, who cometh in the name of the Lord.* The disciples attending Jesus, echoed back the salutation—*Hosanna to the Son of David; blessed is he who cometh in the name of the Lord;*

Lord ; Hosanna in the highest. When he came to Jerusalem, all the city was moved, saying, *¿ Who is this?* The multitude answered—*This is Jesus the prophet of Nazareth.*

Jesus now enters the temple, purges it of the various articles of commerce which he found there, and reproves the traders for turning it into a house of merchandize. Awed by the acclamations of the multitude, they submitted to his authority.

While he was in the temple, the blind, lame, and sick, in great numbers, were brought to him to be healed. The youth, who attended the passover, as they usually did from the age of twelve years, were astonished at the works which he performed. When they observed, how the blind, who had been led groping along, now dismissed their guides, and walked whither they would— how the cripples, who had been laid down at his feet, rose up and walked nimbly away—how the dumb, on a sudden, burst forth into praise; and the deaf, catching the song, joined their joyful voice—they felt the power of conviction, and proclaimed him the promised Messiah.

The scribes and Pharisees, seeing his wonderful works, and hearing the acclamations of the children, were much displeased; but being restrained, by fear of the multitude, they made no violent opposition. They only expostulated with him—*¿ Hearest thou what these say ?* Insinuating, perhaps, that the children ascribed to him glories, which he had no right to claim; or that

they

they uttered things which they did not understand. He answered them by a passage from the eighth Psalm. "¿ Have ye never read—*Out of the mouth of babes and sucklings thou hast ordained praise?*"

That Psalm was probably composed by David, on the victory which was obtained over the Philistines, when he slew the giant of Gath. And the expression may be intended to celebrate the power of God, in accomplishing so great an event by so feeble an instrument. Or, it may allude to the songs, in which the women, coming out of the cities with their children, celebrated this wonderful victory. By applying to the present case these words of David, Jesus signified, that the meanest of God's works display his power; and as the Father receives praise from the least of his creatures, so the Son disdains not the honours offered him by little children. In the present instance, their praise was peculiarly beautiful and pertinent, as it shewed that Christ's miracles were so illustrious, as to strike even youthful minds with wonder and conviction. The praise of the Redeemer, on this occasion, might, with singular propriety, be said, to be perfected out of the mouth of babes.

From the passage now illustrated, some instructions may be collected especially pertinent to the young.

1. We here see, that real piety is not confined to men of years, or of learning. It sometimes
makes

makes a lovely appearance in children and youth.

While the Pharisees and doctors of the law rejected the Redeemer, praise to him was ordained out of the mouth of babes. Those wonderful works, which the former perversely imputed to the power of Satan, struck the latter with conviction, that Jesus was the Christ. Those doctrines of grace, which awakened the indignation of the one, touched the hearts of the other with admiration, and tuned their lips to praise. The priests and scribes enjoyed the fairest opportunities to hear the doctrines, and behold the miracles of Jesus, and to observe in him the fulfilment of the prophecies concerning the Messiah. But their pride, ambition, and selfconfidence, rendered them blind to the evidence of truth, and insensible to the power of argument. These tender minds, in which such perverse affections had not begun to operate, felt conviction, and embraced the truth, on the first proposal of its evidence.

Christ crucified, was to the Jews a stumbling block, and to the Greeks foolishness; but to them who were called, the power and the wisdom of God. Meek and humble minds discern that wisdom, and feel that power in religion, which the vain and selfrighteous will not confess. Not many wise men after the flesh, not many mighty, not many noble, are called; for God hath chosen the foolish things of this world to confound the wise; the weak things to confound the mighty; and things which are not, to bring to nought

things

things which are, that no flesh should glory in his presence.

True religion in the heart depends not on superiour abilities, but on a teachable and humble spirit. Our Saviour has instructed us, that if we would enter into his kingdom, we must humble ourselves, and become as little children. The Apostles direct us, to receive with meekness the engrafted word, which is able to save our souls; to lay apart all guile and hypocrify, and, like newborn babes, to desire the sincere milk of the word, that we may grow thereby.

You see, then, my young hearers, the wisdom of an early attention to religion. Certain *natural* qualities, favourable to religion, you have now; but you will not carry them with you through life. In the first stages of youth, there is a desire of knowledge, a sensibility of mind, a modesty and docility of spirit, which you will not retain after you have accustomed yourselves to the ways and manners of the world. When pride and hardness of heart shall have supplanted these natural dispositions; and when the perplexity of worldly cares and designs shall have banished all religious concern, you will, with greater difficulty and reluctance, bow to the gospel of Christ. If, before you can enter into the kingdom of God, you must be brought to the tempers and dispositions of children—must, in a sense, come back to what you are now, Is it not best to enter into the kingdom now, while you are children, and

before

before you have outgrown the difpofitions which at prefent favour your entrance?

Your *natural* humility, tendernefs and teachablenefs, are not real holinefs; but they are certainly more favourable than the oppofite tempers, to the introduction of real holinefs. The fcripture reprefents them fo, and urges you to take the benefit of them, while you may.

2. We fee that religion, in its main fubftance, is adapted to the capacity of the young.

The Jewifh children were eafily convinced, that Jefus of Nazareth was the promifed Meffiah. It required no laboured reafoning, or depth of learning, to fee, that no man could fpeak as he fpake, or do the works which he did, except God were with him.

The fyftem of religion contains, indeed, many things above the comprehenfion, not only of children, but of mortals. Thefe, however, are not the moft effential things. What immediately relates to our duty, and concerns our falvation, is level to common capacities. The Apoftles, confidering themfelves as debtors both to the wife and unwife, ufed great plainnefs of fpeech. They wrote to young men and little children, as well as to aged men and fathers; and they wrote with perfpicuity.

Think not, then, ye youths, that you may, for the prefent, poftpone religion, as a matter beyond your capacity. In the Saviour's day, there were children, out of whofe mouths praife was perfected.

¿ Does not every thing which you see, teach you, that there is a God; that he is powerful, wife and good; and that you are daily dependent on him, and indebted to him?—¿ Do you find any difficulty in underſtanding good and evil, and in determining what you ought to do, and what you ought to avoid?—¿When you have ſinned, and doubtleſs you know that you ſin often, Is it not a plain caſe, that God is diſhonoured and offended, and that you muſt, by repentance, apply to him for pardon? The goſpel teaches you, that God has ſent his Son into the world to redeem ſinners, by ſuffering death for their ſins. ¿ Is not this an encouragement to your hope, and a motive to your repentance?— ¿ When you read the hiſtory of your Redeemer's life, and obſerve the meekneſs, humility, patience, goodneſs and benevolence, which appeared in him, Are you not pleaſed with the example, and convinced that you ought to imitate it?— ¿ When you are told, that you have immortal ſouls, which muſt live in another world, and be happy or miſerable there, according to the courſe which you now purſue, Are you in doubt to judge what is meant by all this, or what manner of perſons you ought to be?

Theſe are the great things, which immediately concern you; and I queſtion not, but you well underſtand them. I am ſure, that by attention, you may underſtand them. The obligations of religion then lie on you, as well as on others.

Think not to excuse yourselves from it, as a matter too high for you. Improve the advantages given you; gain the knowledge which you may, and act according to the knowledge which you have, and you will doubtless meet the approbation of your God.

3. From the example before us, we learn, that great benefit may accrue to youth, from a stated attendance on divine institutions.

At the time of the passover, these children met with Jesus in the temple.

The passover was instituted in commemoration of the deliverance of the Jews from Egypt, and in prefiguration of the redemption of mankind by Jesus Christ. One design of this festival was, that when children in time to come should inquire, what was meant by this service, the parents should instruct them, how God, by a mighty hand, saved his people from bondage. As soon as children arrived to such an age, as to bring an offering in their hands, they were to appear with their parents at the temple, and there to celebrate the feast. Luke tells us, It was the custom of the feast for children to attend it, when they were twelve years old.

The Jews, though much degenerated in our Saviour's time, generally observed the publick forms of religion. They early brought their children to the passover. Happy it was for many of them, that they were brought to *this* passover. Here they met with the Saviour. They saw his works,

works, and heard his words; their hearts were warmed with love to him, and their mouths were filled with his praise. What a loss they might have sustained, had they been absent now! Christ, at appointed seasons, visited the temple. He honoured divine institutions: They, who would receive his blessing, must honour them too.

Publick worship is as much an ordinance of God under the gospel, as was the passover under the law.

The example of the Jews, in bringing their children to the temple, reproves the neglect of many Christians. ¿Do you imagine, that your children can receive no benefit from the services of the sanctuary? You know not how early the grace of God may open the heart to attend to the things which are spoken, and to receive the influence of divine truths. By a regular and constant attendance, they will be found in the way of God's blessing. If they have not capacity to follow a train of thoughts through a sermon or prayer, yet their minds may be affected with the general solemnity of the appearance. They will grow up with a sense that there is something important in religion. They will be early habituated to religious order. They will, now and then, imbibe a useful sentiment. They will gradually increase in knowledge; and, perhaps, some seasonable admonition may leave an abiding impression.

Consider,

Confider, ye youths, that there is no fmall hazard in an unnecceffary abfence from the place of worfhip, and in a carelefs behaviour there. You fee what certain youths obtained by an attendance at the paffover, and what they would have miffed, if they had refufed to repair to the temple, when Jefus was there, or had been regardlefs of what they faw and heard. If you defire to know your Saviour, and to receive the bleffings of his love, come to the place, where he has appointed to meet you. ¿ Do you think lightly of the ftated worfhip of the Lord's day ? Let me afk you, ¿ Is it not an inftitution of Chrift ; an inftitution, which his difciples obferved, and which he himfelf honoured with his prefence ?— ¿ Is it a light matter to defpife the grace, the authority, and the example of your Redeemer ?— ¿ Do you not believe, that your falvation muft come from him ; that you muft feek it in order to obtain it ; and feek it in the way, which he has prefcribed ? You think, perhaps, that a more private attendance upon him, will be fufficient. This indeed muft be done ; but leave not the other undone. While you neglect publick means, there is little room to hope for his bleffing on private means, and little reafon to believe, that you will regard them. Whatever you may pretend, as long as you are indifferent to the publick inftitutions of Chrift, you will pay no great attention to the more private exercifes of piety.

4. We

4. We are here taught, that the young are under some special obligations to acknowledge and praise the Redeemer. That which was chiefly commended in these Jewish children, was, that they cried in the temple—*Hosanna to the Son of David*. Their regard to the Saviour, led them openly to confess him in a publick assembly.

As Jesus is the author of salvation to sinners, the mediator through whom they must come to God, so faith in him, love and gratitude to him, and an explicit acknowledgment of him, are essential to real religion. These regards and honours to him, are due no less from the young, than from others.

True religion in you, my children, will operate in pious affections and exercises of heart toward your Redeemer. You are a part of the fallen race, which he came to redeem. You have sinned and come short of the glory of God; and your salvation must come through him. He has expressed a particular tenderness and concern for such as you. He became a child, that he might teach you how children ought to walk, and to please God. When he appeared in publick life, he never overlooked those of your age and standing. He gathered the lambs with his arms, and carried them in his bosom. Many of the miracles which he wrought, to confirm the truth of his religion, were in healing the diseases, and relieving the distresses of the young. He directed that children should be brought to him; and those

those who came he graciously received. He owned little ones as his disciples, and denounced his severest wrath against those who should despise them, or lay stumbling blocks in their way. They had a particular share in his prayers on earth, nor can we think they are forgotten in his intercessions above. Many declarations and promises he has made in their favour; and has solemnly charged, not only parents, but ministers, to feed his lambs. In them he encouraged the small beginnings of faith and piety. He was careful not to overburden the feeble, but to assist their virtuous resolutions. In his last sufferings, he remembered children, and spake of them with tender compassion. And, ¿ What think you?—¿ Do you owe nothing to him?—¿ Is he entitled to no regards and honours from you? This Divine Benefactor had you much on his heart when he came from heaven, when he dwelt on earth, when he suffered on the cross, when he arose and ascended to heaven: He has you on his heart still: And, ¿ Will you make him no returns? Give him your hearts, and consecrate to him your lives: He has given *his* life for you. Renounce the vanities and vices of the world: He came to deliver you from this evil world. Confess his name before men: He has not been ashamed to own and commend the youths who believed in him. In a word—by the mercies of Christ I beseech you, that you present yourselves living sacrifices holy and acceptable to him, which is your reasonable service. And be

not

not conformed to this world, but be ye transformed by the renewing of your minds.

We may observe, once more,

V. That youthful piety is peculiarly pleasing to Christ.

When children sung praises in the temple, Jesus vindicated them from the obloquy of the impious scribes, and applauded their faith and devotion, as bringing glory to God. There were multitudes, who, on this occasion, sung the same anthem of praise; but the children he singled out as objects of his special approbation and delight. Piety he loves in all; but in none more than in the young.

Fear not, ye serious youths, that he will despise the day of small things—that he will disdain the praises and prayers offered from your uninstructed tongues. He loves the undissembled language of the penitent and believing heart, however incorrect and imperfect may be the language of the lips. He observes your honest resolutions, hears your humble prayers, and will assist your virtuous endeavours. He will not quench, but fan the smoking flax. He will not break, but support the bruised reed. The good work which he begins, he is ready to complete.

Be encouraged, then, to commit your souls to the care, and to devote your lives to the service, of your Redeemer. ¿When you see how pleased he is with your obedience, Will you deny it to him?— ¿When you observe how he delights in
your

your praise, Will you be silent? The prophet says—*He shall see of the travail of his soul, and be satisfied.* Great were his sufferings for the sins of men. But when he sees the success of them in bringing sinners to repentance and salvation, then he is satisfied; and peculiarly so, when such as you are drawn to him. He has made a general declaration, that those who come to him, he will not cast out; and a particular promise, that they who seek him early shall find him.

Go, my children, and seek him now. But think not at the same time, to indulge the pleasures of sin, and the vanities of the world. No; if you seek him, let these go their way. He bore your sins, that you, being dead to sin, should live unto righteousness.

Learn of him, and you will find that rest to your souls, which is not to be found in the ways of the world. Take his yoke, for it is easy. Submit to the burden which he lays on you, for it is light, and his grace, in the time of need, will sustain you. Trials you may meet with in his service, but he will not forsake you. He will proportion his grace to your temptations, or moderate them to your strength. He will lead you along by such gentle steps, that you will not faint, nor be weary. He will stay his rough wind in the day of his east wind. He will gradually train you up to such strength and fortitude, that you may cheerfully meet every trial appointed you. He considers the weakness of your age, and the feebleness of your

first

first virtuous purposes. He knows your state, and remembers that you are babes. Wait on the Lord, and be of good courage, and he will strengthen your heart. He giveth power to the faint; and to them who have no might, he increaseth strength. When the youths shall faint and be weary, and the young men shall utterly fall, they who wait on the Lord shall renew their strength. They shall mount up with wings as eagles; they shall run, and not be weary; they shall walk, and not faint.

END OF THE SEVENTEENTH SERMON.

SERMON XVIII.

The Necessity of early Religion.

ECCLESIASTES 12, i.

Remember now thy Creator in the days of thy youth.

THIS advice of the preacher supposes the importance of the rising generation. He considered them as worthy of his particular attention; and surely they are worthy of their own. They should not view themselves as insignificant beings, placed in the world only for amusement, pleasure and trifling, but remember, that their own happiness, and the happiness of multitudes around them, and of thousands who are coming after them, much depends on the part which they shall act in life. They can in no way answer the vast design of their intellectual existence, nor sustain the dignity of their rank in the rational creation, without religion. The preacher, therefore, in our text, earnestly admonishes them—*to remember now their Creator in the days of their youth.*

We may observe,

I. God is here exhibited to them in the character of their *Creator.*

As

As creation is the first and most obvious evidence, which they can have of the existence of the Deity, so their first apprehensions of him, and regards to him, are in this character. In calling them therefore to early religion, Solomon, with great propriety, exhorts them to *remember their Creator*.

When they begin to reflect, they find that they can look back but a few months or years; that the other day they had not even an existence; that very lately they rose from nothing, and became such beings as they are. Hence they know, that there must be some invisible power, which made them.

They find themselves placed in a spacious world, and surrounded with a thousand wonders; they behold the heavenly curtains stretched over their heads, and beautified with innumerable lights; they see the earth peopled with various kinds of creatures, and spread with various bounties, for their supply; they observe the rolling seasons, and the daily changes of light and darkness. From hence they have sensible evidence, that there is a superiour Being, who made and upholds them, and all things around them. If they naturally conclude, that *every house is builded by some man;* the conclusion is as natural, that *he who built all things, is God.*

From the inward powers of perception, thought and reason, they know that the Creator must be perfectly wise. ¿ For he who formed the eye,

Shall

Shall not he see?—¿ He who planted the ear, Shall not he hear?—¿ He who teacheth man knowledge, Shall not he know?

When they confider the grandeur of the world, the mighty effects produced before their eyes, and the bountiful supplies afforded to all living creatures, they are at once convinced, that their Creator is infinite in power, rich in goodness, and present in every place.

These sentiments of the Deity easily arise in the mind of every serious and contemplative youth. In the first openings of reason, the young are more given to inquisitive speculation than perhaps some are apt to imagine. The new objects which continually meet their eyes, awaken thought and contemplation in their minds; and if, in this early stage, proper assistance and encouragement were afforded them, they would make easy progress in the knowledge of moral and divine things, and deeply imbibe those sentiments of virtue and religion, which might abide with them through life, and preserve them from the fatal influence of temptation and vice.

We may observe,

II. Solomon here expresses the piety of the young by their *remembering their Creator*.

It is usual in scripture to express the whole of religion by some leading temper or principle; as the knowledge of God, faith in him, love to him, and the fear of him. When a particular virtue or **duty** is enjoined, as a condition of the

divine

divine favour, we must always understand it, as including all those tempers and actions, which are naturally connected with it, or flow from it. To *know God*, is to serve him with an upright heart. To *fear God*, is to depart from evil. The *love of God*, is to keep his commandments. They who have *believed in him*, will be careful to maintain good works.

In the same latitude we must understand *the remembrance* of God. This is not a transient thought, or occasional recollection, that there is a God; but an habitual, influential apprehension of him, and regard to him. It is such a firm belief of his existence, such a just knowledge of his character, such a lively and steady sense of his presence, as shall awaken and preserve suitable affections to him, and produce a correspondent life of humble obedience.

Remembrance is not the learning of something new, but the recollection and retention of something already known. The young are here supposed to have a knowledge of their Creator; to have attended to the evidences of his existence; and to have gained a general acquaintance with his character and will; and they are directed immediately to apply their knowledge to the purpose of real, practical piety.

This is, then, the spirit and meaning of Solomon's address.

"O youth, thou knowest, that there is a God, who made thee, and who created the world, in
which

which thou art placed. And, Wilt thou live unmindful of him? Often confider, what a being he is. Remember that he is a being of infinite power, wifdom, and goodnefs; that he is always prefent with thee, obferving all thy thoughts, words, and actions, and that he will bring every work into judgment, with every fecret thing. Set him always before thine eyes, act under a fenfe of his prefence, call upon him for all that thou needeft, give him thanks for all that thou enjoyeft, acknowledge him in all thy ways, approve thyfelf to him in all that thou doft, and feek his favour with thy whole heart."

We may obferve,

III. Solomon recommends to the young a *direct* and *immediate* application to religion. "Remember *now* thy Creator."

There are few, perhaps, but who intend to devote themfelves to God. The young intend to ferve him in their youth. Though they procraftinate religion today, and think they may fafely do the fame tomorrow, yet they mean not to neglect it through all the period of their youth. They have often been told, and they partly believe, that youth is the moft favourable feafon to begin fo great a work. They know, that they are commanded to engage in it; and they would not *wholly* difobey. But confider, my friends, the fame command, which enjoins you to remember God *in your youth*, enjoins you to remember him *now*. What part of youth you will take for
remembering

remembering God, is no more at your option, than what part of life you will take. You are as expresfsly required to ferve God in youth, as to ferve him at all; and to ferve him now, as to ferve him in youth. You have no more liberty to poftpone religion to the laft ftage of youth, than to the laft hour of life.

Allow me then to inculcate upon you the neceffity of early religion, and your obligation to apply yourfelves to it immediately, and without delay.

1. Let us refume the thought juft now fuggefted, that this is the *exprefs command* of your Creator.

That religion is a matter of indifpenfable neceffity, you will not deny; for you believe, that there is an infinite, allperfect God—that you are moral and accountable creatures—that your happinefs depends on his favour—and that you can fecure his favour only by devoting yourfelves to his fervice.

Now, while you acknowledge that religion is important to mankind in general, you muft acknowledge it to be equally important to yourfelves in particular. For all the reafons in which it is founded, take place with refpect to you; and the divine command, which enjoins it in general, enjoins it *exprefsly* on you. If God had only required his rational creatures to remember him, you muft have confidered yourfelves as coming within the intention of the command. But the matter is not left at large. You are exprefsly

S   and

and particularly pointed out as the subjects of the command—*Remember your Creator in the days of your youth.* Begin a religious life with the first opening of your reason. Devote to God your best days, the flower of your strength. ¿ Is there any room for evasion ?—¿ Is there any subterfuge by which you can withdraw yourselves from the authority of so express a command ? So long as you neglect religion, you live in plain disobedience, not only to the command, which enjoins religion on all men, but to that also which enjoins it distinctly and explicitly on you. And if repentance must respect all known sin, it must, whenever it takes place, particularly respect this youthful delay of repentance. Paul laments, that he was born out of due time. He honours those who were in Christ before him.

2. To convince you farther of the necessity of youthful religion, I would remind you of the means which God has required others to use with you for this purpose.

Your Creator has brought you into existence in a manner favourable to your early nurture and education. He has placed you under the care of those who naturally feel for your welfare. He has, in most express terms, enjoined on them an attention to your moral conduct and religious improvement. As you advance from childhood to youth, you become entitled to more publick instructions. The ministers of religion are to consider you as a part of their charge.

While

While they intreat the aged to be grave, temperate, sober, and sound in faith, they are to exhort the young to be soberminded.

If youthful religion was of little importance, such orders would never have been given. If you had a right to live in the neglect of religion, there could be no reason, why they who go before you, should teach you knowledge, make you to understand doctrine, and give you line upon line, and precept upon precept. The success of their labours depends on your concurrence. Obstinacy and perverseness in you, will defeat their wisest and best endeavours. If they must instruct, warn and reprove, you must hear, learn and obey. If they are to watch over you, you are to watch over yourselves. If they are to commend you to the grace of God, you are to seek unto God betimes. Every precept which you find in the Bible, requiring others to consult your spiritual interest, is an admonition to you of the necessity of early religion, and a call to remember your Creator in the days of your youth.

3. The importance of youthful religion farther appears in the particular promises of grace, which God has made to the young.

The gospel, which teaches us our native depravity, and the necessity of a moral change in our tempers, teaches us also, that to effect this change a divine influence is necessary. Sinners are indeed required to make them a new heart. But whatever means they use for this purpose, it is the grace of God, which gives them succefs. And not only so, but the first convictions and awakenings, by which sinners are excited to the use of the appointed means of religion, are the effects of God's preventing grace. *Behold*, says the Saviour, *I stand at the door and knock; if any man hear my voice, and open the door, I will come in to him, and sup with him.* It is not the sinner's towardly disposition, which first invites the Saviour to knock; but his knocking which first awakens in the sinner a disposition to open. The first motion is from the Saviour; not from the sinner.

Now it is to be remembered, that God has given particular encouragement of success to them who seek him early. To them he will pour out his spirit, and make known his words. To them he is peculiarly near, and of them he will be found. Wherever he sends his word, he sends the influence of his spirit to accompany it. The gospel is called the ministration of the spirit; and men are said to receive the spirit in the hearing of faith. This gracious influence is especially promised and vouchsafed to the young. This is God's promise to his covenant people—*I will pour my spirit on thy seed, and my blessing on thine offspring.* There is undoubtedly a time, when the spirit of grace strives with them, to awaken serious sentiments, convictions, and resolutions, and to excite their attention to their immortal interest. He may strive with sinners in a more advanced age:

But

But in youth he fails not to strive often and earnestly. There are some, whom God gives over to a reprobate mind. But these are such as have rebelled and vexed the Holy Spirit. There are some, from whom the things of their peace are hidden. But there was first a day of visitation.

Remember, my young friends, the peculiar advantages which attend this early period of your life. You not only enjoy the external means of religion, but in addition to these, there are some attendant influences of the Spirit, of which you are the subjects. And let me ask you, ¿ Have you not experienced them ?—¿ Can you not recollect some sensible convictions of conscience—some deep remorse for your youthful follies—some sober resolutions for a virtuous life, which have been excited in your attendance on the appointed means of religion ?—¿ Are not these the fruits of that promise of the spirit, which God has made to the young ? This is the voice of divine wisdom ; and it is directed particularly to the young—*If thou criest after knowledge, and liftest up thy voice for understanding ; if thou seekest her as silver, and searchest for her, as for hidden treasures, then shalt thou understand the fear of the Lord, and find the knowledge of God. Turn ye at my reproof ; behold I will pour out my spirit unto you.*

How precious is this opportunity ! You have not only the means of religion in common with others ; but calls and encouragements peculiar to yourselves. Say not, There is nothing, which you

you can do. Impotent you are in yourselves. But you are not left to yourselves. Under the instructions of the word, and the strivings of the Spirit, there is something which you may do. Imagine not that all your prayers and endeavours are abomination to God. Those prayers and endeavours, to which you are excited by the convictions and strivings of the spirit of God, are not to be called by this name. God does not abhor the work of his own spirit. I beseech you, neglect not this season. ¿When will you find another as good? You may, perhaps, still enjoy some of the same means; but you will not enjoy them all. Parental instructions, admonitions, and restraints, will soon cease. You will gradually outgrow your native tenderness and sensibility. Vicious indulgences will introduce a hardness and obstinacy of heart. And, what is especially to be regarded, you will soon get beyond the encouragement arising from the promises made peculiarly to the young. There is indeed always room for the awakened and thoughtful to hope in God's mercy. But the encouragements given especially to the young, you can apply no longer than while you are young. In a little time you will have no more right to them than your grandsires have now. You will have lost the benefit of them. Your hope must be drawn from more general declarations of God's mercy. ¿Is it nothing to throw by an encouragement, which God has vouchsafed peculiarly to you?—

¿Is

Is it not your wisdom to improve an opportunity so kind and favourable as this?

You cannot possibly get forward to mature age, in a state of impenitence, without aggravated guilt. The guilt of abusing youthful advantages, and of opposing the spirit of God, will pursue you through all the stages of an ungodly life. If you believe that, in the work of your salvation, you are dependent on the grace of God, attend to it at this time, when you have the express offers of his grace. You know not, but when this season is past, his grace may be forever withdrawn.

4. The various contingences, which attend futurity, prove the necessity of early religion.

If religion is necessary to your eternal happiness, it demands your immediate attention. Rash adventures in matters of everlasting importance, ought never to be made. The frailty and uncertainty of human life are plain to your observation, and ought to be familiar to your thoughts. The continuance of reason depends on God's good pleasure; not on your intentions. What changes of condition await you, and how soon you may be placed beyond the enjoyment of the means of salvation, you know not. Nor can you tell what temptations and inticements may meet you, when you step forward on the stage, mingle in the affairs, and associate with the men of the world. If the principles of virtue are not early fixed in your hearts, the dangers before you may be fatal. There is such a thing as the final withdrawment of God's grace, and a heart hardened through the deceitfulness of sin. We hope this not to be the case of the young. But the highminded and presumptuous youth, knows not how soon it may be his case.

You see then, that you have no security of any opportunity but the present. All before you is darkness and uncertainty. If you consider religion as necessary, it is your wisdom to engage in it immediately. Remember now your Creator, before the evil day comes. Put not far from you this evil day. Give glory to God, before he cause darkness, and before your feet stumble on the dark mountains; lest, while you look for light, it be turned into the shadow of death.

5. Besides those solemn arguments, which are taken from another world, the scripture often urges youth to early religion by arguments taken from this world; which, though far less important in themselves, are adapted to influence tender minds just opening to worldly prospects.

Come, ye children, says David, *hearken unto me, and I will teach you the fear of the Lord. ¿ What man is he that desireth life, and loveth many days, that he may see good? Keep thy tongue from evil, and thy lips from speaking guile. Depart from evil and do good; seek peace and pursue it.* In the writings of Solomon, similar observations often occur.—*My son, forget not my law, but let thine heart keep my commandments; for length of days, and long life, and peace shall they add to thee. Honour the Lord*

Lord with thy substance, and with the first fruits of all thine increase; so shall thy barns be filled with plenty.—Happy is the man that findeth wisdom— Length of days is in her right hand, and in her left hand riches and honour; her ways are ways of pleasantness, and all her paths are peace.

Virtue has her native charms, which, properly displayed, will command esteem even from those who have not chosen her for their companion. But her charms never appear to greater advantage, than when displayed in the character of the young. ¿ Did you ever see a youth, who, impressed with the fear of God, and a sense of futurity, carefully shunned the follies and vices of the world, and steadily pursued the path of wisdom—whose natural gaiety was tempered with a religious gravity—whose language, though cheerful, was always discreet; and whose manners, though social, were strictly chaste and pure—who had prudence to decline the known occasions of evil, resolution to withstand a bold temptation, and fortitude to reject a wicked inticement—who could, on proper occasions, mingle with his youthful companions, and yet have no fellowship with their unfruitful works, but rather reprove them—whose governing aim was to act right, without the vanity of human applause—and who, while he maintained a virtuous character, ever preserved a modesty and humility becoming his age?—¿ Did you ever see such a youth? Tell me, if you did not esteem him; if you did not covet his reputation, and almost

most envy his happiness. ¿ Have you ever seen a contrary character? and, ¿ Did you not despise and condemn it? Believe then, that the virtuous youth has favour and good understanding in the sight of God and men.

As you are rational beings, you have a part to act in the world. You are to be members of society, and to take a share in the common concerns of human life. It is not your wish, nor was it the Creator's design, that you should pass through life solitary and unconnected. No man lives merely to himself. Early piety will lay a foundation for your future dignity and usefulness. Religion has something to do in every station, and in every calling; nor can you properly fill your circle without it. Whatever may be the business assigned you, truth, justice and benevolence, are the principles which must govern you. These you ought early to possess, that you may always feel their influence. A habit of duplicity, fraud and unrighteousness, formed in youth, will operate in the concerns of manhood, and soon plunge you into infamy and ruin. If you now banish religion from your thoughts, you banish all reasonable hope of worldly reputation and prosperity, as well as of future glory.

Think not, however, that the chief reward of piety is in this world. It will indeed bring you *many* blessings, and secure you from *many* evils; but still you are in a world of mortality and change.

Disappointment,

Disappointment, pain, sickness, sorrow and death, await the saint in common with others: But he has consolations, to which the guilty can make no claim. Peace of conscience, and hope in God. a persuasion that all things are meant for his good, and the prospect of immortal glory beyond the grave, are comforts which delight his soul in the day of affliction and in the approach of death. Since no man can escape these events, it is every man's wisdom to be prepared for them. Religion is the only preparation; religion in youth is seasonable preparation. If it would be desirable to escape afflictions; next to this, at least, it is desirable to be prepared for them. Your preparation cannot be too soon, for the necessity may be near.

You will, I presume, set out in life with a desire of usefulness. To crawl obscurely through the world, like a mere reptile, only to eat and sleep, and breathe and die, is too despicable an idea for a rational being. To live only that you may disturb the peace, wound the feelings, injure the characters, and corrupt the manners of mankind, is too near an imitation of infernal spirits, not to be abhorred in your thoughts. ¿Is it then your aim to spend life with dignity to yourselves, and usefulness to others; to enjoy peace of mind while you live, and good hopes when you die; to be had in honourable remembrance among those who survive you; and to meet the smiles of angels, and the approbation of the Judge of all?

Remember

Remember now your Creator in the days of your youth. Know the God who made and preferves you, whofe mercy is your hope, and whofe favour is your happinefs; ferve him with a perfect heart, and with a willing mind. If you feek him, he will be found of you; if you forfake him, he will caft you off forever.

However indifferent this advice may feem now, the day is coming, when you will feel its importance. As you are now climbing the hill, and rifing to maturity, worldly profpects open and expand to your view, and you promife yourfelves a delightful and profperous journey through life. But, believe me, you will foon pafs the fummit, and find yourfelves treading the downward path: Then your worldly profpects will fhorten and fhorten, and the fhadows will ftretch over your heads; and when you fink into the vale of old age, your worldly profpects will difappear. Happy then, if you have better profpects in God.

Hear now the conclufion of the whole matter. *Fear God, and keep his commandments; for this is the whole duty of man.* **For God** *will bring every work into judgment, with* **every** *fecret thing, whether it be good, or whether it be evil.*

END OF THE EIGHTEENTH SERMON.

SERMON XIX.

The Youth assisted in forming his religious Sentiments.

PROVERBS 2. x, xi, xii.

When wisdom entereth into thine heart, and knowledge is pleasant unto thy soul, discretion shall preserve thee, and understanding shall keep thee; to deliver thee from the way of the evil man; from the man that speaketh froward things.

SEVERAL of the first chapters of this book, and this in particular, where our text is, are expresly addressed to the young: And the declared intention of them is, *to give wisdom to the simple, and to the young man knowledge and discretion.* That by wisdom and knowledge we are here to understand the principles and dictates of virtue and religion, is so well known to all who are acquainted with the writings of Solomon, that there is no need of adducing instances to prove it.

Religion is founded in *knowledge*, and therefore it is called by this name. He who acts religiously, acts understandingly. When knowledge

edge is pleasant to his soul, understanding will keep him.

The young, however, are to consider, that there are instructions, which cause to err from the words of knowledge. Solomon therefore urges the necessity of *discretion and understanding, to deliver them from the way of the evil man, the man who speaketh froward things; who leaves the paths of uprightness to walk in the way of darkness; who rejoices to do evil, and delights in the frowardness of the wicked.*

The serious youth will then inquire. How he shall distinguish between truth and errour; between the path of uprightness and the way of darkness?

My design is to answer this inquiry. And I solicit the attention of my young hearers, while I lay before them some plain rules for forming just opinions in matters of religion.

I. Let your minds be impressed with this sentiment, that there is such a thing as religion; and that it is of *serious importance.*

While you are inquiring what religion is, resolve to embrace it, and to walk agreeably to it. *Wisdom must enter into your heart; knowledge must be pleasant to your soul, that it may deliver you from the way of the evil man.*

If you consider religion merely as a matter of speculation and amusement, you will fall in with those opinions and usages, which best please your humour and inclination; or which are recommended by your favourite company and connexions; or rather, you will receive no opinions
heartily

heartily but those which relax the obligations of virtue.

When you see men trifling in religion, turning with every tide, and veering about with every wind of doctrine; when you hear them talk lightly about the concerns of futurity, and arguing in support of notions which favour a licentious life; when you observe them pleased in throwing off those principles, which are the greatest restraints from vice, and the most powerful incentives to virtue; whatever degree of ingenuity, and whatever taste for reading they discover, you may certainly conclude, that they are not inquiring after truth; but are contriving to satisfy their conscience in a course which they are determined to pursue.

The reason why many run into errours in religion, is, because knowledge is not pleasant to their souls; the love of wisdom has never entered into their hearts.

Religion, in its great and essential truths and duties, is so plain, that to understand it, there needs only serious inquiry, guided by a sense of its importance.

Look around, and you will see that there is a Deity daily present with you and working in your sight. Look into yourselves, and you will perceive that you are free and accountable creatures. You must then be under some obligations to this supreme Deity. And these obligations are religion.

The

The obligations of creatures to their Creator, and the duties of moral beings defigned for immortality, muft be infinitely important; and therefore all your religious inquiries fhould be conducted with the greateft ferioufnefs and integrity.

II. Always remember, that religion is *agreeable to the nature of God*. As it is a fervice which you owe to him, **your** ideas of it muft correfpond with his moral character.

Holinefs, juftice, truth, mercy, and goodnefs, are perfections of the Deity; and in **an** imitation of thefe perfections religion primarily confifts.

The gofpel requires, that you become partakers of a divine nature—that you be renewed after the image of him who created you—that you be followers of God as dear children—that you be holy; as he is holy; righteous, as he is righteous; merciful, as he is merciful; **and perfect**, as he is perfect. You muft then, in **all your** religious inquiries, keep **the divine** character in your mind, **and** admit for truth nothing which evidently contradicts it, or reflects difhonour upon it.

Purity in heart, rectitude in your intentions, fincerity in your profeffions and in all your language, juftice and probity **in your actions**, mercy to the unhappy, forgivenefs and love of enemies, **and** good will to all men, are the principal lineaments and features in a religion which God will accept. Other things are neceffary as aids to religion; but thefe muft always be regarded as the great and weighty matters.

III. To

III. To judge what religion is, you must always consider, that it is a *rational thing*.

As it is appointed by a **God** of wisdom, you may conclude, that it bears obvious marks of his wisdom; and as it is designed for intelligent creatures, you may be assured, that its doctrines and precepts are adapted to your understanding, judgment, and conscience. There may be doctrines in it beyond the discovery, and above the comprehension of your reason; for even in the natural world you meet with a thousand unsearchable wonders; but the doctrines of religion, when they are once discovered, and when the evidence of them is stated, will appear reasonable to be believed, and plain, as far as they concern your practice.

Religion, indeed, consists much in the exercise of the *affections*; as fear and hope, love and hatred, sorrow and joy. But these affections can no farther bear a part in religion, than they are under the direction of the understanding. They must not be the fortuitous sallies of a blind and heated imagination; but the calm and rational exercises of an enlightened and well instructed mind.

The religious man knows why he is affected in such a manner—why he hopes or fears—why he loves these objects and hates the contrary—why he is grieved, and why he rejoices. Farther than there is a *reason* for these affections, there can be no *religion* in them.

It is possible, that one may be under painful apprehensions of future punishment, and yet have no disposition to repentance. If his terrours arise, he knows not why, or from what; if he has no idea, what it is that exposes men to the wrath of God, and no sense of any thing in himself, that deserves it, there is nothing in all his terrours, which partakes of the nature of religious conviction, or that leads to real amendment. True conviction is a knowledge of sin by the law, a knowledge of one's own sin, by comparing himself with the law, and a knowledge of the exceeding sinfulness of sin, as a transgression of the law.

Religious *hope* is not a blind and hasty confidence of future happiness, but a rational and scriptural expectation of it, founded in the gracious promises of God, and appropriating these promises by a sincere and deliberate submission to the terms of them.

The pious man *loves God*, from a believing view of him, as a holy, just, good, and excellent being; and he *hates sin* from a sense of its contrariety to the will and character of God, and its inconsistency with his own perfection and happiness.

Holy *joy* springs not from an accidental flow of the animal spirits, but from an experimental evidence of our sincerity, and of our consequent interest in the favour of God.

True religion is *devout*, but not *superstitious*. It will excite you to frequent converse with God,

and

and to a diligent attendance on all the inftituted forms of worfhip; but it will not allow you to reft in thefe exercifes, as the great, or the only things required. It will regard them, not as fubftitutes for holinefs, or compenfations for the want of it, but as means to promote the exercife of it in the heart, and the practice of it in the life. To attend on the inftitutions of God with engagednefs of affection, and purity of intention, is *devotion*. To lay the principal weight on the ceremonial part of religion, or on devices and inventions of men, is *fuperftition*.

True religion is *affectionate*, but not *enthufiaftick*.

It is affectionate or fenfible, in oppofition to *ftupidity*; but not wild in oppofition to reafon. There may be a rational affent to the truths of religion, without a heart to feel them, or be governed by them. This is *ftupidity*. True faith is accompanied with a fenfe of the importance of the things believed. Where this fenfible belief takes place, there will be virtuous refolutions and holy affections—there will be forrow for fin, hope in God's mercy, gratitude to the Redeemer, admiring thoughts of the gofpel falvation, earneft defires of an intereft in it, and humble joy in the evidences of a title to it. Thefe are rational exercifes of mind, and they belong to true piety.

But then to make the *whole* of religion confift in inward emotions—to confider the occafional flow of paffion as a fign of grace in the heart— to depend on our lively feelings as indications of the divine will—to determine our duty, or our state, by impressions made on the imagination—and implicitly to follow every powerful impulse, or sudden suggestion, in opposition to the dictates of reason and the voice of revelation, this is to supplant religion by *enthusiasm*.

Though every degree of this spirit may not be inconsistent with integrity, yet the full dominion of it will exclude religion.

Bear it then in your minds, that religion is a *reasonable service*. Employ your reason in judging what is right; and, that you may be furnished for judging, apply to the word of revelation.

IV. Religion must be a work suited to the *nature* and *condition* of man.

God treats all creatures as they are; and requires of them according to what he has given them. He requires not of men all the same things which he exacts of angels; nor would he tolerate in angels the same things which he pardons in men; for he knows our frame; he remembers that we are dust.

Man consists of a material body, and a rational mind. While he dwells in the body, he must take care of its concerns, and provide for its support. His religion therefore cannot *wholly* consist in the spiritual exercises of angels, or in such a refinement and elevation of spirit, as would entirely detach him from the world: For this would be inconsistent with his present condition and connexions. As he is to consult the health and
comfort

comfort of his body, and contribute to the happiness of those around him, so industry in his calling, prudence in his business, frugality in the use of his substance, temperance in the enjoyment of divine bounties, belong to religion in the present state.

You must be weaned from the world by the *moderation*, not wholly abstracted from it by the *extinction*, of your earthly affections. The former is necessary to fit you for heaven. The latter would unfit you for the world before it is time to leave it.

The mind, however, is far the superiour part. This will always claim your chief attention, that you may enlarge its capacity, furnish it with knowledge, rectify its mistakes, eradicate evil habits, introduce and improve virtuous principles, restrain the passions, and prevent them from enslaving the nobler powers.

The duties relating to the body, and the mind, though different in themselves, are nearly connected, and mutually subservient. You cannot complain, that worldly business calls you off from the care of your souls; nor under pretence of engagedness in your salvation, can you excuse your neglect of secular duties. Every duty claims its place, and an attention to each, in its place, will facilitate the practice of the others.

You ought farther to consider your *moral condition*.

You are fallen creatures; but placed under the hopes of pardon and life through a Mediator. And religion includes in it such tempers and duties, as correspond with such a condition.

The gospel plan is founded on the supposition of a fact, which experience and observation cannot but acknowledge; that all have sinned, and come short of the glory of God. Revelation teaches us, that God, in compassion to our apostate race, has sent into the world a glorious Saviour, who, by assuming our nature, and suffering in our place, has opened a way for the exercise of pardoning mercy to repenting sinners.

The religion of an innocent creature, consists in a continued obedience to the will of God. But the religion of a sinner must begin in repentance of sin, and return to God. Your first care then, must be to know yourselves, and to obtain God's grace for the renovation of your souls, and his mercy for the remission of your sins. Your acceptable application to God, can be only in the name of the Saviour, whom he has ordained, and by an attendance on the means, which he has appointed. You must compare yourselves with his word, encourage serious convictions and virtuous resolutions, shun known temptations and dangerous connexions, attend on the institutions of the gospel, frame your ways to turn to the Lord, and seek his favour, until you find.

Viewing yourselves as fallen creatures, you will see these to be reasonable exercises, and necessarily

essarily belonging to religion. Every thing, therefore, which tends to pride and selfconfidence, and which encourages boasting and ostentation, is contrary to the nature of true religion. This will always be modest and humble. It will dispose you to judge of yourselves with caution; to judge of others with candour.

V. You must always remember that religion is a *benevolent* and *useful* thing; and that, wherever it takes place, it makes men *better* than they were before.

It consists not in empty noise and vain show; but in solid virtue and substantial goodness. That cannot be religion, which leaves men as they were, or makes them worse, or which only supplants one vice by introducing another; but that which makes them *new* creatures. Paul says of Onesimus—*In time past he was unprofitable, but now profitable. The works of faith are good and profitable to men.*

Religion does not essentially consist in little niceties and trifling distinctions, which neither influence the heart, nor concern the practice; nor in the observance or rejection of particular rites and forms, which a man may use or disuse without prejudice to real virtue in himself or others; nor in a zealous attachment to, or angry abhorrence of, this sect, or that church, in which, as in most other fields, there are some tares and some wheat; but in something more excellent and divine. That, in a word, is true religion, which makes a *good man*—which renders one pious toward his God—conformed to the pattern of his Saviour—benevolent to his fellow men—humble in his temper and manners—peaceable in society—juſt in his treatment of all—condeſcending in caſes of difference—ſtrict in the government of himſelf—patient in adverſity—and attentive to his duty in all conditions and relations of life. When you ſee ſuch a character, you may believe, that religion is there. When you find this to be your character, you may believe, that wiſdom has entered into your heart.

You are to diſtinguiſh between truth and errour, and to embrace the one and reject the other. But never lay great wait on things, which have no relation to practice; nor make light of great things, which are immediately connected with duty.

If you ſee a man meek, humble, peaceable, ſober and benevolent, careful to practiſe piety himſelf, and to promote it among others, you may think him religious, though you ſuppoſe him to have adopted ſome groundleſs opinions. If you ſee one contentious about religion, condemning all who think not as he does, buſy in ſowing the ſeeds of diſcord, and in cauſing diviſions among brethren, and more zealous to make proſelytes to his own party and opinion, than to make good men of his proſelytes; whatever you may think of his heart, you will at leaſt conclude, that his zeal is not according to knowledge.

Judge

Judge then of the truth and importance of doctrines by their practical tendency and observable effects. If an opinion is proposed to you, inquire, what influence it would naturally have. ¿ Would it awaken in you a more serious concern about futurity, give you a deeper sense and stronger abhorrence of sin, make you more careful in duty, and more watchful against temptations ?—Or, on the other hand, ¿ Would it render you more thoughtless and secure, more pliant to the customs of the world, and more regardless of moral obligations ?—An honest answer to these inquiries will determine the truth and importance of most doctrines, concerning which any doubts may arise. For as the design and tendency of the gospel is to make men better, so, if any doctrine has a contrary influence, you may conclude, either that it is not a doctrine of the gospel, or that it meets with a temper exceedingly perverse.

VI. **Judge of** things doubtful *by things which are plain.*

The great precepts and the leading doctrines of Revelation are easy to be understood.—*The scriptures are given by inspiration of God, and are profitable for doctrine, reproof, correction, and instruction in righteousness; and they are able to furnish* not only *the man of God,* but the *pious youth, unto every good work.* Timothy, *from a child, understood the holy scriptures. The way of holiness, is a high way,* a path so plainly drawn in the chart of the divine word,

word, that *the wayfaring man, though a fool, shall not err therein.*

There are also many obscure passages, which are differently understood even by the learned; and which, by the young, perhaps, cannot be understood at all. But ever make plain things the rule by which to govern your conduct, and the standard by which to prove what is doubtful. Never interpret the latter in contradiction to the former; but either understand them in a sense agreeable to plain scripture, or leave them as they are. You never will suffer for want of the knowledge of a dark text, as long as you act in obedience to those which are plain.

VII. If a matter proposed to you, in a way of instruction or advice, appears doubtful, *suspend your resolution, until you have made farther inquiry.*

When you feel a disposition to receive, or to reject the proposed advice, examine what is your view and design. ¿ Is it that you may stand approved to God ? or, ¿ That you may gratify some humour and passion of your own ? If you reject it, ask yourselves, whether you are rationally convinced, that it is wrong in itself, injurious to your character, and dangerous to your virtue; or whether you only view it as contradicting some favourite habit, pleasure or pursuit. If your inclination is to adopt the instruction given you, examine from whence this inclination arises. ¿ Does it arise from conviction of the truth and importance of the matter in question ? or, ¿ From

its

its agreeableness to that manner of life, which you choose to follow, and from its tendency to secure you against the just reproaches of your conscience?

In forming your judgment concerning religious truth, and moral obligation, never suffer lust, passion, prejudice, or social connexion, to have any influence. Examine and decide calmly and dispassionately. Consider, what you approve, and what you condemn in others—what advice, in a serious hour, you would give to a friend—if you were a parent, what counsel and instruction you would inculcate on a son or daughter, whose reputation and happiness you was anxious to promote—suppose yourself near the closing scene, and think, what you would approve or condemn in so solemn a period. Judge in this manner, and you will seldom judge wrong. A judgment and resolution, formed with these cautions, you may venture to follow. They will not lead you astray.

I would not forget to recommend, nor should you neglect to maintain a continual intercourse with your Maker.

As religion is the obligation, which you are under to him, solicit his grace to lead you into just sentiments of it, and to impress these sentiments deeply on your hearts. Aware of the dangers which attend the present stage of your life—aware of the seductions of a deceitful heart, and the temptations of a guilty world, seek wisdom from

from the Father of lights—seek direction from him, who teaches the meek his way—seek protection from him, whose eye beholds the state, and whose ear attends the prayer of the humble.

If thou criest after knowledge and liftest up thy voice for understanding; if thou seekest her as silver, and searchest for her, as for hidden treasures, then shalt thou understand the fear of the Lord, and find the knowledge of God. For God giveth wisdom; out of his mouth cometh knowledge and understanding; he layeth up sound wisdom for the righteous; he is a buckler to them who walk uprightly; he keepeth the path of judgment, and preserveth the way of the saints. Thus shalt thou understand righteousness, judgment and equity; yea, and every good path.

END OF THE NINETEENTH SERMON.

SERMON XX.

Samson shorn of his Locks.

JUDGES, 16. xx.

The Philistines be upon thee, Samson.

AND, ¿ What then ?—¿ What can the Philistines do to Samson, the man of invincible strength ? He has proved himself more than a match for a thousand of them. He once entered alone into one of their principal cities, slew thirty men, took their spoil, and went off in safety. He afterward, at another place, spread among them a more extensive slaughter. He, with only the contemptible weapon of a jaw bone, smote to the ground a thousand men, and laid them heaps upon heaps. The gate posts of Gaza he plucked up with his hands, and carried them off on his shoulders, with the gate, bar and all. Consenting to be bound with strong cords, green withes, and new ropes, in succession, he snapped them asunder, as a thread of tow ; and when his enemies, thinking him in their power, shouted against him, he rose, and fell upon them with prodigious haveck. And, ¿ What can they do to him now ?
Alas !

Alas! Samſon has ſlept in the lap of a harlot, and his ſtrength is gone! His enemies now ſeize him, put out his eyes, bind him in fetters of braſs, and make him grind in the priſon. Fatal change! The diſmal effect of breaking the ſacred vow of Nazariteſhip, and yielding to the power of luſt.

Samſon's prodigious ſtrength was not a natural endowment, always at his own command: It was an immediate gift, vouchſafed on ſpecial occaſions, and, on thoſe occaſions, obtained by prayer to God. In his exertions, it is ſaid—*The ſpirit of God came upon him.* When his ſtrength failed, it is ſaid—*The Lord departed from him.*

From his infancy, he had been dedicated to God, as a Nazarite forever. He was ſeparated to the ſervice of God, under an obligation to abſtain from wine, and every ſenſual indulgence, which might, in any degree, unfit him for the ſervice to which he was devoted. He was raiſed up to be the deliverer of the Jews, now under the oppreſſion of the Philiſtines, and to be their chief magiſtrate in the adminiſtration of their civil government. That he might better diſcharge the duties of his exalted ſtation, he was required to be a Nazarite as long as he lived. The badge and token of his dedication, was his hair growing in its natural ſtate. By the divine law, a Nazarite was forbidden to cut his hair, or ſhave his head. Samſon's bodily ſtrength had no *natural* connexion with the growth of his hair: It was a privilege annexed to the religious obſervance of

his

his vow. When, in confequence of his violating this bond, he loft the badge, he loft alfo the benefit of his Nazaritefhip. God withdrew the fpecial aid which once he afforded him, and left him to his natural weaknefs. The **lofs of his hair** was followed with the lofs **of** his ftrength, **as a** moral, not as a natural effect; and only becaufe *that* was the fruit **of his own** guilty indulgence. Had his hair been taken from **him by force or** accident, without a previous fault **of** his own, and while he was in the ftrict obfervance of his vow, there is no reafon to **conclude that the fame** effect would have enfued.

Whether Samfon was **a man of** real piety, **is** a queftion which the **hiftory of** his life feems not clearly to decide. The ftrongeft argument in his favour, is the honour done him by the Apoftle to the Hebrews, who **has given him a place in** his lift of believers.

However this may be, he was evidently **a man of** a mixed character.

He believed **in the true God**—regarded **his** governing **providence**—often addreffed him in prayer—received communications of fupernatural ftrength; which he fenfibly **acknow**ledged—and, until he was overcome by the inticements of an artful woman, he carefully preferved the external token of his feparation to the fervice of God. But, on the other hand, we find him, early in life, feeking a marriage contrary to the advice of his parents, and to the law of his God. This marriage

is

is indeed said to be of the Lord—not commanded, but permitted of the Lord in his wise providence—but, though God was wise in his permission, Samson was not wise in his choice. Afterward we find him in the company of a known prostitute—yielding to female charms—making and attending festivals, in which he would naturally meet with temptations to violate his vow of abstinence from wine. And it is probable, that he at length fell under the power of a depraved appetite ; for that he should sleep so soundly, as not to be awakened by the operation of the razor on his head, can hardly be accounted for, but by supposing a degree of inebriation, which Josephus affirms to have been the case.

These stains we discover in his character—not to mention his last act, which perhaps may be justified on the principle of regard to the liberties of his country ; for doubtless there are cases, in which men may expose themselves to probable, if not to certain death, for the general safety of their nation.

But, though we see in this hero, great and inexcusable faults, still it is to be remembered, that, while he lay in confinement, he had time for reflection and repentance. And the return of his strength, with the future growth of his hair, affords a probable argument of the sincerity of his humiliation, in that painful period.

But whatever may be his religious character, the errours of his life, and the calamities which
they

they brought on him, will suggest to us some useful warnings and instructions.

By a conduct inconsistent with his solemn dedication to God, he lost his strength—not only the strength of his body, but, which was of more importance, the strength of his mind, and of his virtue; and suddenly, in the torpor of an artificial sleep, he fell under the power of his enemies. He lay down a freeman, and awoke a captive and a slave. While he thought his strength remained, he attempted to exercise it for his deliverance—but in vain—he was weak as another man.

I. We are here taught, that the young should ever act under a sense of their religious dedication to God.

Samson was, by his parents, consecrated as a Nazarite. Their act he considered as binding on him, because it was in consequence of a divine command.

It is sometimes asked, ¿ How are children bound by an act of their parents, to which they have never consented, and of which they are not even conscious?

But, ¿ Can you tell me, how Samson was bound by the act of *his* parents?

You will say, " It was the authority of God, which obliged him to be a Nazarite, and which obliged his parents to set him apart in this character."

It is well answered. Remember, too, God requires the Christian parent to bring up his children

dren in the knowledge and practice of the religion of the gospel; and to make an early dedication of them to him, in a particular instituted form, as an acknowledgement of his obligation thus to educate them; and as a token of their future obligation, to walk worthy of their Christian education. To ask then, how a parent's act binds his children, is only to ask, ¿ How they are bound by the command of God? A question which surely needs no answer.

If you have been dedicated to God, it is because you are bound to live to him. Your obligation to virtue does not originate from your baptism; but the reason of your baptism is founded in your obligation to virtue. If you live in opposition to the will of God, you contradict the great design, for which you have been consecrated to him.

Samson was much more concerned to keep the *token* of his Nazaritism, than to observe the *duties* of it. He never voluntarily parted with his locks; but he often violated that purity of life, to which his parents had consecrated him, and which his locks denoted. An inconsistency this, which is not uncommon. Few would, in a formal manner, renounce their baptism; but thousands live contrary to it. While they choose to be considered in the character of baptised Christians—in the character of disciples of Christ, whose name has been called on them, and on whose name they call, they indulge those corruptions

of

of heart, and impurities of life, which his gospel expresly forbids. But, ¿ Will their baptism save them, while in works they deny it? It verily profiteth, if they obey the gospel. Otherwise, in effect, it becomes no baptism. He is not a Christian, who is only one outwardly, in name and form. He is a Christian, who is one inwardly, in heart and spirit, whose praise is not of men, but of God.

The parent is solicitous, that his children should be baptised, and visibly introduced into the church and kingdom of Christ. But if he is not as solicitous to furnish their minds with religious knowledge, and form their lives to virtuous manners, he is no more consistent with himself, than Samson's parents would have been, to have consecrated him as a Nazarite, and then fed him with wine, and cut off his hair.

II. We see in the case of Samson, the unhappy effects of sensuality.

By the law of Nazaritism, he was bound to special purity of life: From this purity he early began to depart: The consequence was, he fell into temptation and a snare, and involved himself in misery and ruin.

The youth should come forward into the world, with an apprehension of the various dangers to which his virtue is exposed. There are dangers arising from the gaiety of his spirits, the warmth of his passions, the vivacity of his imagination, the flattering charms of outward objects, the examples of the world, the enticements of wicked men, and, perhaps, of those whom he makes his intimate friends. Sensible of these dangers, he should arm himself with the strongest resolutions; watch the first approach of temptation, and early repel it, before it has taken possession of his mind. He should stand peculiarly on his guard against the fascinating influence of the pleasures of sense. These, when they have gained dominion, will claim unlimited obedience, and induce an absolute slavery. They take away the heart, stupify the conscience, obliterate the sentiments of honour, enfeeble every virtuous resolution, subjugate the noblest powers of the soul, and drown men in destruction and wretchedness.

Samson, long celebrated for his singular strength and courage, sunk, at last, by his criminal indulgence, into the most despicable weakness of mind, as well as body, and fell an impotent captive into the hands of his enemies: And they, who once trembled at his arm, now triumphed in his weakness.

See the man, who rent a lion, as he would a kid—who plucked up the gates of Gaza—who, submitting to be bound with cords, burst them, when his enemies shouted, and, with a contemptible weapon, spread slaughter among them at his pleasure; see him now listening to the enticements of a lewd enchantress, betraying to her the most important secrets of his soul, yielding himself to her power, when she had given him full reason to distrust her fidelity; and thus deprived of his

strength,

strength, and made the sport of his inveterate foes. Alluding to his catastrophe, Solomon says, "Hearken to me, O ye children, and attend to the words of my mouth. Say unto wisdom, Thou art my sister, and call understanding thy kinswoman, that they may keep thee from the stranger who flattereth with her words. Let not thine heart decline to her ways, go not astray in her paths; for she hath cast down many wounded; many strong men have been slain by her. Her house is the way to hell, going down to the chambers of death."

In language equally strong and expressive, he warns the youth of the fatal effects of intemperance. "Be not among wine bibbers; among riotous eaters of flesh; for so shalt thou come to poverty, and be clothed with rags. Thou shalt have woe, disease, sorrow, contention, and wounds without cause—thine heart shall utter perverse things—thou shalt be as he who lieth down in the midst of the sea, or sleepeth on the top of a mast. They have beaten me, shalt thou say, and I felt it not: ¿When shall I awake? I will seek it yet again."

III. The case of Samson shews us the fatal consequences of criminal connexions.

From this cause the errours and calamities of his life took their rise. Our virtue, honour, and happiness, depend on nothing more, than the character of the friends whom we choose, and the company which we keep. Sensible of this, David

vid resolved, that he would say to evil doers, Depart from me; and would be the companion of them who feared God, and observed his commandments.

The youth, who has enjoyed the benefit of a virtuous education, will form some virtuous resolutions. While he hears parental instruction, or while he indulges his serious thoughts in solitude, he feels these resolutions operating powerfully in his mind. He thinks he shall easily retain them. When first he happens into licentious company, the conversation which he hears, and the examples which he sees, shock his mind. But, in the mean time, some circumstance may occur to invite him again into similar company. He goes, however, with a resolution to keep himself clear of the vices which he sees. By degrees the scene is familiarized. Vice seems to divest itself of some part of its deformity, his watch is slackened, and his resolution droops. He sees, perhaps, in an ungodly companion, some agreeable accomplishments, which half conceal the deformity of the character. As he attaches himself more closely to the person, he has less power to resist the influence of the example. He can now with patience, and by and by he will with pleasure, hear those virtuous principles and manners bantered and ridiculed, which once he regarded with veneration. Thus gradually and insensibly, he is drawn off from the virtuous course, which it was his early resolution to pursue.

The youth, who has not wisdom to shun a vicious connexion, has seldom resolution enough to withstand the temptations which attend it. Though he may carry a good resolution into bad company, he will hardly be able to bring it off entire and unbroken. The first step to security, is to retreat from the path of danger. They who deliberately enter upon it, whatever good resolutions they form, are usually beguiled along, until they have advanced so far, and find their way so much embarrassed, that they have but little heart to return. "Hear, O my son," says Solomon, "and receive my commandments, and the years of thy life shall be many. I have taught thee in the way of wisdom, and led thee in right paths. When thou goest, thy steps shall not be straitened; when thou runnest, thy feet shall not stumble. Enter not into the path of the wicked, go not in the way of evil men; avoid it, pass not by it, turn from it, and pass away."

IV. We see the meanness of vice, and in what a despicable light it places the man who yields to it.

While Samson, with the character of the hero, preserved that of the Nazarite, and employed his great strength in vindicating the liberty of his country, and chastising the insolence of her enemies, we view him with esteem and admiration. But when we see this mighty man sinking away into the softness of effeminacy, yielding himself a slave to lust and appetite, and putting that strength, which was the gift of God, unto the hands

hands of one, whose only aim was to betray it to the common enemy; when we see him shorn of his locks, and led off blind and impotent, what different sentiments we feel! If we behold him with pity, it is pity mixed with contempt.

Similar spectacles, however, are too often to be seen. If the man of superiour powers, and a virtuous education, yields himself a slave to passion and appetite; if by criminal indulgences of any kind, he debilitates his body, and beclouds his intellects, destroys his health, and wastes his substance, and, from the dignity of a man, sinks down to the meanness of an animal, he is like Samson shorn of his locks, while he slept in the arms of pleasure. If ever he awakes, he will feel with shame and regret the disgraceful change.

The youth, who aims at honour and reputation, must maintain his virtue. Let not mercy and truth, purity and sobriety, ever forsake thee; bind them about thy neck, write them on the table of thine heart, take them with thee in all thy walks, make them thy companions in all companies, and thy guards in all temptations; so shalt thou find favour and good understanding in the sight of God and men.

V. We see how naturally sin brings trouble in this world, and what reason there is to believe it will bring misery in the next.

There was such a natural connexion between Samson's iniquity, and the calamities which ensued, that he could not but ascribe them to himself.

self. His unlawful commerce with a daughter of an idolatrous people (for such, undoubtedly, was the person with whom he was now connected) drew him, as the Jewish historian supposes, into frequent violations of his vow of Nazariteship. Enticed and overcome by her deceitful arts and urgent solicitations, he disclosed the secret of his strength; and, in a profound sleep, the effect of previous excess, he lost the token of Nazaritism, with which his strength was connected. With his strength he lost his freedom and his eyes; and he, who lately was judge in Israel, is now a slave in a Philistine dungeon.

The man of strictest virtue, is, in this state, liable to adversity; nor can we, from the calamities which a man suffers, conclude him to be a transgressor. But when calamities, by direct and natural steps, follow, after manifest iniquity, we must view the former as the proper fruit and punishment of the latter.

Though rewards and punishments are not exactly and constantly dispensed here, yet there are many cases, in which they take place in a degree, to awaken men's attention to the different consequences of virtue and vice, and to convince them that righteousness tends to life, and that he who pursues evil, pursues it to his death.

When they see the connexion between sin and punishment here, they ought to extend their views to the world of retribution, where, on the children of disobedience, the wrath of God will come

come to the uttermoſt. He makes their ſins to fall upon them in this world, to remind them, that theſe ſins, indulged until death, will find them out in the next. If there is a natural connexion between vice and miſery, viſible in many inſtances now, it is preſumption and madneſs for the ſinner to flatter himſelf that he can ever be ſecure from miſery without renouncing his ſins.

It often proves a mercy to mankind, that vice is productive of preſent miſery, becauſe thus its progreſs is retarded, and in ſome inſtances, tranſgreſſors are thus reclaimed. This ſeems to have been the caſe with our fallen hero. While he indulged, with profound ſecurity, the luxuries of life, he forgot the vow which ſhould have bound him to the ſtricteſt purity; and to what depth he might have fallen, if nothing had diſturbed his guilty ſlumbers, we cannot tell. But awakened by the inſulting alarm—*The Philiſtines be upon thee*; and, after a fruitleſs effort, finding himſelf in their power, and his former ſtrength departed; experiencing the ſad change from a hero to a ſlave, and the ſudden tranſition from a ſeat of judgment to a dungeon, he began, we may ſuppoſe, to reflect on the errours of his life, and eſpecially on his late criminal conduct, which had produced ſo diſmal a reverſe; and in his darkſome ſolitude, exerciſed that deep repentance, which entitled him to the divine favour, and to the return of the ſupernatural gift which had forſaken him.

Affliction

Affliction is the common means of repentance. When transgressors are bound in fetters of iron, and holden in cords of affliction, God sheweth them their works, openeth their ears to discipline, and commandeth that they return from iniquity.

It is happy for some to be denied the means, and cut off from the opportunities of former indulgences. Samson, in prison, had it no longer in his power to pursue a habit, which was dangerously gaining influence upon him. He here renewed his Nazariteship, which had been, for a time, interrupted; and he returned to the purity which that required. Though he could not offer sacrifice for the expiation of his guilt, as the law in this case enjoined, yet, no doubt, by repentance, prayer, and a fresh dedication of himself, he sought and obtained pardon of God; and therefore, as the token of his Nazariteship returned, the privilege annexed to it, returned also. By sin we provoke God to withdraw his presence; by repentance we recover his favour. Reflecting therefore on the fatal effects of transgression, let offenders dedicate themselves to God with deep repentance, and stronger resolutions of virtue and obedience. Thus God will have mercy on them, and abundantly pardon them.

END OF THE TWENTIETH SERMON.

SERMON XXI.

Reflections on Abraham's Artifice with Abimelech.

GENESIS, 20. x, xi.

And Abimelech said unto Abraham, What sawest thou, that thou hast done this thing? And Abraham said, because I thought, surely the fear of **God** *is not in this place; and they will slay me for* **my** *wife's sake.*

ABRAHAM, having occasion to remove from Mamre toward the southern part of the land of Canaan, to a place called *Gerar*, of which Abimelech was king, adopted, for the security of his life, the same expedient which he had once before used in Egypt. He desired his wife to disguise the relation between them, and to call him her brother, and he also agreed to call her his sister, lest some of the people, tempted by her beauty, should kill him for her sake.

From so good a man, and one who had so often experienced the divine protection, we should not have

have expected an artifice like this; especially as the result, on a former trial, had taught him how unnecessary it was. But the best men have their weaknesses; and in men, whose faith is ordinarily strong, fear will sometimes prevail.

Abimelech, supposing Sarah to be only Abraham's sister, sent and took her into his house, with an intention, not to dishonour her, but to make her his wife.

Before he had accomplished this design, God, by a dream in the night, warned him of the dangerous step which he was meditating, and directed him to restore the woman to Abraham, whose wife she was.

The king, after professing the innocence of his intentions, calls for Abraham, and thus expostulates with him on the unjustifiable deception which he had used. ¿ " What hast thou done to us ? and, ¿ What have I offended thee, that thou hast brought on me, and on my kingdom, a great sin ?" i. e. exposed us to a great scandal and calamity. " Thou hast done deeds to me, which ought not to be done. ¿ What sawest thou, that thou hast done this thing ?" Abraham answers, I did this, " because I thought, surely the fear of God is not in this place, and they will slay me for my wife's sake." However, he says, the relation which they had professed, was not altogether fictitious ; for " she was the daughter of his father, though not the daughter of his mother." She was his father's grand daughter ; and, in the

language

language of scripture, grandchildren are often called children. *Sarai*, who in the eleventh chapter is called *Iscah*, was daughter to *Haran*, Abraham's elder brother. It seems, by this account, that *Terah*, Abraham's Father, had two wives, from one of whom was born *Haran*, the father of Lot and Sarai, or Iscah, and from the other was born Abraham. So that she was daughter to Abraham's half brother. And with such a niece, it was, in those days, thought not unlawful to marry.

But though Abraham's account of their relation, was, according to the language of the times, literally true; yet his concealment of the more delicate and important relation, could not, on the reason assigned, be justified. For surely he ought not to have gone voluntarily among a people, where he apprehended no regard would be paid to the conjugal rights: Or, if he was called in providence to sojourn among them, he might have trusted to divine protection.

This incident, in the history of Abraham's life, will afford us some useful observations.

I. The atrocious nature of the sin of *adultery*, which consists in violating connubial rights, is here represented in a very striking manner.

Though Abraham supposed that there was no sense of God and religion among the people of Gerar, yet he seems not to have entertained the least suspicion that they would insult the honour of his family, either by rape or seduction. His apprehension was, that they would *kill him* for
his

his wife's fake. He imagined, that no man could be so abandoned, as to take his wife from him, or debauch her, while he was alive; but he was much afraid, there were men bad enough to murder him, that they might have liberty to enjoy her.

Abraham evidently considers *adultery* as a crime far more horrid in its nature, and far more contrary to the dictates of natural reason and conscience, than even *murder* itself. His whole conduct, in this, and the former instance, is grounded on the supposition, that a ruffian, who is bloody enough to assassinate an innocent man, yet may not be so brutal as to violate a married woman. The man who can do the latter, in a deliberate and customary manner, is undoubtedly capable of any kind of wickedness, to which he feels the smallest temptation.

Murder is generally considered as one of the blackest crimes of which a man can be guilty. But it is observable, that, by the divine law, the same penalty is annexed to adultery, as to murder: And, perhaps, of the two, it is the greater crime. It certainly indicates a more depraved state of mind. Murder may be the effect of high provocation, or sudden passion. The other proceeds from a settled, habitual viciosity of heart. And in its consequences no species of villany can be more mischievous—more fatal. It is contrary to the peace and order of society—both of particular families, and of larger communities. It is an unprovoked, and irreparable injury to men, in those rights of which they are most jealous. It robs them of that comfort and enjoyment, which they value no less than life, and without which life is hardly supportable. It extends its baleful effects to the innocent offspring, and dooms them, without their fault, to infamy and misery. It is a violation of the most sacred and solemn **vows.** It tramples in the dust the honour and the happiness, not of a single person, or family only, but of many persons, and of divers families. It awakens grief, anxiety, and perpetual jealousy; excites hatred, malice, and revenge; sometimes leads to the deliberate murder of the tender offspring, and of the injured party; and, on the other hand, provokes to the violent assassination of the infamous invader. In a word, it involves in it the guilt of injustice, fraud, cruelty, and perjury; yea, and murder too, if not in the immediate act, yet in the **remoter** effects, as it taints and poisons the sweetest joys of life.

Such is the horrid criminality of this evil, that every resolved **offender** must be viewed as thoroughly depraved, **and** presumptuously wicked, and be held in detestation and abhorrence by all the lovers of virtue, and friends of human society. His concern for the rights of mankind is absorbed in his own lawless gratifications. His regard to the Deity is totally lost in sensuality. His social and benevolent affections are extinguished in the polluted sink of brutal indulgence.

Such

Such a depraved libertine cannot be supposed to possess a single principle of virtue or honour; or to be secure from any vice, if only a temptation should offer itself. Joseph, solicited to this crime, rejected the proposal with the strongest abhorrence.—" My master," says he to the lewd enchantress, " knoweth not what is with me in the house, and hath committed all that he hath into mine hand, neither hath he kept back any thing from me, but thee, because thou art his wife, ¿ How then can I do this great wickedness, and sin against God ?" His words import, that a man, who feels in his heart any fear of the presence of God, or any regard to the rights of his fellow men, cannot deliberately perpetrate so vile an action.

David, in his penitent reflections on this sin, and the murder which followed, prays—" Create in me a clean heart—deliver me from blood, thou God of my salvation. Thou desirest not sacrifice ; else would I give it. The sacrifices of God are a broken heart."

In the case of Abimelech, God says, " The woman, whom thou hast taken, is a man's wife ; and unless thou restore her, thou shalt surely die." From this moment he indulged not a single thought of retaining her in his house. And such a sense had his people of the sacredness of the conjugal relation, that, when they heard of the unhappy errour, into which their prince had fallen, they were in painful anxiety for the consequences,

W

sequences. To wipe off, as far as possible, the reproach brought on the community by this transaction, the king avowed the innocence of his intentions, immediately restored to Abraham his wife, made him a liberal donation of servants, flocks, and herds, and gave him the fullest assurance of future security in his kingdom. The whole transaction shews the utter abhorrence which this people had of the crime under consideration.

This crime has been held in detestation by almost all nations, in all ages of the world. By the ancient laws of *Draco* and *Solon*, the husband of an adulteress, if he detected her in her guilt, might immediately kill both the criminals, or stigmatize them, or put out their eyes, or might exact of the adulterer a heavy fine. But, by the law of Moses, they were both to be put to death with publick infamy ; and, in ordinary cases, there was no dispensation.

I proceed to observe,

II. That a sense of virtue and religion is sometimes found where we least expect it.

How different was the true character of the people in Gerar, from that which Abraham's jealousy had drawn for them ? There was much of the fear of God among them, though he had imagined there was none at all.

It appears, from this short history, that the prince of the country was a man of great virtue. He was not an idolater, but a worshipper of the

true

true God, as was also Melchizedek the priest. He was not a stranger to divine Revelations, though favoured with them in a lower degree than Abraham. As God, on the occasion here mentioned, communicated to him his will in a dream, so there is no doubt, but, on other occasions, he had been favoured with divine discoveries. He seems not to have been unacquainted with this manner of receiving intimations of the divine pleasure. He acknowledges a supreme governour of the world, and regards him as a being of almighty power, and of perfect rectitude and goodness. He expresses a benevolent care for the safety of his people, and a just concern, lest they should suffer by his mistake. He professes an integrity of heart in what he had done, and God approves the profession. He readily obeys the divine command in restoring the woman he had taken; and while he reproves Abraham for the needless artifice which he had used, he gives back his wife uninjured, accepts his intercession for himself and his people, and, retaining no unsuitable resentment, dismisses him with generous presents, and with full liberty to dwell in his territories.

Though it is not probable, that all the people were equally virtuous with the prince, yet a sense of justice, and a regard to the common rights of mankind, evidently belonged to their general character. Abimelech appeals to Abraham, whether he had seen, since he had been in the country,

country, any thing, which could be matter of complaint, or could require such deception as had been used: Abraham pretends nothing more, than a previous jealousy, that the fear of God was not in that place.

We see then, that to condemn sects or communities in the gross—to censure and reprobate men on mere suspicion—to conclude that there can be no religion among those who enjoy not advantages equal to our own, is rash and unjustifiable. Where external advantages are less, internal assistances may, for aught we know, in some instances be greater.

To suppose that they, who enjoy a standing Revelation, should receive immediate discoveries from God, in the things of religion, would, indeed, be absurd; for, on this supposition, the standing Revelation becomes useless. God never communicates to men, in an immediate way, those things which they may learn by means already in their hands.

Cornelius is favoured with a vision from heaven; but this vision gives him no instruction in the way of salvation; it only directs him to send for an Apostle, who should teach him things, by which he might be saved. If we, who enjoy the gospel revelation, laying this aside, depend on discoveries of truth made to us in another manner, we are guilty of the greatest insult on the authority of God, and the highest affront to his goodness; and we judge ourselves unworthy of
eternal

eternal life. Where God has given means, he requires the use of them, as the condition of his favour.

But we cannot hence determine, but that God, by his good spirit, may so assist, direct, and enlighten the minds of some who enjoy not our external means, that they will make improvements in knowledge and virtue far beyond the exertions of simple nature. We see, in the instance under consideration, that a people, among whom Abraham imagined there was no knowledge or fear of God, were led to worthy conceptions of his character and government, and to a just regard for the rights of mankind.

Let us beware, lest some, who never have enjoyed means and advantages like ours, rise in the judgment against us, and condemn us by their superiour attainments in virtue. The Jews, who rejecting the instructions of heavenly wisdom, still continued in their sins, our Saviour warns, that the men of Nineveh, who repented at the preaching of Jonas, and the queen of the south, who came from far to hear the wisdom of Solomon, will stand as witnesses against them at the last day.

Jesus often found, among Gentiles and Samaritans, those examples of faith, piety and goodness, which he found not among the Jews, the highly favoured, and highly professing people of God.

Exemplary piety sometimes appears, where we should last have sought it: and the grossest instances

stances of vice are too often seen in men, whose education, advantages and profession, had given us quite different expectations. Many, who are last, shall be first; and the first shall be last. Let us not condemn others for their want of privileges, but beware, lest we be condemned for our abuse of them. How God will deal with those who enjoy not our light, it is not easy for us to decide. But how he will deal with us, if we walk not in the light, there remains no doubt.

III. The case, under consideration, teaches us that the indulgence of too bad an opinion of mankind, is of dangerous consequence to ourselves and others.

Had Abraham entertained a just opinion of the prince and people of Gerar; or taken pains to become acquainted with them, before he listened to the secret whispers of jealousy, he would have shunned so dangerous an artifice, as to disguise his relation to his wife, and would have prevented the mischiefs which ensued, and the still greater mischiefs, which threatened his own family and the house of Abimelech. It was a special divine interposition, which averted consequences of the most serious nature.

Caution and circumspection in our intercourse with mankind, are always prudent, and may often be necessary. An implicit, unguarded confidence, will expose us to many inconveniences, and may involve us in ruin. The advice which our Saviour gave his disciples, deserves attention

in

in times less dangerous than those. *Be wise as serpents and harmless as doves. Beware of men.* Put not confidence in every one. Expose not yourselves to unnecessary dangers. But ever maintain your innocence. Injure no man; and then, as far as prudence can secure you, let no man injure you.

But we must not carry our caution to a total distrust of mankind, nor treat them with such apparent jealousy, as would naturally provoke their resentment; neither ought we, in our concern for our own security, to pursue unwarrantable measures, or neglect the plain calls of duty.

By extreme caution, men often run into the mischiefs which they aim to avoid; and by excessive jealousy bring on themselves injuries, which were not before intended. By indulging too ill an opinion of those around them, they contract a sourness of temper, a reservedness of behaviour, an unsociableness of manners, which injure their own feelings, obstruct their usefulness, and disgust those with whom they converse. Good Elijah, in an evil day, met with so many obstructions and discouragements in his endeavours to reform the nation, that he gave over his labours, and retired to a cave. While he was there, indulging a gloomy imagination, he concluded that there was no piety in the land, and no safety for him. " Lord," says he, " they have pulled down thine altars, and slain thy prophets, and I only am left, and they seek my life." But,

¿ What says the divine answer? " I have reserved to myself seven thousand men, who have not bowed the knee to Baal."—" ¿ What dost thou here, Elijah?

His ill opinion of the world first urged him into a cave; and, in this retirement, the gloom increased, until his jealousy condemned mankind without reserve.

While we mingle with the world, we should keep ourselves unspotted from it. But to shun the pollutions of it, we must not withdraw from all intercourse with it. The Christian is to keep himself from an untoward generation, and to be blameless and harmless, and without rebuke in the midst of the ungodly and profane, holding forth the word of life, that others may be gained by his good conversation.

IV. It is proper farther to remark, that, in the best men, there may be great infirmities and failings.

None is more celebrated than Abraham for the eminence of his piety, and the strength of his faith. He was strong in faith, giving glory to God. The greatness of his faith appeared, in his leaving his native land at the divine call, and going forth to sojourn in a strange country—in his steady observance of the worship of God, in all places where he sojourned—in his pursuing the enemies who had conquered and plundered the country of Sodom, recovering from them the spoils which they had taken, and restoring them to the proper owners—in his reliance on the divine

vine promise concerning his seed, at a time of life, when, according to the course of nature, no issue could be expected—in his obeying the painful command, to offer up that son in whom his seed was to be called; and in his reasoning from past experience that God was able to raise him from the dead, from whence he had already received him in a figure.

Could we imagine that such a man as this would, on any occasion, betray symptoms of timidity, or discover a distrust of God?—But this same patriarch, when he went to sojourn in Gerar, dared not own his relation to his wife, lest the men of the place should kill him for her sake. Where is now the faith and fortitude, which, at other times, he discovered, when difficulties pressed, and dangers threatened him?—His faith now languished; his fear prevailed; and, in a time of imaginary danger, he adopted a method of conduct which exposed him to the reproof of the very persons, who, he imagined, had not the fear of God.

Let him, who thinks that he stands, take heed, lest he fall.

Even they whose faith is strong, must guard against the prevailing influence of fear, and call into exercise that confidence in God which is the best security against the terrours of the world.

In times of apparent danger, and threatening temptation, they have need to be peculiarly watchful. Let them deliberately inquire, whither

Providence

Providence calls them; and, having found the line of their duty, purfue it with calm refolution, and fteady reliance on the divine protection.

We are never fo fafe, as when we invariably follow the path of virtue and integrity. He who walks uprightly, walks furely; but he who perverts his way, fhall fall. Duplicity and artifice, to avoid an evil, will but embarrafs us the more. It was only a fpecial, gracious interpofition, which prevented moft fatal confequences, from the patriarch's unworthy device.

While we aim to act with integrity ourfelves, let us remember the weaknefs of human nature, and treat with candour the failings of our fellow men. We fee weaknefs and errour in fo good a man as Abraham. We are to look for perfection in none. Nor ought we, for particular faults, to withdraw our charity from men of general integrity and virtue. The candour of Abimelech was great and noble. While he reproved Abraham in one inftance, of unworthy conduct, he acknowledged him as a good man and a prophet of God. He fought his prayers, and folicited his friendfhip, being perfuaded, that God was with him. We may reprove a good man's faults; but for particular faults, which are an exception from a general character, we muft condemn no man's perfon. Let us walk in that charity, which hopeth all things; for this will cover a multitude of fins.

END OF THE TWENTY FIRST SERMON.

SERMON XXII.

The Kingdom of God without Observation.

LUKE, 17. xx, xxi.

And when he was demanded of the Pharisees, When the kingdom of God should come; he answered them and said, The kingdom of God cometh not with observation: Neither shall they say, Lo here; or, lo there; for behold, the kingdom of God is within you.

THIS phrase, *the kingdom of God,* is frequently used in the new testament; and it signifies either that state of glory, to which good men will be exalted in the future world, or the gospel dispensation, and the church of God in this world. The latter is the more common acceptation, and evidently intended in the text. The question of the Pharisees, ¿ *When shall the kingdom of God appear?* manifestly respected the kingdom of the Messiah, or that dispensation which he was to introduce. Christ, in his answer, uses the phrase in the same sense, only correcting

recting their mistake concerning its nature, and the manner of its introduction and establishment.

At the time of our Saviour's appearance, there prevailed a general expectation of him. This expectation was grounded on the prophecies, which had expressly foretold the certainty, and accurately stated the time of his coming. But the prophecies, which described the *manner* of his appearance, were grossly misapprehended by most of the Jews, and especially by the Pharisees. The grand and lofty figures representing the power of his doctrines, they understood as expressing the majesty of his temporal dominion, and the splendour of his earthly court.

They demanded of Jesus, *when the kingdom of God should come*; meaning, when would the Messiah come to erect his kingdom in Judea, and to deliver the Jews from the oppressions of a foreign power. Jesus had declared himself to be the promised Messiah. But there was nothing in his condition, which answered to *their* ideas of his temporal reign. Instead of that wealth and power, that splendid court and numerous host, with which they expected he would be attended, they saw him poor and humble, and only accompanied with a few disciples of ordinary birth and character. They therefore demand of him, " ¿ When is that kingdom of God to be erected, which the scripture foretels ?"—¿ Are you the Messiah ?— ¿ Where is your kingdom ?—¿ Can you be the important person, who is the subject of so many
notable

notable predictions?—¿ Was all that pomp of prophetick language wasted only to point out a man like you?

Jesus tells them, they wholly misunderstood the intention of prophecy, which was to foretel, not a temporal, but a spiritual kingdom. *The kingdom of God cometh not with observation*, or with external parade and show; but with moral and internal power and influence. Neither shall men have occasion to say, *Behold, it is here;* or *behold, it is there*. It will not, as you imagine, be confined to Judea, or to any particular place:—*For behold, the kingdom of God is within you*, or *among you*: And it will be extended wherever my doctrines are preached. *It will reach from one part under heaven, unto the other part under heaven.* So he adds, verse 24.—This kingdom is already begun among you, being preached by me and my disciples, and confirmed by the evidence of my works; and soon it will spread around, and bless other nations of the earth. Seek it not in this, or in that particular place; know that it is come to you already: Submit now to its authority; secure its blessings, where ye are.

The illustration of these words—*The kingdom of God cometh not with observation*, will lead us to some important thoughts on the nature and design of the gospel, and prepare our way for some useful reflections.

1. The *manner*, in which the gospel was first *introduced*, was without external show and ostentation.

Worldly

Wordly kingdoms are usually erected and supported by the power of arms. The princes of the world, the better to command the respect and obedience of their subjects, are distinguished by riches, splendour and equipage. But the kingdom of Christ was introduced without any of these forms of pomp and grandeur.

He came, meek and lowly, publishing peace, and bringing salvation to mankind.

John, his forerunner, appeared in the wilderness, preaching repentance, and warning men to flee from the wrath to come. His humble habit, and austere manner of life, were suited to the doctrine which he preached.

Jesus himself was born in an obscure family, and educated in a manner below the common rank of people. He grew up as a root out of dry ground. There was in him no form or comeliness to captivate the admiration of earthly pride. He entered on his publick ministry with solemn fasting; and was consecrated to his work by the washing appointed for the priests under the law. To prove his divine authority, he performed many miracles; but these were of the mild and benevolent, not of the showy and ostentatious kind. He exerted his heavenly power, not, as a worldly conqueror would wish to do, in overturning kingdoms, and spreading destruction among his enemies; but in relieving the distressed, feeding the hungry, healing the sick, and giving sight to the blind. He was not attended with armed bands

bands to defend his person, but with a few disciples to assist in spreading his doctrines. He laboured, not to raise himself to wealth and power, but to promote truth and righteousness among our degenerate race. He displayed his dignity, not in revenging injuries, but in continual exercises of mercy and forgiveness; and gained subjects, not by the force and terrour of the sword, but by the persuasive influence of reason and goodness. He closed the scene, not by dealing death among his enemies, but by dying for their salvation. His last prayer was, not for vengeance, but for pardon to those who compassed his death. And when he ascended on high, the language of his lips was in blessings of peace, not in imprecations of wrath.

2. The *external dispensation* of Christ's kingdom is without ostentation.

His laws are plain and easy to be understood, and delivered in language level to common apprehension. The motives, by which obedience is urged, are pure and spiritual, taken not from this, but the future world. His institutions are few and simple, adapted to our condition, and suited to warm and engage the heart.

When the law was given from Sinai, the people prayed—*Let Moses speak, and we will hear; but let not God speak, lest we die.* The pomp and majesty, with which the law was proclaimed, struck them with terrour. They desired to receive it in a gentle manner. In the gospel dispensation

pensation, God has condescended to the weakness of our nature. In these last days he has spoken to us by his Son, who is indeed the brightness of his glory, but has veiled this glory in human flesh, being made in all things like unto us, that he might be a merciful high priest. And those whom he has appointed to administer the affairs of his government, are men of like passions with ourselves. The Apostle says, *We are ambassadours of Christ, as though God did by us beseech you; we pray you in Christ's stead, be ye reconciled to God.* In regard of the mildness of the gospel dispensation, compared with the law, the Apostle says to the Hebrews—*Ye are not come to the mount, which might be touched,* the sensible, tangible mount—*and which burned with fire, nor unto blackness, and darkness, and tempest, and the sound of a trumpet, and the voice of words, which they who heard could not endure; but ye are come to mount Sion, and the city of the living God, the general assembly and church of the first born, to God the Judge of all, and to Jesus the mediator of the new covenant: We have received a kingdom, which cannot be moved. Let us therefore have grace, whereby we may serve God acceptably with reverence and godly fear.*

3. The *virtues,* which the gospel principally inculcates, are without observation, distant from worldly show, and independent of worldly applause.

The kingdom of God is righteousness, and peace, and joy in the Holy Ghost. The religion of Christ
consists

consists not in those actions, which glare in the eyes of the world, and strike the minds of men with admiration ; such as courage in war, conquest over enemies, acquiring territory and spreading dominion ; but in sincere piety, humble devotion, lively faith, strict sobriety, patient self-denial, extensive charity, and contempt of the world. These are modest virtues, remote from ostentation. They seek not applause from men, but only the silent approbation of God and the heart.

The kingdom of God is received with *faith*. This is the great principle of obedience. This was the doctrine with which Jesus began his ministry—*The kingdom of God is* at hand *; repent ye, and believe the gospel.*

Faith is not only a persuasion of the truth, but also a submission to the authority of the gospel. As it supposes a conviction of personal guilt and unworthiness, so it implies a godly sorrow for sin—a reliance on the mercy of God, through the Redeemer, for pardon—a desire of his sanctifying and assisting grace—and a resolution to walk in newness of life. It is accompanied with a hatred of sin, a watchfulness against it, and earnest breathings after holiness. These operations of faith come not with observation. Though they are powerfully felt in the believing soul, they are not seen by others. They become visible only in their effects.

Where the kingdom of God takes place, there is a great change in the *temper* and *disposition* of the mind.—*If any man be in Christ, he is a new creature;* and this is a humble creature. We must receive the kingdom of God as little children—as new born babes.—*Except ye be converted,* says the Saviour, *and become as little children, ye shall not enter into the kingdom of heaven; but whoso shall humble himself as a little child, the same is greatest in that kingdom.* The gospel, where it comes with power, mortifies the pride of the heart, humbles the soul at the foot of a sovereign God, casts down imaginations, and every high thing which exalts itself against the knowledge of God, and brings into captivity every thought to the obedience of Christ.

The subjects of this kingdom exercise a temper of *selfdenial*. *Whosoever will come after me,* says Christ, *let him deny himself, and take up his cross, and follow me.*—This selfdenial principally consists in the denial of *ungodliness* and *worldly lusts*. They who are under the dominion of sin, make provision for the flesh to fulfil the lusts thereof. They contrive the means of gratifying pride, ambition, covetousness, and sensual desires. But when the kingdom of God takes place in them, they no longer live to the lusts of men, but to the will of God. They keep under the body to bring it into subjection. They abstain from the appearance of evil, and especially watch against their own iniquity. They maintain a warfare with

with themselves, and with the world; and seek grace that they may cleanse themselves from all filthiness of the flesh and spirit, and may perfect holiness in the fear of God.

The kingdom of God in the soul *subdues worldly affections*. As it is not of this world, but from heaven, so the subjects of it seek the things which are above, not the things which are on the earth.

Worldly affections, reigning in the soul, are inconsistent with the religion of Christ. He came to deliver us from this evil world. Faith in him overcomes the world. They who trust in riches cannot enter into his kingdom. He has chosen the poor in this world, rich in faith, to be heirs of the kingdom which he has promised; and he has declared, that only to the poor in spirit the blessings of it belong.

The kingdom of God is a kingdom of *peace* and *love*. It not only calls men into a state of peace with God, but requires them to live in peace with one another. Benevolence, condescension, meekness, forbearance, and inoffensiveness, are distinguishing virtues of Christ's disciples. A temper of charity is the grand qualification for a subject of his kingdom. This is the end of the commandment, and the bond of perfectness. For this we are called into his kingdom; and then only we walk worthy of our calling, when we walk in all lowliness, longsuffering, and meekness, forbear one another in love, and keep the unity of the spirit in the bond of peace. There is nothing more offensive to the Prince of

Peace, than contentions, animosities, and tumults among his subjects. There is no law of his kingdom more fully expressed, more frequently repeated, and more solemnly enforced, than that which requires us to love one another, and to study the things which make for peace. We are commanded to mark and avoid them who cause divisions and offences. Mutual love and condescension, are the marks by which Christ's disciples are to be known among men.

Charity is a humble, modest virtue. It makes no ostentation. Contentions and disputes are noisy and tumultuous. They make uproar and confusion. But love is still and silent. It does good without sounding a trumpet. While it scatters blessings with one hand, the other scarcely knows what is doing. It prays for, and forgives offenders in secret, and makes no proclamation. It bestows favours on little ones, on persons of obscure condition. Such favours seldom come to publick notice. They fall not under the observation of the world.

4. As the temper of the gospel, so also *the operation of the divine spirit*, in producing this temper, is without observation.

A divine influence is necessary to form the hearts of fallen men to the love of religion. This influence is afforded, wherever the gospel is dispensed. But this is a secret influence: It comes not with observation. It is something, which the human eye cannot see. They who are the subjects

jects of it, cannot directly and immediately distinguish it from the rational operations of their own minds. They know it rather by its holy fruits, than by sense and consciousness. Our Saviour says, It is as *the wind, which bloweth where it listeth, and we hear the sound thereof, but cannot tell whence it cometh, nor whither it goeth.* This influence, like the gospel itself, is soft, mild, and gentle. It is not a tempest, an earthquake, or fire; but a small, still voice. It is a spirit of power, but yet a spirit of love, and of a sound mind. The fruits of it, like its nature, are kind and benevolent. They are love, joy, peace, long-suffering, gentleness, meekness, and goodness. The wisdom of the world is attended with strife and confusion: But the wisdom from above, is pure, and peaceable, gentle, and easy to be entreated, full of mercy and good fruits.

5. The *blessings* of God's kingdom are chiefly invisible, and without observation.

The rewards which the gospel promises are not earthly and temporal, but heavenly and spiritual. They are not external power, wealth, and honour; but inward peace, hope, and joy here, and everlasting felicity hereafter. In this world, the good Christian is subject to the same outward calamities which attend others. But he has consolations, which spring only from religion, and which a stranger intermeddles not with. He rejoices in the approving testimony of his conscience; in hope of the glory of God; and in the happy influence of his afflictions, which work patience, give him experience, enliven his love to God, and confirm his heavenly hope. The Apostle says—*We are troubled on every side, yet not distressed ; perplexed, but not in despair ; as sorrowful, yet always* **rejoicing** *; as poor, yet making many rich ; as having* **nothing***, yet possessing all things.* It is the power of religion in the heart, which enables the Christian, in all his trials, thus to triumph in Christ Jesus.

We see in what respects, the kingdom of God comes without observation. How happy is the state of the sincere Christian ! He has a kingdom within him. He may be poor and despised in this world. He may suffer a variety of adversity and distress ; but he is a subject of the King of faints. He receives continual supplies and consolations from heaven. He has peace of mind, and hope toward God. He is an heir of everlasting glory. Blessed are the poor in spirit, for theirs is the kingdom of heaven.

END OF THE TWENTY SECOND SERMON.

SERMON XXIII.

The Kingdom of God without Observation.

LUKE, 17. XX, XXI.

And when he was demanded of the Pharisees, When the kingdom of God should come; he answered them and said, The kingdom of God cometh not with observation: Neither shall they say, Lo here; or, lo there; for behold, the kingdom of God is within you.

IN what respects the kingdom of God, or the gospel dispensation, comes without observation, **we** have shewn in a preceding discourse. We will now attend to the reflections and instructions which our subject offers to **us**.

1. If the kingdom of God is now among us, we are all, without exception, bound to acknowledge it, and submit to it.

As Jesus declared himself to be the Messiah, who, according to the prophecies of scripture, was to come into the world, the Pharisees demanded of of him, when his kingdom was to begin. He answered them, that it was begun already. He was now working miracles to prove his heavenly mission. He was now preaching the way of salvation for sinners. He was now proclaiming peace to them, and stating the terms of their acceptance. The kingdom of Messiah, foretold by the prophets, was now among them. It only remained for them to bow down in humble submission to its laws, and secure the happiness which it promised.

Wherever God sends his gospel, there he erects his kingdom, and calls men to become the subjects of it. And it is at their peril, if they reject it. When Jesus came, preaching the gospel of the kingdom of God, he said to the people—*The time is fulfilled, and the kingdom of God is at hand: Repent ye, and believe the gospel.*

We are not to suppose, that it is at our option, whether we will enter into this kingdom, or not. We are indispensably bound to receive it. Among the various forms of human government, we may choose the one which pleases us best. A people may adopt that constitution, in which they can agree and unite. If particular members of a community disapprove the constitution, which is chosen and ratified, they have a natural right to repair to some other society, whose government suits them better. But the kingdom of God is not to be viewed in this light. It is not a mere form, which men may take, or let alone at pleasure, and

which

which derives its authority merely from human consent. It is a kingdom of righteousness; and its authority is absolute and universal.

God is the supreme Lord of all worlds. He has a sovereign right to our obedience. His wisdom has framed the order, his will has established the authority, and his goodness has made to us the discovery of his kingdom; and it is a kingdom which cannot be moved. Our rejection of it must be accompanied with the highest guilt, and our disobedience will be followed with the most amazing punishment.

Some seem to imagine, that if they profess themselves the subjects of this kingdom, they come under higher and stricter obligations than others; and that there are then duties incumbent on them, in which before they had no concern. Under this delusive imagination, many, it is probable, decline to make any profession at all, that they may feel themselves more at liberty to walk according to the course of the world.

But the truth is, the kingdom of God is come nigh to us; it is among us; and we are all bound to profess obedience, and yield it too. We have no more right to reject God's kingdom, when it is offered, than we have to withhold obedience when we have promised it. A profession is not the assumption of arbitrary obligations, but an acknowledgment of real ones. A profession of obedience is required; and he who refuses it, is guilty of the same contempt of divine authority,

as

as he who refuses obedience after he has professed it.

The gospel dispensation is sometimes called *a covenant*. Now, because the validity of covenants between man and man, depends on mutual consent and agreement, we are apt insensibly to fall into this conception of the *divine* covenant. But we should remember, that God is a sovereign; that we stand not on the ground of equality with him, as we do with men; that his wisdom is perfect, and his authority supreme; and *his covenant he commands us*. Wherever he reveals and proposes it, the obligations of it take place. Whether we consent or not, still we come within its authority. Though our consent is necessary to our enjoying the saving benefits of it, yet it is not necessary to our coming under its commanding power.

Whatever excuses may be made for the heathens, who have never known the gospel, these excuses cannot be admitted in our case, because **God** has placed us in a very different condition from theirs; and we cannot put ourselves in their condition, if we would.

The wickedness of those who profess the gospel, is indeed highly aggravated. But the aggravation arises from the *enjoyment*, rather than from the *profession* of the gospel. *This is the condemnation, that light is come into the world, and they have loved darkness rather than light, because their deeds are evil.* Their guilt is aggravated, not in comparison with the guilt of those who enjoy the gospel,

pel, and yet refuse to profess it; but rather in comparison with the guilt of those, who have never known the gospel, nor had an opportunity to profess it.

Our Saviour, alluding to the state of the Jewish nation, who received their kings by an appointment from Rome, illustrates the kingdom of God, or the gospel dispensation, by a parable of a certain nobleman, who went into a far country, to receive to himself a kingdom, and to return. This nobleman, at his departure, committed to his servants the care of his money, with a direction to occupy it for him, until he came back. These servants had professed a regard for his person, and an attachment to his interest, and with them he trusts his riches. But there were some of his citizens who hated him, and sent a message after him, saying—*We will not have this man to reign over us.* When he returned, having received the kingdom, he first called his servants to a reckoning, among whom was found one who had neglected to improve his Lord's money. This negligent servant fell under his severe displeasure. He said to them who stood by, *Take from him the pound—for from him who hath not,* or improveth not what is committed to him—*shall be taken away even that which he hath.* But, ¿What became of those, who would not that he should reign over them?—¿Were they excused? or, ¿Was their punishment alleviated, because they had never professed themselves his servants? No:

After

After sentence on the unfaithful servant, the king says—*But those mine enemies, who would not that I should reign over them, bring hither, and slay them before me.*

In the parable of the wedding feast, there were some who made light of the king's invitation, and injuriously treated the messengers who brought it. Among those who accepted the invitation, there was one found without a wedding garment. This unworthy guest was bound, and cast into outer darkness; and against those who rejected the invitation, and abused his servants, the king sent forth his armies, and destroyed them, and burnt up their city.

You see then the indispensable obligation of all, to whom the gospel comes, to profess their belief of, and subjection to it. ¿ Do you decline to make a religious profession, from an apprehension, that after this, the guilt of your sins will be aggravated? Know, that whether you make a profession or not, the guilt of your sins is already aggravated, from the advantages under which the gospel has placed you.—*They who know their Lord's will, and do it not, shall be beaten with many stripes.* It is vain to think of securing yourselves, by pleading that you are not of the number of professors; for God has not left it to your choice, whether you will be of that number, any more than he has left it to your choice whether you will love and fear him. You have no more right to live at large, and unconnected with the Christian church, than you have to be unjust, profane, or intemperate.

temperate. No caution of this kind can avail to alleviate your guilt. Yea, the very pretence confutes itself; for, while you deliberate how to sin with safety, you discover a heart set in you to do evil.

2. We learn, that it concerns every one, not only to submit to God's kingdom, but to submit to it *immediately*. There is no occasion for delay.

Imagine not that the kingdom of God comes with such observation, that there are only particular *times* when you may enter into it. It is come nigh to you. Its laws are now stated, and its blessings proposed; and you may submit to these laws, and secure these blessings now, as well as hereafter. You are not to wait for a more favourable opportunity; but to embrace the present. The Apostle says—*We have received a kingdom, which cannot be moved.* It is a steady, as well as a perpetual kingdom. Its laws are always the same—its blessings are continually offered—its grace is ever free.—*Let us have grace, that we may serve God acceptably, with reverence and godly fear.*

You are not to suppose, that God grants his spirit *only* at certain seasons; that then it comes as a violent shower, with such observation, as distinguishes this from all other seasons; and that these are the only seasons of salvation.—He stretches out his hand, all the day long, even to the disobedient and gainsaying. His spirit strives with sinners, while his longsuffering waits. The stiffnecked and perverse, *always* resist the Holy Ghost. He *now* commands all to repent, and invites all to receive

the

the bleffings of his grace. We are to hear his voice, while it is called *today*. *Now is the day of falvation, and the time of acceptance.* We are not **to delay**, under an apprehenfion that God will be more gracious, the operations of the fpirit more powerful, or our hearts better difpofed, at another time, than this. We are to improve *this* time, *this* day, as the only feafon, which is ours; remembering, that God waits to be gracious, and **exalts** himfelf that he may have mercy.

We are here taught, that we have no occafion to run from place to place, in order to find the grace of God, for we may obtain it in any place, where his Providence calls us.

We are not to imagine, that the fpirit of God is poured out in fuch, or fuch a place, and no where elfe; and that, in order to obtain a portion of the fpirit, we muft go to fuch a place, hear fuch a preacher, or join with fuch an affembly. The kingdom of God comes not with obfervation; neither fhall men have occafion to fay, *Lo, it is here*; or, *lo, it is there:* For the fpirit is not confined to certain places; its influences are not at human difpofal, nor do its operations come with publick obfervation. The gofpel is a miniftration of the fpirit. Where God fends the former, he fends alfo the latter. You are to receive the fpirit in the hearing of faith. Its influence on the heart is not like an overbearing ftorm, but as the gentle rain on the tender herb, and the dew on the grafs.

We

We are to attend on the ordinances which God has appointed, in the place which his providence points out, hoping for a blessing in the way which his wisdom has prescribed. Here we are to lift up holy hands, not doubting of his readiness to give his spirit to them who ask him, in this place, as well as another. If they say—*See here, or, see there ; go not after them, nor follow them, for the kingdom of God is among you.* God grants his grace in his own way ; and when in his way we seek, we may be sure to find.

4. We learn from our subject, that true religion is not ostentatious. It seeks not observation.

The true Christian is exemplary, but not vain. He is careful to maintain good works, but affects not an unnecessary show of them. He does nothing through vain glory, but thinks and acts with lowliness of mind. He will not put himself forward, or take upon him to censure and dictate. Conscious of his numerous imperfections, he hopes humbly, reproves gently, hears reproof patiently, judges charitably, and shews out of a good conversation his works with meekness of wisdom.

Real religion begins in selfabasement, in a conviction of sin, sense of unworthiness, and reliance on free mercy. The same humble temper, in which it begins, accompanies its future works. The Christian, after his highest improvements, remembers what he was once, a guilty creature, exposed to wrath. He considers, that from this

deplorable

deplorable condition he was recovered by the sovereign grace of God. He reckons not himself to have already attained, or to be already made perfect; but he presses toward the mark for the prize of the high calling. He glories not in his attainments, but laments his deficiencies. When he compares himself with other Christians, he is inclined to hope them better than himself. His language is not—*God, I thank thee, that I am not as other men; but, God be merciful to me a sinner.* In the performance of duty he seeks not the observation of men, but the approbation of God. If he perceives a regard to human applause creeping in, and mingling itself with spiritual duties, he abhors himself, laments the remaining corruption of his heart, prays for grace to cleanse him from it, and keeps his soul with greater diligence. If he sees reason to rejoice in a consciousness of his integrity, he acknowledges with the Apostle—*By the grace of God, I am what I am.*

5. It appears, that they only are the true subjects of God's kingdom, who have experienced its power on their hearts.

A religion, that is merely external, will carry none to the world of glory. Let us then inquire, what influence the gospel has *within* us.

We profess to believe its divinity and importance. ¿Have we felt its transforming power?— ¿Are we governed by its doctrines, and conformed to its precepts?—¿Have we received the kingdom of God as little children, with a meek, humble,

humble, teachable, and obedient spirit?—¿ Have we been taught by the grace of God to deny ourselves?—¿ Are our wills subjected to God's authority, and our affections raised to heavenly objects?—If we are strangers to this internal operation of the gospel, then it has only come near to us; but we have not received it.—¿ How great is our guilt?

To us the word of salvation is sent; and it will not return empty. It will not leave us, as it found us. It will have some mighty effect. If it is not a favour of life unto life, it will be a favour of death unto death. If we treat with contempt the gospel of the grace of God, our condemnation will be more dreadful than if we never had known it. We are then in a most solemn situation; guilty, and worthy of death—under the offer of pardon—on trial whether we will accept it. The issue of our probation will be an exceeding and eternal weight of glory, or everlasting misery, aggravated beyond conception by a contempt of offered salvation. Behold, ye despisers, and wonder, and perish—God will perform a work, which you will not believe, though one declare it to you.

6. As the kingdom of God comes not to the heart with observation, we are incompetent judges of the characters of others.

It is a great thing to know our own hearts; impossible for us to know the hearts of others. God only knows the hearts of all the children of men,

men. Therefore judge nothing before the time, till the Lord come, who will bring to light the hidden things of darkness, and make manifest the counsels of the heart. And happy they, who then shall have praise of God. In the mean time, let us not judge and condemn one another; but judge this rather, that no man put a stumbling **block, or occasion to fall,** in his brother's way. Why should we judge and set at nought our brother? We must all stand before the judgment seat of Christ. Since we cannot look into the hearts of our brethren, **we must** hope all things, **and** leave the decision of their state to him, whose judgment is according to truth. We are not to exclude men from our charity and fellowship on mere suspicion, **or for want of the** highest evidence of sincerity; but whoever professes subjection to the kingdom of Christ, and contradicts not that profession by an ungodly life, him we must receive as a fellow citizen with the saints, and of the household of God. Let us therefore be likeminded one toward another, according to Christ Jesus; and receive one another as Christ also received us, to the glory of God. Let us comfort and encourage one another, as fellow workers to the kingdom of God, unite **our** influence to increase the number of his subjects, and to enlarge the extent of his kingdom on earth, and, in all things walk worthy of him, who has called us to his kingdom and glory.

END OF THE TWENTY THIRD SERMON.

SERMON XXIV.

Innumerable gone to the Grave, and every Man drawing after them.

JOB, 21. xxxiii.

And every man shall draw after him, as there are innumerable before him.

THE main purpose of Job's discourse in the preceding verses, and indeed through a great part of this book, is to shew, that no judgment can be formed of men's characters by the present dispensations of Providence toward them; for good men often meet with great calamities in the course of their life; and some are early cut off by the hand of violence; and wicked men, on the other hand, as often prosper in their worldly designs, live to old age, and go down to the grave by a natural death; and consequently we must look for another state, in which an equitable distribution of rewards and punishments may take place.

He particularly observes concerning death, which is the greatest of worldly evils, and the most dreaded by the sons of men, that it is appointed, not as a punishment merely for a few distinguished offenders, but as the common lot of all; and therefore from the time, manner, and circumstances of a man's death, we can conclude nothing concerning his character.

When we see one, by any means, or at any age, brought to the grave, we may properly make the same reflection which Job makes in our text—*Every man shall draw after him, as there have been innumerable before him.*

Such an event, however common, is very solemn. It admonishes us of the mortal condition of the human race, and of our own mortality in particular.

Job observes, that *innumerable* have already been brought to the grave. This was true in his day: It is more emphatically true now.

The numbers, which have mingled with the dust, since man was first placed on the earth, exceed all computation. The human race has existed almost six thousand years. Before the flood the succession was less rapid, and probably the world less populous, than it is now. Procreation seems to have begun later in some proportion to the greater length of life. In the antediluvian genealogy no mention is made of a parent younger than sixty five years. But still, as the longevity of men, in that period, gave time for numerous families to spring from each progenitor, we must suppose, that the numbers, which were born

and

and died, in the space of sixteen hundred years, were vastly great.

For a few generations after the flood, human life was still prolonged to a considerable extent. But it is now more than three thousand years, since it has been reduced to its present scanty measure. The earth is supposed to change its inhabitants, at a medium, three times in a century. The change, in this part of the world, is not so rapid; but applied to the world in general, perhaps the estimate is not far from the truth. The number of people on the globe, at any one time, cannot possibly be ascertained to any degree of exactness. But it must doubtless amount to many hundreds of millions. Some have reckoned about nine hundred millions. Probably this calculation does not exceed the truth. Now suppose so many souls passing off this stage, and as many coming on, thrice in the space of one hundred years, which will be nearly eighty thousand in a day; and suppose this to have been the rate of succession for several thousand years past, and you will easily conceive the propriety of the expression—*Innumerable have gone before us.* The numbers, which have already lived and died, utterly surpass our comprehension.

The fate of past generations will be the fate of the present, and the future. When we see a man go down to the grave, this is a natural thought— *Every man will draw after him.* Had we no other evidence of our mortality, but what arises from

the

the multitudes which have died before us, this would be sufficient to put it beyond a doubt.

Our knowledge of future events, in the natural world, chiefly depends on observation and experience. That which has uniformly been the course of things, in former time, we expect will be their course in time to come. That the sun will rise again, after it has set—that summer will succeed to winter—that harvest will follow seed-time—that fire will warm us, and our food will strengthen us, we conclude with a sufficient degree of certainty, because this has ever been the steady course of nature. And experience gives us the same evidence, that we must go down to the grave, for innumerable have gone before us. For many thousand years there has not been an instance of a man's living to any considerable length of time, in this world. When we look around, we find but here and there one but who was born within seventy or eighty years; and much the greater part within half that time. To expect immortality here, would be as absurd, and as contradictory to all human experience, as to expect perpetual summer, or unchanging sunshine. And to conduct as if we were never to die, is as irrational as it would be to order our affairs in summer, on the presumption that there is never to be another winter.

Though no man needs evidence to convince him, yet every man needs warnings to remind him, of his mortality. Providence, therefore, so

orders

orders events as to give us continual admonitions of this serious and most interesting change. Every death which we see, though it can hardly be called a proof of what is already as evident as possible, yet is a fresh call from God to the sons of men, to think of, and prepare for, their own approaching death.

Admonitions of this kind are of all the most solemn and impressive, because they not only *tell* us, but *shew* us, that we must die. And that they may be suited to persons of every age and condition, may come with greater power, may strike the mind with some solemnity, and may not lose their effect by growing too familiar, God is pleased to send men to the grave by different means, in a variety of ways, in every period of life, and under the greatest imaginable diversity of circumstances. In almost every death, there is something new and affecting. Job observes in the preceding verses—*One dieth in his full strength, being wholly at ease and quiet, his breasts are full of milk, and his bones moistened with marrow: Another dieth in the bitterness of his soul, and never eateth with pleasure. They shall lie down alike in the dust, and the worms shall cover them.*

To dwell on the proof of so obvious a truth, would be a misspense of time. More useful will it be to entertain and apply the instructions and reflections, which it suggests to us.

1. In the mortality of the human race, we have a clear demonstration of a future state.

The frame of our bodies, and the powers of our minds, speak forth the wisdom of the Creator; for we are fearfully and wonderfully made. Perfect wisdom has some worthy end in all that it does, some good design in every thing which it makes. But, ¿ For what purpose could man be be made, if death terminates his existence? Here is a numerous race of creatures, which, in the present state, answer no end equal to the dignity, or suitable to the capacity of their nature. They have reason, memory, forethought, and reflection. They can look within and around, can contemplate the earth, and the heavens, can conceive immortal desires, and form eternal designs. They have fears of future evil, and hopes of future good. They can discern between right and wrong, approve the one, and condemn the other. By study and application, they can improve their knowledge, enlarge their powers, and extend their prospects. But, ¿ To what purpose is all this, if they have no existence beyond this poor, mortal state?—¿ Are their desires and hopes, their fears and apprehensions, merely imaginary?—¿ Are they made with a sense of good and evil, and with the powers of reflection and forethought, only to vex and torment them?—¿ Are they to be struck out of existence almost as soon as they come into it, without opportunity for their minds to open, spread, and reach their just perfection?—¿ Can it be suspected, that an allwise Creator would make a race of intelligent, moral beings,

to

to come on this stage, and pass off again by millions, in such rapid succession, for ages and ages together, when there is no rational or moral purpose to be answered?—Would he give an intellectual existence to creatures merely for an animal and momentary life; merely to sport for a day, like those swarms of insects, which play in a summer's sun, and then vanish into eternal nonexistence? This is a supposition so contradictory to our ideas of creating wisdom, that we at once reject it. Let us then accustom ourselves to regard and improve this state as preparatory to another. Let every death, which we behold, remind us of a future world, and awaken us to make effectual provision for the important hour, when we must take our departure hence for an everlasting state.

2. What an evil and bitter thing is sin, which has brought into the world innumerable deaths!

Revelation teaches us, that *by one man sin entered into the world, and death by sin, and so death passes upon all men, for that all have sinned.*

Man was originally made for immortality. And though we cannot suppose, that, in case of innocence, he would always have lived in this world, in a state of continual increase, because then the earth must, in time, have been surcharged with inhabitants; yet his remove from this to a more perfect state, would certainly have been in a manner very different from death; perhaps by such an easy translation as that of Enoch and Elijah. It was by sin, that death made its gloomy

entrance

entrance into the world, and gained its dreadful dominion over the human race. And the sin, by which it entered, was the first offence of the first human pair. It is not each man's personal transgression that subjects him to death; for death is common to all—to good and bad—to young and old—to them who have sinned, and to them who have not sinned by actual disobedience. Every man must go down to the grave, whither innumerable have gone already. It is then only one single sin, which has made this awful havock.—*By one offence, death reigns.—By one offence judgment is come on all men.* One transgression has filled the world with deaths, in ages past; nor is its baleful influence spent.

¿ Shall we then, like fools, make a mock of sin ?—¿ Shall we think it a light and trifling matter to offend the great and holy God, to transgress his laws, and run in the face of his warnings and threatenings ?—¿ Shall we dare any longer to continue under the guilt of all our personal sins? Think what innumerable deaths one sin has produced, and then say, whether it be safe to live any longer exposed to the punishment, which our innumerable sins deserve.

How infinitely it concerns every son of Adam now to take the benefit of the glorious redemption purchased by the death of a Saviour!

The Son of God has come down to our world, and taken our nature, that he might suffer death for our redemption. It was not the intention of his death to exempt us from dying; die we muſt ſtill; but to deliver us from the awful conſequences of death—from eternal death. Let the conſideration of the great evil of ſin, manifeſted in the univerſal mortality of the human race, excite us immediatly to fly from ſin by repentance, and to the Saviour by faith, that we may obtain a diſcharge from our guilt, and a title to that glorious reſurrection and happy immortality, by which death is ſwallowed up in victory.

If a ſingle ſin deſerves ſuch numberleſs deaths, how amazing muſt be the deſert of all our ſins, and how amazingly will this deſert be increaſed, if, to all our other ſins, we add this the greateſt of all ſins, an obſtinate and contemptuous rejection of the Saviour! His death is an atonement for other ſins; but, ¿ What other atonement will you find for the ſin of finally refuſing this? If we ſin wilfully after we have received the knowledge of the truth, there remaineth no more ſacrifice for ſin; but a fearful looking for of judgment.

3. Our ſubject may give us ſome faint ideas of the grandeur of the final judgment.

The ſcripture aſſures us, that, as there will be a righteous judgment, ſo it will be *univerſal*, extending to all—to quick and dead—to bond and free—to great and ſmall. That earth and ſea will give up their dead—that all who are in their graves ſhall come forth, and thoſe who are alive, and remain, will be collected with them before the throne of the Son of God, who will render to

every

every one according to the deeds done in the body. On that great day, what an amazing multitude will be aſſembled! Not merely the people of a particular country—not only the numerous millions, which now ſwarm on the globe—not only the countleſs myriads, which have peopled it for nearly ſix thouſand years paſt; but all who ſhall be called on this ſtage, in the unknown ſucceſſion of future generations, till time ſhall be no more. *Theſe, all* theſe ſhall be collected in one grand aſſembly, to attend their final trial, hear their righteous ſentence, and receive their eternal deſtination. Yea, not only the human race, but thoſe legions of evil ſpirits, which left their firſt habitation, and are now reſerved in chains, under darkneſs, to the judgment of the great day, will then be brought forth, and adjudged to the full meaſure of their torments. And to add to the majeſty and ſolemnity of the ſcene, thouſands of thouſands, ten thouſand times ten thouſand, an innumerable company of angels, will give their attendance, and wait around the fiery throne, as miniſtering ſpirits, to teſtify their approbation of the equity of the proceſs, and carry into execution the orders of the Judge.

The contemplation of this great and awful judgment, at which we muſt aſſuredly make our appearance, and in which we ſhall have an infinite concern, may juſtly fill us with amazement, awaken our moſt ſolemn attention, and make us careful what manner of perſons we are.

Beware

Beware of hypocrify; for there is nothing covered, which fhall not be revealed. Be afraid of fecret fins, for thefe will be brought into judgment. The hidden things of darknefs will be expofed in the light, and the counfels of all hearts made manifeft before the affembled world.

4. How vain and trifling are our earthly interefts and poffeffions!

We are only pilgrims, paffengers, tranfient, fugitive mortals. The generations of men are paffing in quick fucceffion, and there is no abiding. ¿What have we in this world, that can be worth the name of property?—¿What folly to be anxious about our worldly condition; or to take much thought what we have, or what we want, what we get, or what we lofe?

How many millions have lived in this world, each of whom had fomething which he called his own! What ftruggles and contefts have there been about this tract of territory, and that fpot of ground—this lump of ore, and that glittering ftone! The fame worldly and contentious fpirit remains. We have our refpective claims, right or wrong. One boafts of his fuperiority; another complains of his want: One defpifes a poor neighbour; another envies a rich one: One facrifices eafe and confcience to gain more wealth; another, to gratify vanity and lufts, fpends what his father gained.

How bufy are mankind; and yet how trifling their defigns and purfuits! But foon death breaks
all

all their purposes, and frustrates the thoughts of their heart. In a few days, we who now live, shall have as little concern with the world, as those who lived before the flood. What one calls *his*, and another calls *his*, soon will belong neither to the one, nor the other, but to some successor, as mortal as himself, who must again leave it to the man who comes after him; and he still is mortal. Thus it passes from mortal to mortal, till it shall be lost in the wreck of nature.

Learn then to moderate your worldly affections. Be patient in want, beneficent in fulness, contented whether in fulness or want. Place your affections on things above, and lay up durable riches in the heavenly world, where, on your arrival, you will find them secure, and ready for enjoyment.

5. Our subject teaches us, what reason we have to pity, console and succour the afflicted.

A world of mortality must be a world of sorrow. Here is not only pain and distress of body; but, that which is often more painful and distressing, the loss of most pleasant and intimate friends, on whom the bigger half of life's joys depended. When a mortal, in the midst of his expected days, is torn from his near connexions, how many hearts bleed with the wound. There you will see a solitary companion, and here disappointed parents; helpless offspring on one hand, and weeping brethren on the other. The fall of such a man, like the fall of an uprooted tree,

tree, spreads wide ruin around, and rifles the bloom of all who are near.

When we see, what we often see, numbers distressed by the death of one, let us reflect, that their distress may soon be ours. The man, who died last, was not the only one who was mortal. Every man must draw after him, as there are innumerable before him. We have not a friend on earth, who is not as mortal as he was—not a friend on earth, but may soon leave us in sorrow and anguish. Let us then bring home to our hearts the sorrow of our neighbours, take a sensible share in it, and remember those who are in bonds, as bound with them ; and those who suffer adversity, as being ourselves also in the body.

6. We are taught the danger which attends too strong a reliance on earthly friends.

Every man must go down to the grave. Cease then from man, whose breath is in his nostrils ; for wherein is he to be accounted of. Trust in the Lord forever, for with him is everlasting strength.

The loss of friends, is a call from heaven to raise our thoughts and affections there. When our earthly dependence sinks under us, we must lean more fully on the power and wisdom, the mercy and faithfulness of God. In him we must seek our comfort in every adversity. The world, which is itself so full of trouble, cannot be a source of comfort in trouble. Our comfort we must seek in another place ; our refreshments we must

must draw from another fountain. A settled persuasion, that a God of infinite wisdom, power and goodness, governs the world; that he orders all events, and extends his care to all creatures; that we are interested in his favour; and, all things, under his direction, will work for our good; that heavenly joys will soon recompense all our earthly sorrows; this is the only sure principle of comfort, hope and courage, in our worldly afflictions.

Let us then be quickened to a life of undissembled religion, which is necessary to our comfortable passage through this world, and our happy entrance into a better.

Religion exempts no man from affliction, or from death; but it does more; it gives him substantial comfort in affliction, and sure preparation for death, and thus turns both to his advantage.

Since religion is so supremely necessary, life so precarious, and death so surely approaching, let us call off our thoughts from this world, and direct them to our future and everlasting concerns. This is the dictate of reason, of scripture, and of providence. Let us realize human frailty, pity those in adversity, and stand prepared for similar trials. Let not the prosperous flatter themselves, that they never shall be moved, nor the young and vigorous imagine, that their mountain stands strong. The day is hastening, when the strong must bow themselves. Health, strength, youth, and vigour, when death approaches, can make no resistance.

fiftance. Virtue, ufefulnefs, helplefs dependents, and weeping, praying friends, cannot procure an exemption from the grave.

Whatever your hands find to do, do it with your might; there is no work in the grave, whither ye are going. Let your repentance be fpeedy, that death may not prevent it; let your hope be well founded, that death may not difappoint it; and let it be improved, and confirmed by the conftant exercife of piety, that your departure may be comfortable, your entrance into heaven abundant, and your reward rich and glorious.

END OF THE TWENTY FOURTH SERMON.

SERMON XXV.

Reflections on Harvest.

JEREMIAH, 5. xxiv.

Neither say they in their heart, Let us now fear the Lord our God, that giveth rain, both the former and the latter rain in his season: He reserveth unto us the appointed weeks of the harvest.

AMONG the many instances of the great corruption and degeneracy of the Jews, enumerated in this chapter, one of the plainest, is their inattention to, and disregard of, the constant government of God's providence, when there were the most obvious and familiar proofs of it daily before their eyes. They paid their devotions to inanimate idols and imaginary divinities, and renounced the worship and service of that almighty and most glorious Being, whose hand created, and still sustains, the whole frame of nature, and whose goodness supplies the wants of every living creature.

" Hear this, O foolish people," says God by his prophet, " a people without understanding, who have eyes, and see not; who have ears, and hear not :—¿ Fear ye not me ?—¿ Will ye not tremble

at

at my prefence, who have placed the fand for the bound of the fea, by a perpetual decree, that it cannot pafs it ; and though the waves thereof tofs themfelves, yet can they not prevail ; and though they roar, yet can they not pafs over it ?"

The reftraint of the ocean, that tumultuous body of waters, which the Jews, living near the Mediterranean, had frequent opportunities to obferve, is often mentioned in fcripture, as an effect of God's watchful providence, and an evidence of his mighty power. This is felected from among the numerous proofs of God's government, not becaufe it is more immediately his work, but becaufe the grandeur and majefty of the fcene ftrikes the mind with a deeper and more awful fenfe of his continual fuperintending influence, than moft other appearances in the natural world.

The direction of the feafons, the interchanges of rain and funfhine, and the timely returns of harveft, are, if not fo grand, yet as plain and convincing proofs of God's providence, as the control of the ocean. To this God appeals in the text, and complains, that while his people partook of his bounty, they regarded not his hand. "But this people hath a revolting and a rebellious heart : They are revolted and gone ; neither fay they in their heart, Let us now fear the Lord, who giveth us rain, the former and latter rain in his feafon, and referveth to us the appointed weeks of the harveft."

There is frequent mention of the *former*, and the *latter* rain. The one came on juſt after feed time; the other, not long before harveſt, and is called, "the latter rain of the firſt month," or the month in which harveſt began. The fruitfulneſs of the feafon depended much on theſe rains, which feem to have been periodical in that country. If either of them failed, the harveſt was fmall.

The meſſage contained in this chapter, was probably delivered to the people about the time of harveſt. In fome preceding years, the crops had been cut ſhort by unfavourable weather, as well as by the incurfions of enemies. It is faid, in the third and fourth chapters, that for the wickedneſs of the people, " the ſhowers had been withheld, and there had been no latter rain—all the birds of heaven were fled, and the fruitful field was become a wilderneſs." The failure of the harveſts, in feafons paſt, had given them anxious apprehenfions for the next. But having, beyond all expectation, received timely rains, they beheld their fields covered with corn, and their paſtures clothed with flocks. And yet they remained as regardleſs of the divine government as before; Neither, faid they, let us now fear the Lord, who gives us rain in feafon, and beſtows upon us the rich, but unexpected bleſſings of harveſt.

There are two obfervations fuggeſted to us in our text.

I. That

I. That the regular return of harvest is a demonstration of the existence and providence of God.

II. That the time of harvest naturally calls us to pious meditations and reflections.

I. The regular return of harvest is an obvious proof of the existence and providence of God.

The Jews, who, with this evidence before their eyes, feared not God, are called " a foolish people, and without understanding.

The fruits of the earth, so necessary to the support of animal life, depend on causes beyond the reach of human power. Our labour in the culture of the soil, is useless and vain without a friendly disposition of the seasons. But in the direction of the seasons, we can have no more influence than in the creation of worlds. There is nothing within the sphere of human agency, that in the least contributes to hasten or restrain the showers of heaven, to increase or moderate the heat of the sun, to continue or change the course of the winds. The whole management of the natural world is in hands superiour to ours—in the hands of an invisible, almighty Being. The invisible things of God are not more clearly seen from the creation of the world, than from the productions of nature. Had we been present, when God laid the foundation of the earth, we could not have had more convincing evidence, than what we now have in the stated returns of seed time and harvest, that there is a Being who fills,

fills, sustains, and rules the universe—who is above all, through all, and in us all.

The prophet remarks, that God reserves to us the *appointed weeks* of harvest.

That we may order our affairs with discretion, the world is governed by general, established laws. If the seasons should be thrown into confusion, or their regular succession frequently interrupted, there would be an end of human prudence and activity: We could never judge how to plan and pursue our business; when to sow our seed, or look for a harvest; and what provision to make, in one season, for our support till the return of the next. But as the system of God's government is uniform and steady, or subject only to small and occasional variations, we are able to form and prosecute our necessary designs with success.

We see that the seasons are ordered with wisdom superiour to ours. If we had power to influence them, yet we have not skill to guide them. Experience convinces us, how erroneously we have judged: But all our experience has not enabled us to judge perfectly for the future. A plentiful harvest often follows seasons; which to us appeared unfavourable; and the fruits of the earth as often are cut short after promising prospects. There are many things in the natural world, so entirely out of our sight, that it is impossible for us to determine the manner in which it is best the seasons should be ordered. The
weather,

weather, which we think unkind, may be neceſſary to the removal or prevention of evils, unknown to us, which might be fatal to the fruits of the earth :—That which is unfriendly to particular ſoils, may be adapted to general fertility :—That which produces a ſcanty harveſt, in one ſeaſon, may conduce to the fruitfulneſs of ſucceeding years.

Harveſt, in its appointed weeks, teaches us the goodneſs of God.

" He has not left himſelf without witneſs, in that he does good, gives us rain from heaven, and fruitful ſeaſons, and fills our hearts with food and gladneſs." We learn God's goodneſs from the effects of it, which we behold ; and the bleſſings of it, which we enjoy. When we ſee a man of wealth diſperſing abroad his charities among the indigent, we admire the goodneſs of his heart, and rejoice in his ability. Much greater evidence have we of the goodneſs of God, " who cauſes the graſs to grow for the cattle, and herb for the ſervice of man ; who gives to the beaſt his food, and to man wine which cheers, and bread which ſtrengthens his heart ; who crowns the year with bleſſings, and whoſe paths drop fatneſs."

God has made us dependent on his care for all our ſupplies ; and our neceſſary ſupplies he gives us, while we truſt his care in the exerciſe of prudence and induſtry. " Truſt in the Lord and do good : So ſhalt thou dwell in the land, and ſhalt be ſurely fed."

That divine promise, delivered to the world four thousand years ago, that "seed time and harvest, cold and heat, summer and winter, shall not cease," we see continually verified; and hence we learn, that the God who governs the world, is constant to his word. If particular countries have, at times, felt the distresses of famine, yet of seed time and harvest there has never been such a *general* failure, as looked like an infraction on the truth of this ancient promise. Every harvest is a new instance of God's faithfulness, a new performance of his promise, and a new encouragement to our faith in his providence and word.

As the return of harvest gives us such immediate sensible evidence of the existence, providence, wisdom, bounty, and faithfulness of God; so,

II. It naturally calls us to pious meditations and reflections.

It was an instance of great stupidity in the Jews, that they said not, "Let us now fear the Lord, who reserveth to us the appointed weeks of the harvest."

1. The seasons are so ordered, as to remind us of the *shortness of human foresight*.

From past experience we expect a harvest in its appointed weeks: And rarely is our expectation frustrated. But the event is not always adjusted to the measure of our hopes. It often falls short, and often exceeds them. That rain and sunshine are necessary to the fruitfulness of the earth, we know by constant observation. But what

what proportion of drought and moisture, of heat and cold, is most friendly to vegetation, and most conducive to plenty, is a matter in which we often misjudge. The management of the seasons, however, is in unerring hands. Rational beings, in the care of infinite wisdom and goodness, are always safe, while they proceed in the line of their duty; and never ought they to indulge anxiety. With him who governs futurity, they may calmly trust all events. "Take no thought for your life," says the divine Saviour, "what ye shall eat, or drink, or put on. Behold the fowls of the air; they neither sow, nor reap, nor gather into barns, yet your heavenly Father feedeth them.— Are ye not much better than they? Your Father knoweth that ye have need of these things. Seek ye first the kingdom of God, and these things shall be added."

2. Our *dependence* is apparent, as in many other things, so especially in the return of harvest.

Now we see the fruits of the earth brought to maturity, and provision made for our support through the succeeding year. This is not the work of man, but of the great Governour of Nature, whose bountiful designs nothing can defeat. Our industry and prudence must do their part; but it is God alone who succeeds our labours. The friendly showers, and the quickening sunbeams are not under our command. Hail storms, mildews, and devouring insects, are not subject to our will. If God send his blessing,

none

none can revoke it. If he withhold his smiles, our toil is fruitless. If he commissions storms or winds, frosts or insects, to lay waste our fields, our hopes are cut off. "These things are turned about by his counsels, that they may do whatsoever he commandeth them upon the face of the world."

At the time of harvest, it becomes us to reflect how insufficient we are to perfect our own designs, or to prevent the evils which may defeat them; and thus learn, in all our ways, to acknowledge God.

3. The scripture speaks of harvest as a season of *gratitude* and *joy*.

To express the happiness of mankind under the kingdom of the Messiah, the prophet says—"They joy before thee, as the joy of harvest." By the same allusion the Psalmist describes the felicity of the Jews in their national deliverance from captivity.—"They that sow in tears, shall reap in joy. He that goeth forth and weepeth, bearing precious seed, shall doubtless come again with rejoicing, bringing his sheaves with him." Particular festivals were instituted in the divine law, to be observed as testimonies of gratitude for the blessings of harvest. "Thou shalt keep the feast of harvest, the first fruits of thy labours, which thou hast sown in thy field, and the feast of ingathering in the end of the year, when thou hast gathered in thy labours out of the field— none shall appear before me empty. The first fruits

fruits of thy land thou shalt bring into the house of God."

We are daily loaded with benefits, which call for daily returns of gratitude. But harvest is such a rich and plentiful blessing, as we cannot every day receive. This is given only in the *appointed weeks*. If it should then fail, famine, distress, and mortality, must ensue; for according to the settled course of nature, it can no more be procured, till the stated period returns. No wisdom or power of man can hasten it. Such a blessing, so evidently from a divine hand, so necessary to human support, and so absolutely beyond our command, ought to be received with fervent sentiments, and lively expressions of thanksgiving and joy. With what a flow of gratitude the Psalmist comes before God on such an occasion as this! " Praise waiteth for thee, O God, in Zion. Unto thee shall the vow be performed—Thou makest the outgoings of the morning and of the evening to rejoice. Thou visitest the earth, and waterest it. Thou preparest them corn, when thou hast so provided for it. Thou waterest the ridges thereof abundantly. Thou settlest the furrows thereof, and makest them soft with showers. Thou blessest the springing thereof. Thou crownest the year with thy goodness, and thy paths drop fatness. They drop upon the pastures of the wilderness, and the little hills rejoice on every side. The pastures are clothed

with

with flocks; the valleys also are covered over with corn; they shout for joy; they also sing."

4. Harvest teaches us *diligence* and *frugality*.

This is heaven's reward to human industry. "The earth, by the blessing of God, brings forth herbs meet for them by whom it is dressed."

God supplies our wants, not by an *immediate* providence, but by succeeding our prudent labours. According to the ordinary course of his providence, "he becometh poor, who dealeth with a slack hand, but the hand of the diligent maketh rich."—"He who will not plow by reason of the cold, shall beg in harvest, and have nothing."

Every returning harvest is a fresh reward of the husbandman's labours, and a new encouragement to future industry.

Various are the circumstances under which God places mankind; but in regard of his blessing on their prudent labours, he treats them with an equal hand. This is what no man can engross to the prejudice of another; but all may alike enjoy. There are some less important things, which God permits men to appropriate. One may possess a more extensive tract of soil than his neighbours: He may call distant lands his own, which he has never seen, and which his sons will not see after him: He may claim more numerous herds and flocks, or count over larger parcels of shining metal, than most others can acquire, or than he himself can use. But the grand things on which life and happiness depend, God has

has not trusted to human disposal. He keeps them in his own hands, and distributes them with equal bounty. Rain, air, and sunshine, are alike free to all. The rain falls in as bountiful showers, and the sun shines with as lively beams on the poor man's garden, as the rich man's manor. The air as sweetly refreshes, and the winds as kindly fan the peasant, as the prince. How poor soever one may be in regard of those trifles, in which property consists, he has as ample a share in the great bounties of Providence, as sure a prospect of God's blessing on his labours, as high encouragement to industry in his calling, as the wealthiest possessor on the globe.

Harvest calls to frugality, as well as industry. Blessings bestowed by a divine hand, are to be used according to the divine will. Those precious fruits of the earth, which are dealt out only at certain seasons, and which, by no art or industry of man, can at other seasons be obtained, should be applied to honest and virtuous purposes; not wastefully consumed in criminal indulgences. What would you think of a beggar, who immediately perverts to intemperance the charitable allowance made him for his necessary subsistence? The same must you think of those, who by a prodigal mispense of the blessings of one harvest, reduce themselves to want before the return of another.

5. Harvest inculcates *benevolence*.

Religion

Religion confists in an imitation of God's moral character, especially of his diffusive and disinterested goodness. Fruitful seasons are instances of his goodness, and calls to imitate him by doing good to those around us. " Give to him who asketh of thee," says our Saviour, " and from him who would borrow of thee, turn not thou away— Do good, that ye may be the children of your Father, who is in heaven ; for he maketh his sun to rise on the evil and on the good, and sendeth rain on the just and the unjust."

The system of nature gives us daily lectures on benevolence. The world subsists by a reciprocation of benefits, and interchange of kindnesses. The clouds send down, in showers, the water, which by gentle exhalations they receive from the earth. By the medium of rains, the sea remits, to recruit the streams, that water which they had poured into his bosom. The air, by its constant motion, agitates the herbs and flowers of the field, and thus quickens the circulation of their fluids, and contributes to their growth. The flowers and herbs, thus moved and enlivened, emit their balsamick sweets to perfume and enrich the air. The sun sheds his beams on the earth and other revolving worlds ; these reflect his beams, which, after various repercussions from globe to globe, may return back to their source, and yield their assistance to repair his perpetual wastes. Man bestows his labour on the soil ; and, the soil repays his labour by the sustenance which it gives him.

him. He employs the beasts in his service, and, in his turn, he serves the beasts with that food, which they alone could not procure for themselves. This is the constitution of nature; and, What can be its moral design, but to teach men their obligation to promote each other's happiness, the happiness of society, and of the race, by mutual offices of kindness? The bodies of the system tend toward each other, and move in their orbits, by the great law of attraction. The members of society should be directed in their courses, and drawn to one common centre, the general happiness, by the grand law of benevolence.

6. Harvest reminds us of the *shortness of life*, and calls us to the *diligent improvement of our time*.

How fast one harvest rolls on after another!— How swiftly the intervening months have flown away! A few harvests more, and time will have reaped the earth of all its present growth, and a new one will succeed. As one harvest follows another, so passes one generation of mortals, and another comes. Let harvest then awaken our attention to the future world, and excite our speedy preparation for that happy clime, where seasons no more walk their rounds, and age no more succeeds to age—where the blest inhabitants abide secure, and whatever numbers enter, still there is room— where one perpetual summer smiles, immortality glides in a constant stream, the trees of life are always verdant, and yield their fruits every month—where will be no more toilsome labour,

poisonous

poisonous curse, nor wasting disease; but life, without decay—fulness, without fear of want—rest, without interruption—and joy, without mixture of grief.

Harvest is an industrious season. When this calls, time is precious. It is always precious. We have a business before us which loudly demands our diligence. Harvest is the time to provide for approaching winter. Life is the time to prepare for the eternal world. Lay up for yourselves a good treasure against the time to come. Provide for yourselves bags which wax not old, a treasure in heaven, where neither moths corrupt, nor thieves break through and steal. How industriously you labour for the meat which perishes! How anxious you appear to sustain a body, which, after all you can do, is mortal still! Rather labour for the meat, which endures to eternal life, the meat which alone can nourish the immortal soul. Food and raiment are needful for the body; seek them you may; but rather seek the kingdom of God, and these things will be added.

7. Harvest should be a season of *selfexamination*.

We are God's husbandry. Much has he done for us.—¿ What could he have done more?—¿ Have we answered his cost? When we see our fields fruitful under our culture, it is proper to inquire—¿Whether we are as fruitful under the culture of the divine hand?—¿ Whether we have abounded in the fruits of righteousness, in proportion to the blessings which we have received from heaven?

heaven. If we bear no fruit, we shall soon be rejected. God has let us alone this year. But behold, the ax is laid to the root of the trees; every tree that beareth not good fruit, will be hewn down and cast into the fire. The field, which bringeth forth herbs, meet for him by whom it is dressed, receiveth blessing from God. But that which beareth thorns and briars, is nigh unto cursing, whose end is to be burned.

Lastly. Harvest reminds us of our obligation to *faith* and *patience*.

We have a kind of natural faith, which, standing on the ground of past experience, looks forward with expectation of a future harvest. Let Christians, enlightened by Revelation, look beyond this world to things unseen; and, relying on the promise, truth, and grace of God, anticipate the blessings of the heavenly state. In full persuasion of the glory revealed, let them patiently endure the trials, and cheerfully perform the duties, allotted them in the present world. Let them not be weary in welldoing, but abound in the work of the Lord, knowing, that in due time, they shall reap, if they faint not; and if they sow bountifully, they shall reap also bountifully.

They have need of patience, that, after they have done the will of God, they may inherit the promises. Behold, the husbandman waiteth for the precious fruit of the earth, and hath long patience for it, till he receive the early and the latter rain. Be ye also patient, stablish your hearts, for the coming of the Lord draweth nigh. God is not unrighteous to forget your work of faith, your labour of love, and your patience of hope: Give diligence, therefore, to the full affurance of hope to the end; and be not flothful, but followers of them, who through faith and patience, inherit the promifes.

www.ingramcontent.com/pod-product-compliance
Lightning Source LLC
Chambersburg PA
CBHW031415230426
43668CB00007B/311